Praise for *The Book Lover's Cookbook*

"Trying to inspire your children to read more? Plan a few meals around passages from your or their favorite books with help from *The Book Lover's Cookbook*."
—*The Philadelphia Inquirer*

"Two Utah bookaphiles concoct a savory cookbook . . . This is a most appealing volume for those legions of book group members who may well enliven some future gatherings with the peach pie inspired by Toni Morrison's *The Bluest Eye*."
—*Seattle Post-Intelligencer*

"A culinary delight."
—*The Arlington Advocate*

"This literary feast links nearly two hundred recipes with the books in which the dishes appeared. Treat yourself to a bran muffin from Oscar Wilde, peach pie from Toni Morrison or 'Anne's Anodyne Liniment Cake' from *Anne of Green Gables*. Book-group hosts can rely on this volume as they anguish over what to serve."
—*Chicago Tribune*

"I have about three bookshelves filled with cookbooks at home, but I can't say I've actually 'read' any one of them—until now. . . . The anecdotes in between are delicious."
—*Green Bay Press Gazette*

"A fun read for any bibliophile-cum-foodie."
—*Publishers Weekly*

"A couple of Utah-based writers have the perfect gift for all of us:
The Book Lover's Cookbook . . . is a lovingly crafted collection of excerpted passages from
works of fiction and nonfiction matched with recipes for the particular foods they
mention. . . . This delightful book is bound to encourage both experiments in the kitchen
and forays into new works of literature."
—*Contra Costa Times*

"Sprinkled throughout are marvelous anecdotes about writers and writing—perfect
appetizers that add lots of flavor to this mouth-watering main course."
—bookreporter.com

"Will spur vivid memories for those who have been avid readers since childhood . . .
You will finish devouring *The Book Lover's Cookbook* wanting more for your plate."
—*Pittsburgh Tribune-Review*

"With roots in literature and cooking, *The Book Lover's Cookbook* has attracted a
variety of readers, including many book groups who like to read and make the
recipes for their meetings."
—*The Salt Lake Tribune*

"Books and food together—what's not to like?"
—*The Herald Journal* (Logan, Utah)

THE BOOK LOVER'S COOKBOOK

THE

BOOK LOVER'S

COOKBOOK

Recipes Inspired by Celebrated

Works of Literature, and the

Passages That Feature Them

Shaunda Kennedy Wenger

& Janet Kay Jensen

BALLANTINE BOOKS • NEW YORK

A Ballantine Book
Published by The Random House Publishing Group

Copyright © 2003 by Shaunda Kennedy Wenger and Janet Jensen
Reader's Guide copyright © 2005 by The Random House Publishing Group, a division of Random House, Inc.

Published in the United States by Ballantine Books, an imprint of The Random House Publishing Group,
a division of Random House, Inc., New York, and simultaneously in
Canada by Random House of Canada Limited, Toronto.

Owing to limitations of space, permission acknowledgments can be found on pp. 309–317,
which constitute an extension of this copyright page.

Ballantine and colophon are registered trademarks of Random House, Inc.
Reader's Circle and colophon are trademarks of Random House, Inc.

www.thereaderscircle.com

Library of Congress Cataloging-in-Publication Data

Wenger, Shaunda Kennedy.
The book lover's cookbook : recipes inspired by celebrated works of literature and the passages that feature them /
Shaunda Kennedy Wenger and Janet Kay Jensen.—1st ed.
p. cm.
1. Cookery. 2. Cookery in literature. 3. Food in literature. I. Jensen, Janet Kay. II. Title.

TX714.W347 2003

641.5—dc21   2003052134

ISBN 0-345-46546-6

Manufactured in the United States of America

4   6   8   9   7   5   3

First Edition: October 2003
First Trade Paperback Edition: April 2005

Text design by Liney Li

For my three little dumplings: Joanna, Nathan, and Eric—SKW

For my family: Miles, Kevin, Emily, BJ, Marica, and Jeff—JKJ

When I get a little money I buy books;

and if any is left I buy food and clothes.

—*Desiderius Erasmus*

CONTENTS

∽

APPETIZERS, BREADS,
. . . . AND OTHER FINGER FOODS 167 . . . .

"As God is my witness, I'm never going to be hungry again."

☙ **Margaret Mitchell,** *Gone with the Wind*

ACKNOWLEDGMENTS

This cookbook would not be possible without writers who breathe life, healthy appetites, and impressive cooking skills into their characters, fictional people who seem as real as the neighbor next door. To writers who offer new ways of looking within ourselves, we thank them for touching our lives. To those authors who actively participated in our project by helping us develop recipes or contributing their own recipes or anecdotes, we offer our warmest thanks and appreciation: Isabel Allende, Joan Bauer, Elizabeth Berg, Maeve Binchy, Carolyn Campbell, Kay Chorao, Sandra Dallas, Jim Fergus, Connie May Fowler, Patricia Gaffney, Judith Guest, Jane Hamilton, Joanne Harris, Barbara Kingsolver, Sue Miller, Laura Numeroff, Richard Peck, Jodi Picoult, M. L. Rose, Gwyn Hyman Rubio, Janet Stevens, James Alexander Thom, Jamie Langston Turner, and Camron Steve Wright.

Nor would this book be possible without readers who connect with the written word and then with each other across the pages of books. We all cherish these connections . . . Connections made through an unexpected conversation with a stranger holding a familiar book . . . Connections made over warmed foccacia bread at book club meetings . . . Connections made with our children, tucked in with the lingering words of *Goodnight Moon* . . . Without a doubt, these connections mix flavor into our lives as surely as garlic adds flavor to chicken.

We are truly thankful for the connections and friendships we found with our agent, James Vines; our editors, Maureen O'Neal and Joan Mendenhall; and Ballantine permissions manager Lorraine DeMarino. Without their vision, enthusiasm, and support, this book would not be in your hands or propped open on your kitchen counter. We also thank for their assistance in bringing this material together: Elizabeth Herr, Margaret Gorenstein, Nancy Delia, and Sue Waryn.

We are grateful to other individuals who contributed directly to this project with recipes, suggestions, or encouragement: Mary and Jim Kennedy, Erin Kennedy O'Boyle, Dennis Wenger, Miles Jensen, Becky Yeager, Jane Kiick, Lisa Saraiva, Laura Rahe, Janelle Grantham, Helen Jordan, Krista McHugh, Gretchen Spieler, Patrice Moss, Holly Thomas, Judy Wenger, Nancy Koenig Peckham, Sammie and Dee Justesen, Nadene Mattson, Charlene Hirschi, all the dear friends in our Logan book clubs, and the Cache Valley Chapter of the League of Utah Writers.

Shaunda extends love and appreciation to her mother, who never turned down young helping hands in the kitchen, and to her father, who jazzed up his first "gourmet" meals with ketchup. *Thank you both for instilling curiosity, humor, and confidence that have extended beyond the kitchen and into life.*

Janet extends gratitude and love to her late parents, Darwin and Lorene Craner. *They introduced us to the best of literature, fostering love and respect for the written and spoken word. For advice and recipes throughout the years, thanks to my sisters, Anne and Ellen, dear friends who will always be better cooks than I am.*

INTRODUCTION

Jo Becker makes chili with a murderer, Oliver Twist's request for more gruel starts a riot, and Ma Joad agonizes over not being able to fill the bellies of hungry children who watch her family eat stew. When characters deal with food, whether they're eating, cooking, dreaming, manipulating, or suffering, they step off the page and connect with the reader. These connections can evoke feelings of pleasure, admiration, revulsion, or disgust depending on the situation.

Food scenes offer a universal platform that can foster connections between the reader and the character. Some food scenes bring such strong feelings of nostalgia, the experience between the fiction of the story, the reality of the present, and the memories of the past blur to the point where we question, *Could I have known this author? Could I have known this character?* These very questions arose from reading *While I Was Gone*, planting the seed for *The Book Lover's Cookbook* during the pantry hunt for that vegetarian chili recipe made so many years ago with friends in a three-story East-coast house.

We delved back and forth between library and kitchen, amazed at the wealth of literature that offered scrumptious derivations in food and pleased to find authors who cared enough to feed their characters well. Ultimately, we ate well right along with them when we extended our lives into *The Accidental Tourist* and sat down to a Leary family dinner or realized that customers who ate at Moro's Restaurant unwittingly supported organized crime in *Dark Lady*. Some characters shared recipes for generations to come. Others jealously guarded them from prying eyes. In our favorite stories, friendships were forged over pie crusts, comfort was served in a bowl of macaroni and cheese, and romance sparkled over a first dinner date.

In our quest to develop recipes, we experienced our own culinary triumphs and disasters, which oddly tended to validate our own lives as life mirrored fiction. Of course, we were firmly planted in reality. Library fines accumulated. Family members balked at times with either: "Your office looks like a war zone!" or "What's burning?" (Rest assured, most of the time they said, "Smells good.")

The Book Lover's Cookbook celebrates the best of food and literature. We hope you enjoy cooking with your favorite authors and characters.

Janet Jensen   Shaunda Wenger

BREAKFASTS

Breakfast at six-thirty. Skim milk, crusts, middlings, bits of doughnuts, wheatcakes with drops of maple syrup sticking to them, potato skins, leftover custard pudding with raisins, and bits of Shredded Wheat.

Breakfast would be finished at seven.

From seven to eight, Wilbur planned to have a talk with Templeton, the rat who lived under his trough.

E. B. WHITE, *CHARLOTTE'S WEB*

About the jelly beans. On the Cheerios. I know this is probably not recommended by nutritionists. But I had never tried it before. And you never know. Somebody has to do the field-testing. The jelly beans were better than raisins, actually. If you want to check it out, I suggest the Jelly Belly brand, which comes in forty official flavors. My choice was a combination of apricot, banana, watermelon, and root beer. If you want a little zing in the mix, throw in a few jalapeno-flavored ones. A little wow! in the Cheerios. A little whoopee in the minimum daily requirement.

ROBERT FULGHUM, *UH-OH*

Pancakes

✧

When Black Mumbo saw the melted butter, wasn't she pleased! "Now," said she, "we'll all have pancakes for supper!"

So she got flour and eggs and milk and sugar and butter, and she made a huge plate of most lovely pancakes. And she fried them in the melted butter which the Tigers had made, and they were just as yellow and brown as little Tigers.

And then they all sat down to supper. And Black Mumbo ate twenty-seven pancakes, and Black Jumbo ate fifty-five, but Little Black Sambo ate a hundred and sixty-nine, because he was so hungry.

❧ Helen Bannerman, *The Story of Little Black Sambo*

PANCAKE?

Who wants a pancake,
Sweet and piping hot?
Good little Grace looks up and says,
"I'll take the one on top."
Who else wants a pancake,
Fresh off the griddle?
Terrible Teresa smiles and says,
"I'll take the one in the middle."

❧ Shel Silverstein, *Where the Sidewalk Ends*

Stack of Pancakes

2 eggs, separated

2 tablespoons sugar

2 cups all-purpose flour, sifted

2 tablespoons vegetable oil

1 tablespoon applesauce

4 teaspoons baking powder

½ teaspoon salt

2 cups milk

¼ teaspoon vanilla extract

Bananas

Maple syrup

Beat the egg whites and sugar together in a large bowl. Add the egg yolks, flour, oil, applesauce, baking powder, salt, milk, and vanilla and mix until the batter is nearly smooth. Some small lumps will remain. Spoon the batter onto a greased hot griddle heated to about 375° (medium-high heat), making pancakes a manageable size. Flip each pancake when the batter is bubbled over the entire top and the edges are slightly dry (should take about 2 to 3 minutes). Cook the bottom until golden brown, about 1 minute.

Serve topped with butter or margarine, sliced bananas, and maple syrup.

MAKES ABOUT 8 PANCAKES

VARIATION: Stir 1 cup of fresh blueberries into batter for blueberry pancakes.

Just the knowledge that a good book is awaiting one at the end of a long day makes that day happier.

Kathleen Norris

4

Alternative Crepes

1½ cups all-purpose flour
½ teaspoon baking powder
2 cups milk
½ teaspoon vanilla
1 tablespoon sugar
½ teaspoon salt

2 large eggs
2 tablespoons butter or
    margarine, melted
Bananas, strawberries, and
    mango, sliced
Blueberries, raspberries

Combine all the ingredients, except fruit, together in a large bowl and beat the batter until it is nearly smooth. Heat a greased, 8-inch crepe skillet to 400° or begin warming a large, greased frying pan over high heat with a tablespoon of butter or margarine. Spread the batter out in the pan to a ⅛-inch thickness, so that the finished crepe will be thin. Flip the crepe when the batter on top is completely bubbled and the edges are slightly dry, about 2 minutes. Cook the bottom until golden brown, about 1 minute. Place the crepe on a warmed plate. Repeat with the remaining batter. Wrap your choice of fresh fruit inside the crepes (sliced bananas, strawberries, mangos, blueberries, raspberries). Serve with maple syrup.

MAKES EIGHT 8-INCH CREPES

Slapjacks

As Ichabod jogged slowly on his way, his eye, ever open to every symptom of culinary abundance, ranged with delight over the treasures of jolly autumn. On all sides he beheld vast stores of apples, some hanging in oppressive opulence on the trees, some gathered into baskets and barrels for the market, others heaped up in rich piles for the cider press. Farther on he beheld great fields of Indian corn, with its golden ears peeping from hasty pudding; and the yellow pumpkins lying beneath them, turning up their fair round bellies to the sun, and giving ample prospects of the most luxurious of pies; and anon he passed the fragrant buckwheat fields, breathing the odor of the beehive, and as he beheld them, soft anticipations stole over his mind of dainty slapjacks, well buttered and garnished with honey or treacle, by the delicate little dimpled hand of Katrina Van Tassel.

Washington Irving, *The Legend of Sleepy Hollow*

Behold! Ichabod's Slapjacks

2 cups all-purpose flour, sifted
2½ teaspoons baking powder
1 teaspoon salt
1 cup milk
2 tablespoons butter or
    margarine, melted

2 tablespoons honey
2 large eggs, slightly beaten
Butter or margarine
Maple syrup

Combine the dry ingredients in a large bowl. Add the remaining ingredients and mix well, scraping sides. Mixture will be somewhat thick. Spoon batter onto a greased griddle heated to about 375° (medium-high heat), making pancake a manageable size. Flip the pancake when batter is bubbled over the entire top and the edges are slightly dry (should take about 2 to 3 minutes). Cook bottom until golden brown, about 1 minute.

Serve topped with butter or margarine and maple syrup.

MAKES ABOUT 8 SLAPJACKS

Next time you're browsing the shelves in a library, realize you're standing in the midst of a family discussion.

   Kathleen Duey

Waffles

She moved out of bed carefully, so as not to disturb Jesse. He stirred and opened his eyes. "Was it something I said?" he asked groggily.

"You're suffocating me," she whispered lovingly. On the way to the bathroom she had an idea. She'd make Jesse some waffles. Waffles and muffins and bacon and . . . That was probably enough. Oh, and orange juice and coffee. Coffee with cinnamon in it.

Maybe she shouldn't make waffles, though. Her slapstick tendencies had a habit of rearing their ugly heads during waffle preparation. Still, she wanted to do something nice for him. She'd been staring at him for half an hour, and now she'd sort of woken him up . . . All in all, she felt she owed him waffles. That big waffle gesture was the only one that would do. She smiled at her reflection, filled with enthusiasm of bold reserve.

Twenty minutes later, on the way to the hospital, Jesse said, "But why waffles? I don't even really like waffles."

"Look," said Suzanne stoically. "It's already starting to blister." She held up her left hand, with its domestic scar across the knuckles where the waffle iron had landed.

   Carrie Fisher, *Postcards from the Edge*

Waffles

2 eggs plus 1 egg white, beaten
¼ cup sugar
½ cup butter or margarine, melted
¼ cup applesauce, unsweetened
1½ cups all-purpose flour with
    1 teaspoon baking powder

½ teaspoon salt
½ cup plus 2 tablespoons milk
1 teaspoon vanilla
Maple syrup
Mangos, strawberries, or
    blueberries

Mix all the ingredients except syrup and fruit in a large bowl. Spray a waffle iron with cooking spray. Spoon the batter onto the heated waffle iron. Cook the waffle until lightly browned, about 2 minutes. Serve with maple syrup and sliced mangos, strawberries, or blueberries.

MAKES ABOUT 6 LARGE WAFFLES

I suggest that the only books that influence us are those for which we are ready, and which have gone a little further down our particular path than we have gone ourselves.

E. M. Forster

French Toast

c><>

Back in the kitchen, I gulp down another cup of coffee. Then I mix eggs and milk in a blue-and-yellow bowl *that tiny shop in Paris, our weeklong vacation there, I stood at the window one morning after I'd gotten up and he came up behind me and put his arms around my middle, his lips to the back of my neck,* add a touch of vanilla, a sprinkle of sugar. I put the frying pan on the stove *put his lips to the back of my neck and we went back to bed,* lay out two slices of bread on the cutting board. These hands at the ends of my wrists remove the crusts. I'm not sure why. Oh, I know why. Because they're hard.

I sit down at the table. Stand up. Sit down. Concentrate on my breathing, that's supposed to help.

Actually, it does not.

Elizabeth Berg, *Open House*

Samantha's French Toast

c><>

4 eggs, beaten
½ cup milk
½ teaspoon vanilla extract
A sprinkle of sugar

¼ teaspoon cinnamon
6 slices of dense bread
Maple syrup

Mix the eggs, milk, vanilla, sugar, and cinnamon in a shallow, wide-bottomed bowl that is large enough to accommodate a slice of bread. Grease a griddle with melted butter or margarine, or use cooking spray. Heat the griddle to 350° (medium-high heat). Dip a slice of bread into the egg batter, coating both sides. Remove the bread and place it on the hot griddle. Brown the bread on both sides, cooking each side about 2 to 3 minutes.

Serve with maple syrup.

MAKES 6 SERVINGS

VARIATION: Top with maple syrup and berries of your choice: straw-berries, blueberries, or raspberries.

> I hope that it does bring comfort. I hope all my books do.
>
> ⟨ **Elizabeth Berg**

Eggs

"I shall take some up to mother, though she said we were not to think of her, for she'd take care of herself," said Meg, who presided and felt quite matronly behind the teapot.

So a tray was fitted out before anyone began, and was taken up with the cook's compliments. The boiled tea was very bitter, the omelet scorched, and the biscuits speckled with saleratus; but Mrs. March received her repast with thanks and laughed heartily over it after Jo was gone.

⟨ Louisa May Alcott, *Little Women*

Pray don't burn my house to roast your eggs.

⟨ Benjamin Franklin, *Poor Richard's Almanack, 1757*

When Tyler got home, he put a bag of groceries on the counter. The phone rang and he spoke into it with a low voice. "Tomorrow," she heard him say. "Yes. I promise." Edith felt so silly. She wanted to disappear. But she was much too big to disappear. She decided to make the best of it. She cooked an omelet. Edith was good with eggs and butter and her omelets were always tender and brown. "This is a symphony," said Tyler, taking a bite, "a poem and a symphony."

"This is my specialty," said Edith, proud and happy. "One of my specialties." And she ate her omelet with a big spoon.

ᴁ **Abigail Thomas, "Edith's Wardrobe (Negligee)" from *Herb's Pajamas***

Specialty Omelet

2 tablespoons olive oil

½ red or green bell pepper, diced*

½ onion, chopped

15 large black olives, sliced

6 eggs, beaten

¼ cup milk

1 teaspoon garlic

salt and pepper to taste

¼ teaspoon thyme

¼ teaspoon parsley

½ cup shredded cheddar cheese

In a large nonstick skillet, sauté the pepper, onion, and olives in olive oil until tender over medium-high heat, about 2 minutes. Remove the vegetables from the skillet and set aside in a bowl. Mix the eggs, milk, and spices in another bowl. Pour this mixture into the heated skillet. When the egg begins to solidify around the outer edges, lift its edges and tilt pan to allow uncooked egg mixture to slide from top of the omelet to underneath. Continue cooking. Sprinkle vegetables and cheese over the top of the cooking egg mixture. When the top of omelet appears moist and not wet, lift one side of the omelet with a wide spatula and fold it over onto the opposite edge. Cook one more minute, covered. Remove from heat.

Serve with toast and bacon or sausage.

MAKES 3 TO 4 SERVINGS

* Filling for an omelet is entirely a matter of personal taste. Possible fillings include cooked sausage, sautéed mushrooms, chopped tomatoes, shredded Monterey Jack cheese, green onions, fresh chives, broccoli, and cauliflower.

> I really have to believe that the people I'm writing about are real, have their own wills, and I can't simply manipulate them.
>
> ◅ **Peter S. Beagle**

Quiche

◦◊◦

"Real men don't eat quiche," said Flex Crush, ordering a breakfast of steak, prime rib, six eggs, and a loaf of toast.

We were sitting in the professional drivers' section of an all-night truckers' pit stop somewhere west of Tulsa on I-44, discussing the plight of men in today's society. Flex, a 225-pound nuclear-waste driver, who claims to be one of the last Real Men in existence, was pensive:

"American men are all mixed up today," he began, idly cleaning the 12 gauge shotgun that was sitting across his knees. Off in the distance, the sun was just beginning to rise over the tractor trailers in the parking lot.

"There was a time when this was a nation of Ernest Hemingways. *Real Men.* The kind of guys who could defoliate an entire forest to make a breakfast fire—and then go on to wipe out an endangered species hunting for lunch. But not anymore. We've become a nation of wimps. Pansies. Quiche eaters, Alan Alda types—who cook and clean and relate to their wives, Phil Donahue clones—who are *warm* and *sensitive* and *vulnerable.* It's not enough anymore that we earn a living and protect women and children from plagues, famine, and encyclopedia salesmen. But now we're also supposed to be *supportive*. And *understanding*. And *sincere*."

 Bruce Feirstein, *Real Men Don't Eat Quiche*

A Real Man's Quiche

1 package refrigerated crescent
   rolls
3 cups cooked, shredded
   potatoes
3 large eggs, beaten
1 tablespoon chopped green
   onions

1 cup shredded cheddar cheese
1 cup shredded mozzarella cheese
½ cup cooked meat: sausage,
   crumbled bacon, or diced ham

Coat a 9-inch pie pan with cooking spray. Press triangles of crescent roll dough into pie pan, sealing seams, to form a pie crust. Crimp edges. Combine remaining ingredients in a large bowl, stirring gently. Pour the mixture into the crust. Cover loosely with foil and bake at 400° for about 45 minutes. Remove the foil and bake an additional 10 minutes to brown crust. Quiche is done when center is firm.

MAKES 6 TO 8 SERVINGS

Truth is not loved because it is better for us. We hunger and thirst for it. And the appetite for truthful books is greater than ever.

 Saul Bellow

Zucchini

There are few things in life more satisfying than saving money by growing your own vegetables in a little garden. Last night, we had three small zucchini for dinner that were grown within fifty feet of our back door. I estimate they cost somewhere in the neighborhood of $371.49 each. There may be more before the summer's over. Zucchini are relentless once they start coming.

Andrew Rooney, "The $371.49 Zucchini" from *Word for Word*

Priceless Zucchini Bread

3 eggs, slightly beaten

2 cups sugar

1 cup oil

2 cups finely grated zucchini

1 teaspoon vanilla

3 cups all-purpose flour

1 teaspoon salt

1 teaspoon baking soda

2 teaspoons cinnamon

¼ teaspoon nutmeg

½ teaspoon baking powder

½ cup chopped nuts (optional)

Mix together the eggs, sugar, oil, zucchini, and vanilla in a large bowl. Combine the dry ingredients and add them to the zucchini batter and mix well. Stir in nuts, if desired. Pour the batter into two greased and floured loaf pans. Bake for 1 hour at 325°.

MAKES 2 LOAVES

"More, Please!" Chocolate Zucchini Bread

6 egg whites

¼ cup oil

2 cups sugar

1 teaspoon vanilla

2 cups shredded zucchini

1 cup applesauce or 2 mashed
   bananas

2½ cups all-purpose flour

½ cup cocoa

1 teaspoon salt

1 teaspoon baking soda

1 teaspoon cinnamon

¼ teaspoon baking powder

Mix all ingredients in a large bowl. Pour the batter into 2 greased and floured loaf pans. Bake at 350° for 1 hour.

MAKES 2 LOAVES

Books, the children of the brain.

🖋 Jonathan Swift

Muffins, Cakes, and Scones

At that moment Ella, the maid, came in with the coffee pot, and Mrs. Settergren said, "Please come and have some coffee."

"*First!*" cried Pippi and was up by the table in two skips. She heaped as many cakes as she could onto a plate, threw five lumps of sugar into a coffee cup, emptied half the cream pitcher into her cup, and was back in her chair with her loot even before the ladies had reached the table.

Pippi stretched her legs out in front of her and placed the plate of cakes between her toes. Then she merrily dunked cakes in her coffee cup and stuffed so many in her mouth at once that she couldn't have uttered a word no matter how hard she tried. In the twinkling of an eye she had finished all the cakes on the plate. She got up, struck the plate as if it were a tambourine, and went up to the table to see if there were any cakes left. The ladies looked disapprovingly at her, but that didn't bother her. Chatting gaily, she walked around the table, snatching a cake here and a cake there.

"It certainly was nice of you to invite me," she said. "I've never been to a coffee party before."

＊ **Astrid Lindgren,** *Pippi Longstocking*

Pippi's Orange-Cranberry Muffin Cakes

¼ cup butter or margarine

1 cup plus 2 tablespoons sugar

¼ cup applesauce

1 teaspoon vanilla or almond
    extract

¾ teaspoon orange extract

3 tablespoons water,
    3 tablespoons oil, and
    2 teaspoons baking powder,
    mixed together

Zest of one orange, grated

Pulp of one orange, slightly
    chopped

2 cups all-purpose flour with
    2 teaspoons baking powder

¼ teaspoon salt

½ cup fresh-squeezed orange juice

2 cups dried cranberries

Preheat oven to 375°.

Mix the butter or margarine and sugar together in a large bowl. Add the applesauce, vanilla, orange extract, and baking powder mixture and beat well. Add the zest and orange pulp to the batter. Add the flour with baking powder, salt, and orange juice; mix well. Fold in the cranberries.

Spoon the batter into paper-lined or prepared muffin tins. Sprinkle the top of the batter with sugar. Bake for about 25 minutes, or until done. Remove the muffins from the pan and place on a cooling rack. Cool before serving.

MAKES 12 TO 16 MUFFINS

As a child who loved to read, I had trouble finding honest stories. I felt that adults were always keeping secrets from me, even in the books I was reading.

Judy Blume

BLUEBERRIES

"You ought to have seen what I saw on my way
To the village, through Patterson's pasture today:
Blueberries as big as the end of your thumb,
Real sky-blue, and heavy, and ready to drum
In the cavernous pail of the first one to come!
And all ripe together, not some of them green
And some of them ripe! You ought to have seen!"

"I don't know what part of the pasture you mean."

"You know where they cut off the woods—let me see—
It was two years ago—or no!—can it be
No longer than that?—and the following fall
The fire ran and burned it all up but the wall."

"Why, there hasn't been time for the bushes to grow.
That's always the way with the blueberries, though:
There may not have been the ghost of a sign
Of them anywhere under the shade of the pine,
But get the pine out of the way, you may burn
The pasture all over until not a fern
Or grass-blade is left, not to mention a stick,
And presto, they're up all around you as thick
And hard to explain as a conjuror's trick."

    Robert Frost

First-Picking Blueberry Muffins

MUFFIN BATTER:

¼ cup butter or margarine

1 cup plus 2 tablespoons sugar

¼ cup applesauce

1 teaspoon vanilla

3 tablespoons water,
     3 tablespoons oil,
     2 teaspoons baking powder,
     mixed together

2 cups all-purpose flour with
     2 teaspoons baking powder

¼ teaspoon salt

½ cup apple juice

2½ cups blueberries

STREUSEL TOPPING:

½ cup all-purpose flour   ½ teaspoon cinnamon

⅛ teaspoon salt   ¼ teaspoon nutmeg

½ cup quick-cooking oats   6 tablespoons butter

⅓ cup sugar   ⅓ cup powdered sugar

Mix the butter or margarine and sugar together. Add the applesauce, vanilla, and baking powder mixture and beat well. Add the flour with baking powder, salt, and juice; mix well. Fold in the blueberries. Set aside. Prepare topping by combining all the dry ingredients, except powdered sugar, in a medium bowl. Cut the butter into the dry mixture with a fork or pastry blender until mixture resembles crumbs. Finish making crumbly texture by pinching the mixture between fingers.

Spoon the batter into paper-lined or prepared muffin tins. Sprinkle with streusel topping. Bake at 375° for about 25 minutes, or until done. Remove muffins from pan and set on a cooling rack. Sprinkle the muffins with powdered sugar while they are still warm. Cool before serving.

MAKES 12 TO 16 MUFFINS

When power leads man toward arrogance, poetry reminds him of his limitations. When power narrows the areas of man's concerns, poetry reminds him of the richness and diversity of his existence. When power corrupts, poetry cleanses, for art establishes the basic human truths which must serve as the touchstone of our judgment. The artist, however faithful to his personal vision of reality, becomes the last champion of the individual mind and sensibility against an intrusive society and an officious state. The great artist is thus a solitary figure. He has, as Frost said, a lover's quarrel with the world.

ᕙ   John F. Kennedy

ALGERNON: I don't think there is much likelihood, Jack, of you and Miss Fairfax being united.

JACK: Well, that is no business of yours.

ALGERNON: If it was my business, I wouldn't talk about it. [Begins to eat muffins.] It is very vulgar to talk about one's business. Only people like stock-brokers do that, and then merely at dinner parties.

JACK: How can you sit there, calmly eating muffins when we are in this horrible trouble, I can't make out. You seem to be perfectly heartless.

ALGERNON: Well, I can't eat muffins in an agitated manner. The butter would probably get on my cuffs. One should always eat muffins quite calmly. It is the only way to eat them.

JACK: I say it's perfectly heartless your eating muffins at all, under the circumstances.

ALGERNON: When I am in trouble, eating is the only thing that consoles me. Indeed, when I am in really great trouble, as any one who knows me intimately will tell you, I refuse everything except food and drink. At the present moment I am eating muffins because I am unhappy. Besides, I am particularly fond of muffins. [Rising.]

JACK: [Rising.] Well, that is no reason why you should eat them all in that greedy way. [Takes muffins from ALGERNON.]

ALGERNON: [Offering tea-cake.] I wish you would have tea-cake instead. I don't like tea-cake.

Oscar Wilde, *The Importance of Being Earnest*

Consolation Bran Muffins

2 cups bran cereal (Bran Buds,
    All Bran, Bob's Best Oat Bran
    Hot Cereal, Bran Flakes, or
    Oat Bran)
2 cups buttermilk
2 eggs
½ cup vegetable oil
⅔ cup brown sugar, packed
1 teaspoon vanilla
2 cups all-purpose flour
2 teaspoons baking powder
2 teaspoons baking soda
½ teaspoon salt

Mix the cereal and buttermilk in a large bowl; let stand for 10 to 15 minutes until buttermilk is absorbed. Mix in the eggs, oil, brown sugar, and vanilla. Add the dry ingredients and mix well. Grease and flour a muffin pan, or line it with paper muffin cups. Fill the cups two-thirds full with batter. Bake at 400° for 15 to 20 minutes until the muffins are light brown. Remove the muffins from the pan and set them on a cooling rack.

MAKES 24 MUFFINS

Variations:

Add a mashed banana.
Substitute ½ cup applesauce for vegetable oil to reduce fat content.
Add 1 cup raisins or any dried fruit, diced.

Orange-Poppy Seed Tea Cakes

2 eggs plus 1 egg white
2½ cups sugar
⅛ cup vegetable oil
1 cup applesauce
1½ teaspoons vanilla
1½ teaspoons almond extract

3 cups all-purpose flour mixed
    with 1½ teaspoons salt and
    1½ teaspoons baking powder
1½ cups milk
1½ teaspoons poppy seeds
¼ teaspoon grated orange zest

GLAZE:

¼ cup orange juice
¾ cup powdered sugar

½ teaspoon vanilla
½ teaspoon almond extract

Beat the eggs in a large bowl; add the sugar, oil, applesauce, and extracts. Mix well. Add half of the flour mixture and half of the milk. Mix. Add the remaining ingredients. Blend for about 2 minutes until batter is smooth. Spoon the batter into muffin tins lined with paper muffin cups. Bake for 25 minutes at 350°. Cool.

After muffins are cooled, prepare glaze. In a saucepan, stir all ingredients continually over medium heat at a slow boil until thickened. Do not overcook. Immediately drizzle over muffins. Allow glaze to cool and harden.

MAKES ABOUT 24 MUFFINS

The poet's body even is not fed simply like other men's, but he sometimes tastes the genuine nectar and ambrosia of the gods, and lives a divine life. By the healthful and invigorating thrills of inspiration his life is preserved to a serene old age.

  Henry David Thoreau, *A Week on the Concord and Merrimack Rivers*

"You'll have a cup of tea, Mr. Herriot." She said it in a gracious way, not casually, her head slightly on one side and a dignified little smile on her face.

And when I went into the kitchen, I knew what I would find: the inevitable tray. It was always a tray with Mrs. Dalby. The hospitable Dales people were continually asking me in for some kind of refreshment—"a bit o' dinner" perhaps, but if it wasn't mid-day there was usually a mug of tea and a scone or a hunk of thick-crusted apple pie—but Mrs. Dalby invariably set out a special tray. And there it was today with a clean cloth and the best china cup and saucer and side plates, with sliced buttered scones and iced cakes and malt bread and biscuits.

⎰ **James Herriot,** *All Things Bright and Beautiful*

Mrs. Dalby's Buttermilk Scones

3 cups all-purpose flour
⅓ cup sugar
1 teaspoon salt
2½ teaspoons baking powder
½ teaspoon baking soda

¾ cup unsalted butter or margarine
1 cup buttermilk
1 tablespoon heavy cream, for
    brushing
Powdered sugar

Optional fillings: orange marmalade, raisins, dried cranberries soaked in orange juice to soften, strawberry preserves, dried apricots, grated cheddar cheese, chopped golden Delicious apple mixed with melted butter, brown sugar, and chopped pecans

Combine the flour, sugar, salt, baking powder, and baking soda in a large bowl. Add the butter and mix with your fingertips or press butter into flour with a fork until crumbly. Add the buttermilk and mix until combined.

Transfer the dough to a floured board or counter. Tear off 2-inch-diameter portions from the dough and roll the dough out into circles that are about 4 inches in diameter and ¼ inch thick. Place filling of choice in the center. Fold the circle in half and seal edge. Place on a greased baking sheet. Brush the top of scone with cream, and bake at 400° for 15 minutes, or until lightly browned. Sprinkle with powdered sugar while warm, and serve.

MAKES 2 DOZEN SCONES

A poem is never finished, only abandoned.

 Paul Valéry

Yams, Pancakes, and Doughnuts

"Some folks think as how Ah kin fly," grumbled Mammy, shuffling up the stairs. She entered puffing, with the expression of one who expects battle and welcomes it. In her large black hands was a tray upon which food smoked, two large yams covered with butter, a pile of buckwheat cakes dripping syrup, and a large slice of ham swimming in gravy. Catching sight of Mammy's burden, Scarlett's expression changed from one of minor irritation to obstinate belligerency. In the excitement of trying on dresses she had forgotten Mammy's ironclad rule that, before going to any party, the O'Hara girls must be crammed so full of food at home they would be unable to eat any refreshments at the party.

 Margaret Mitchell, *Gone with the Wind*

Mammy's Yams

4 large yams, peeled and cooked
1 13-ounce can pineapple chunks
   or crushed pineapple or
   pineapple tidbits with juice
⅓ cup sugar
⅓ cup brown sugar
¼ teaspoon salt

¼ teaspoon cornstarch
½ cup orange juice (or ¼ cup
   orange juice plus ¼ cup lemon
   juice)
2 tablespoons butter or margarine
Cinnamon
Nutmeg

Cut yams in thick diagonal slices; arrange them in a shallow greased baking dish. Drain pineapple; reserve juice in a small saucepan. Pour pineapple chunks over yams. In a small bowl, combine the sugars, salt, and cornstarch. Add orange juice to the pineapple juice and bring the fruit juices to a boil; gradually add sugar mixture. Stir over medium-high heat until thickened. Stir butter or margarine into this thickened sauce until it is melted. Pour the hot sauce over the yams and pineapple, then sprinkle lightly with cinnamon and nutmeg. Leave the baking dish uncovered while it bakes in a 350° oven for about 30 minutes, or until bubbly.

MAKES 6 TO 8 SERVINGS

Fill 'Er Up Buckwheat Pancakes

1 cup buckwheat flour (not packed)

½ cup oat flour (not packed)

2 tablespoons cornmeal

¼ cup all-purpose flour

2 teaspoons baking powder

1 teaspoon baking soda

¾ teaspoon salt

2 teaspoons molasses stirred into 1⅔ cups milk

3 tablespoons butter or margarine, melted

2 egg yolks

2 egg whites, whipped until stiff but not dry

Margarine

Blueberries

Maple syrup

Combine all the ingredients in order listed, up to the egg whites, and mix well. Fold in the egg whites. Spoon batter onto a greased griddle heated to about 375° (medium-high heat), making pancakes a manageable size. Flip pancake when batter is bubbled and edges are slightly dry (should take about 2 to 3 minutes). Cook bottom until browned, about 1 minute. Serve topped with margarine, fresh blueberries, and maple syrup.

MAKES 8 LARGE PANCAKES

P oetry—and by extension, all writing— becomes "the autobiography of a soul," in which the poet's job is to "see clear to the truth beyond oneself."

 Robert Allen Papinchak, quoting Emily Dickinson

Before twenty more doughnuts could roll down the little chute he shouted, "SAY! I know where the bracelet is! It was lying here on the counter and got mixed up in the batter by mistake! The bracelet is cooked inside one of these doughnuts!"

"Why . . . I really believe you're right," said the lady through her tears. "Isn't that *amazing? Simply amazing!*"

"I'll be durn'd!" said the sheriff.

"OhH-h!" moaned Uncle Ulysses. "Now we have to break up all of these doughnuts to find it. Think of the *pieces!* Think of the *crumbs!* Think of what *Aggy* will say!"

Robert McCloskey, *Homer Price*

Homer's Applesauce Doughnuts

3 tablespoons dry yeast

2 tablespoons sugar

1 cup lukewarm water

1 cup scalded milk (stirring constantly, bring milk just to a boil over medium heat and remove from heat)

¾ cup sugar

3 eggs

8 cups sifted all-purpose flour

½ cup butter or margarine (room temperature)

¾ teaspoon salt

1 teaspoon mace

1 cup applesauce

Vegetable oil for deep-frying

GLAZE:

1 pound powdered sugar

Approximately ¼ cup hot water

1 teaspoon vanilla *or* 1 teaspoon maple flavoring *or* 1 teaspoon lemon juice

In a small bowl combine yeast, 2 tablespoons sugar, and warm water. In a large bowl combine scalded milk and ¾ cup sugar and set aside to cool. When milk mixture is cooled add yeast mixture to it. Using a mixer, add the eggs one at a time, mixing well after each egg. Add half the flour (4 cups). Add butter or margarine, salt, mace, and applesauce and mix well. Mix in remaining flour (4 cups).

Knead the dough until it is elastic and smooth. Place the dough in a large, greased bowl. Flip the dough over in the bowl so its top surface is also greased. Cover the bowl with plastic wrap and allow dough to rise in a warm place until it is doubled in size.

Line baking sheets with lightly floured paper towels. On a lightly floured surface, roll the dough out to a ¾-inch thickness and cut out doughnuts with a doughnut cutter (doughnut holes can also be fried). Place the doughnuts on the baking sheets, at least one inch apart. Heat oil in a deep-fryer (between 275° and 300°). Use enough oil so the doughnuts will float. Line shallow baking pans with 3 layers of paper towels and place cooling racks over them.

Turn the doughnuts upside down, so that the flat side is upward when frying begins. Transfer the doughnuts to the hot oil. Fry the doughnuts until they are light brown on each side, turning them once. Place fried doughnuts on the cooling racks, allowing drippings to drain onto paper towels. While still warm, drizzle the doughnuts generously with glaze. To prepare glaze, whisk ingredients together until glaze attains desired smooth consistency.

Alternatively, roll hot doughnuts in a cinnamon-sugar mixture, coating several times, or roll warm doughnuts in powdered sugar, coating several times.

Makes approximately 3 dozen large doughnuts. These freeze well and can be wrapped in foil and reheated in the oven.

It is certain that no culture can flourish without narratives of transcendent origin and power.

≪ **Neil Postman**

MAIN AND SIDE DISHES

We ate roasted chicken, raised out back the previous summer, and tender potatoes brought by train from the Red River Valley, and gravy stirred up from the cracklings. I suppose it was a meal intended to impress, though you don't think of a woman like Roxanna worrying about how her hospitality comes off; she hadn't seemed at all ashamed about the goats. But she went to a lot of trouble for us, who were after all just one small family paying for a night's room and board. During that meal I saw Dad lean back in his chair and smile over and over again, an expression that aggrieved me somehow; Swede looked often at the windows, and I knew she was growing the storm in her mind, abetting it until the world should be slowed and the roads stopped and us buried at some happy length in the warmth and contentment of this house.

LEIF ENGER, *PEACE LIKE A RIVER*

At least once a fortnight a corps of caterers came down with several hundred feet of canvas and enough colored lights to make a Christmas tree of Gatsby's enormous garden. On buffet tables, garnished with glistening hors-d'oeuvre, spiced baked hams crowded against salads of harlequin designs and pastry pigs and turkeys bewitched to a dark gold. In the main hall a bar with a real brass rail was set up, and stocked with gins and liquors and cordials so long forgotten that most of his female guests were too young to know one from another.

F. SCOTT FITZGERALD, *THE GREAT GATSBY*

How careless they had been of food then, what prodigal waste! Rolls, corn muffins, biscuits and waffles, dripping butter, all at one meal. Ham at one end of the table and fried chicken at the other, collards swimming richly in pot liquor iridescent with grease, snap beans in mountains on brightly flowered porcelain, fried squash, stewed okra, carrots in cream sauce thick enough to cut. And three desserts, so everyone might have his choice, chocolate layer cake, vanilla blanc mange and pound cake topped with sweet whipped cream. The memory of those savory meals had the power to bring tears to her eyes as death and war had failed to do, had the power to turn her ever-gnawing stomach from rumbling emptiness to nausea. For the appetite Mammy had always deplored, the healthy appetite of a nineteen-year-old girl, now was increased fourfold by the hard and unremitting labor she had never known before.

MARGARET MITCHELL, *GONE WITH THE WIND*

Stuffed Chicken

ᴄᴧᴐ

I had been asked what I would like as my last meal if I was going to die. I had replied, "I don't like to think that far ahead, but if I were going to Mars tomorrow I would like to have hot chicken, a chilled bottle of wine, and a loaf of good bread." When I went into the darkened house, I was greeted by the aroma of roast chicken. There was a note on the refrigerator that read, "There is hot chicken in the oven, a cold bottle of wine in the fridge and a loaf of good bread on the cutting board. Thank you for the good times." Now that's the kind of man I wanted to marry and did marry. And if it wasn't for those two damned bad houses, I would still be married to him.

Maya Angelou, "A House Can Hurt, a Home Can Heal," from *Even the Stars Look Lonesome*

Good Times Roasted Garlic Chicken with Mushroom and Black Olive Stuffing

ᴄᴧᴐ

STUFFING:

2 cups toasted whole-wheat or
  bran bread, cubed

½ cup black olives, diced

½ cup mushrooms, chopped

½ cup onion, diced

¼ cup celery, diced with leaves

½ teaspoon garlic powder

1 teaspoon thyme

1 tablespoon fresh parsley,
  chopped

¼ teaspoon black pepper

½ teaspoon salt

2 tablespoons butter or
  margarine, melted

BASTE:

2 cloves of minced garlic mixed with 2 tablespoons melted butter or
    margarine

CHICKEN AND VEGETABLES:

1 whole chicken, about 5 to 6   6 to 8 carrots, rinsed and halved
    pounds
6 small red potatoes, rinsed, with
    skins on

Stir all the stuffing ingredients together. Spoon the stuffing into the cavity of the cleaned roasting chicken and pin the body cavity shut. Enclose
any remaining stuffing in tin foil and place it inside the roasting pan with
the chicken. Add ½ cup water to the pan. Arrange the potatoes and carrots around the chicken. Brush the basting sauce over the outside of the
chicken, potatoes, and carrots. Bake at 375° according to weight (about
1½ hours). Repeat basting of the chicken with drippings after about 45
minutes. Chicken is done when the thigh moves freely in socket or thigh
temperature is 180°. Remove the chicken from the oven and let it sit in
the pan for about 15 minutes before slicing.

Serve with Unbelievable Braided Bread (page 186).

MAKES 6 SERVINGS

I don't know how to paint, dance, or play an
instrument, but I get a thrill out of creating.

    Yann Martell

Oysters

cvɔ

THE WALRUS AND THE CARPENTER

"Oysters, come and walk with us!"
   The Walrus did beseech.
"A pleasant walk, a pleasant talk,
   Along the briny beach;
We cannot do with more than four,
   To give a hand to each."

The eldest Oyster looked at him,
   But never a word he said:
The eldest Oyster winked his eye,
   And shook his heavy head—
Meaning to say he did not choose
   To leave the oyster-bed.

But four young Oysters hurried up,
   All eager for this treat;
Their coats were brushed, their faces washed,
   Their shoes were clean and neat—
And this was odd, because, you know,
   They hadn't any feet.

Four other Oysters followed them,
   And yet another four;
And thick and fast they came at last,
   And more, and more, and more—
All hopping through the frothy waves
   And scrambling to the shore.

The Walrus and the Carpenter
   Walked on a mile or so,
And then they rested on a rock
   Conveniently low:
And all the little Oysters stood
   And waited in a row.

"The time has come," the Walrus said,
   "To talk of many things:
Of shoes—and ships—and sealing-wax—
   Of cabbages—and kings—
And why the sea is boiling hot—
   And whether pigs have wings."

"But wait a bit," the Oysters cried,
   "Before we have our chat;
For some of us are out of breath,
   And all of us are fat!"
"No hurry!" said the Carpenter,
   They thanked him much for that.

"A loaf of bread," the Walrus said,
   "Is what we chiefly need:
Pepper and vinegar besides
   Are very good indeed—
Now, if you're ready, Oysters dear,
   We can begin to feed."

"But not on us!" the Oysters cried,
  Turning a little blue.
"After such kindness, that would be
  A dismal thing to do!"
"The night is fine," the Walrus said.
  "Do you admire the view?"

"It was so kind of you to come!
  And you are so very nice!"
The Carpenter said nothing but
  "Cut us another slice:
I wish you were not quite so deaf—
  I've had to ask you twice."

"It seems a shame," the Walrus said,
  "To play them such a trick,
After we've brought them out so far,
  And made them trot so quick!"

The Carpenter said nothing but
  "The butter's spread too thick!"

"I weep for you," the Walrus said:
  "I deeply sympathize."
With sobs and tears he sorted out
  Those of the largest size,
Holding his pocket-handkerchief
  Before his streaming eyes.

"O, Oysters," said the Carpenter,
  "You've had a pleasant run!
Shall we be trotting home again?"
  But answer came there none—
And this was scarcely odd, because
  They'd eaten every one.

≈⊚   **Lewis Carroll,** *Through the Looking-Glass*

(Stuffed Pig Stomach with) Oyster Filling

1 pig stomach (available at specialty markets)*
1½ dozen fresh stewing oysters with about ½ cup oyster liquid

1 package Pepperidge Farm Bread Stuffing
½ cup onion, diced
½ cup celery, diced
Salt and pepper

Remove the inner lining from the stomach and discard. Rinse the stomach well and soak it in salty water for at least 1 hour. After soaking, drain and rinse the stomach in cold water.

Purée the oysters in their liquid and add them to the bread stuffing. Stir well. Sauté the onion and celery in butter until tender, about 3 minutes. Add the onions and celery to the stuffing and stir to combine. Add salt and pepper to taste.

Fill the stomach with the stuffing and sew the openings shut with a heavy needle and thread. Cook in a covered roasting pan at 350° for about 2 hours.

MAKES 6 SERVINGS

* Alternatively, bake this stuffing in a roasting turkey.

I am a part of all I have read.
   John Kieran

Chestnuts and Stuffing

 otho

"I was looking for chestnuts," I said. I didn't want to say I went walking just to see the woods, to be outdoors in the fall weather. That wouldn't have sounded right.

"Did you find any?" Hank said.

"A few," I said. I didn't want Hank to think I went gallivanting around the woods just to be footloose. After all, I was carrying a baby. I didn't want to tell him I had gone dancing around in the woods with the flying leaves, and that I laid on the mountaintop looking into the sky till it felt like I was falling out toward the stars. The best way I could show him how helpful I was was to keep my mouth shut and fix the turkey.

<a> **Robert Morgan,** *Gap Creek*

"*Meleagris gallopavo,*" he says, and Mr. Banerji leans forward; the Latin perks him up. "A pea-brained animal, or bird-brained you might say, bred for its ability to put on weight, especially on the drumsticks"—he points these out—"certainly not for intelligence. It was originally domesticated by the Mayans." He tells a story of a turkey farm where the turkeys all died because they were too stupid to go into their shed during a thunderstorm. Instead they stood around outside, looking up at the sky with their beaks wide open and the rain ran down their throats and drowned them. He says this is a story told by farmers and probably not true, although the stupidity of the bird is legendary. He says that the wild turkey once abundant in the deciduous forests in these regions, is far more intelligent and can elude even practiced hunters. Also it can fly.

<a> **Margaret Atwood,** *Cat's Eye*

Charles Wallace sat there tucking away turkey and dressing as though it were the most delicious thing he had ever tasted. He was dressed like Charles Wallace; he looked like Charles Wallace; he had the same sandy brown hair, the same face that had not yet lost its baby roundness. Only the eyes were different, for the black was still swallowed up in blue. But it was far more than this that made Meg feel that Charles Wallace was gone, that the little boy in his place was only a copy of Charles Wallace, only a doll.

She fought down a sob. "Where is he?" she demanded of the man with red eyes. "What have you done with him? Where is Charles Wallace?"

"But my dear child, you are hysterical," the man thought at her. "He is right there, before you, well and happy. Completely well and happy for the first time in his life. And he is finishing his dinner, which you also would be wise to do."

◖ Madeleine L'Engle, *A Wrinkle in Time*

Chestnut Stuffing for Meleagris Gallopavo (Turkey)

1 quart whole chestnuts

1 tablespoon butter or margarine

2½ cups bread crumbs

1 egg, beaten

1 cup celery, finely chopped

1 onion, finely chopped

¼ cup butter or margarine, melted

1 teaspoon salt

1 teaspoon sage

1 teaspoon thyme

½ teaspoon marjoram

Pinch nutmeg

Black pepper to taste

Make a crossed gash on the bottom of each chestnut. Place the nuts in a heavy skillet with the 1 tablespoon butter or margarine and shake them over low heat for a few minutes. Place the nuts in a 450° oven for about 10 minutes. Remove the shells and skins with a knife. Cover the chestnuts with boiling salted water and cook until tender. Drain and purée the chestnuts in a food processor. Remove the ground chestnuts, add them to the remaining ingredients and spices, and stir together thoroughly. Place the stuffing in a cleaned turkey cavity. Bake turkey according to weight and method (i.e., roasting pan, turkey bag, etc.).

I like showing Ruthie the books I take out
of the library. Books are wonderful, Ruthie
says, and then she runs her hand over them
as if she could read them in Braille.

    〜 Sandra Cisneros, *The House on Mango Street*

Amish Food

Sarah made enough food to feed the whole Amish community, much less that of her own small household plus one live-in guest. She brought bowl after bowl to the table, chicken with dumplings and vegetables swimming in sauces and meat that had been cooked to the point where it broke apart at the touch of a fork. There were relishes and breads and spiced, stewed pears. In the center of the table was a blue pitcher of fresh milk. Looking at all the rich choices, I wondered how these people could eat this way, three times a day, and not grow obese.

In addition to the three Fishers I'd met, there was an older man, who did not bother to introduce himself but seemed to know who I was all the same. From his features, I assumed he was Aaron's father; and that he most likely lived in the small apartment attached to the rear of the farmhouse. He bent his head, which caused all the others to bend their heads, a strange kinetic reaction, and began to pray silently over the food. Unsettled—when was the last time I'd said grace?—I waited until they looked up and began to ladle food onto their plates. Katie raised the pitcher of milk and poured some into her glass; then passed it to her right, to me.

I had never been a big fan of milk, but I figured that wasn't the smartest thing to admit on a dairy farm. I poured myself some and handed the pitcher to Aaron Fisher.

The Fishers laughed and talked in their Dialect, helping themselves to food when their plates were empty. Finally, Aaron leaned back in his chair and let out a phenomenal belch.

My eyes widened at the breach of etiquette—but his wife beamed at him, as if that was the grandest compliment he could ever give.

I suddenly saw a string of meals like this one, stretching out for months, with me prominently cast as the outsider. It took me a moment to realize that Aaron was asking me something. In Pennsylvania Dutch.

"The chow chow," I said in slow, careful English, following his gaze to the particular bowl. "Is that what you want?"

His chin went up a notch. "Ja," he answered.

I flattened my hands on the table. "In the future, I'd prefer it if you asked me questions in my own language, Mr. Fisher."

"We don't speak English at the supper table," Katie answered.

My gaze never left Aaron Fisher's face. "You do now," I said.

Jodi Picoult, *Plain Truth*

A NOTE FROM JODI PICOULT: When I wrote Plain Truth, *I did research by living on an Amish dairy farm for a while. To pitch in, I spent a great deal of time doing what that family's Amish women did—that is, creating the bountiful buffets of food that fill the table three times a day. Not only was I amazed by the sheer volume of food—I was struck by the way family dynamics were really brought into focus across a meal. It seemed to me that the dinner table would be the ultimate place for a power struggle between Ellie, my narrating big-city lawyer, and the Fishers—the Amish family of the girl she'd been asked to defend against a murder charge.*

Amish Chicken and Dumplings

1 4-pound chicken

1 onion, diced

4 medium potatoes, peeled and
    cut into chunks

2 carrots, sliced

2 stalks celery, diced

Salt and pepper to taste

DUMPLING DOUGH:

2 eggs   2 to 3 tablespoons milk
2 cups flour

Cook chicken in 2 quarts of water until nearly tender. Add onion, potatoes, carrots, and celery and cook until tender. Remove chicken from
broth. Remove meat from bones and set aside. Meanwhile, bring broth
to a boil. Make dumplings by breaking eggs into the flour, working together, and adding milk to make a soft dough. Drop tablespoonfuls of
dumpling dough into the boiling broth and cook for twenty minutes.
Add chicken meat to the broth and serve steaming.

MAKES 4 TO 6 SERVINGS

—Recipe contributed by Jodi Picoult

1-2-3-4 Cake

1 cup butter or margarine   ½ teaspoon salt
2 cups sugar   3 teaspoons baking powder
4 eggs   1 cup sour cream
3 cups flour (or, for chocoholics,   1 teaspoon vanilla
    use 2½ cups flour and ½ cup
    cocoa)

Cream butter or margarine, add sugar gradually and beat until light and
fluffy. Add eggs one by one, beating well after each addition. Sift dry ingredients together. Combine sour cream and vanilla. Add dry ingredients and sour cream alternately to the batter, beating well. Bake in a
greased bread pan at 350° for about 1 hour.

—Recipe contributed by Jodi Picoult

If you wish to learn the highest truths, begin with the alphabet.

꧁ **Japanese proverb**

Dumplings

∽

"But, with all of her spooky ways, there wasn't a better cook in the state of Alabama. Even at eleven, they say she could make the most delicious biscuits and gravy, cobbler, fried chicken, turnip greens, and black-eyed peas. And her dumplings were so light they would float in the air and you'd have to catch 'em to eat 'em. All the recipes that were used at the café were hers. She taught Idgie and Ruth everything they knew about cooking."

꧁ **Fannie Flagg,** *Fried Green Tomatoes at the Whistle Stop Café*

Catch 'Em to Eat 'Em
Chicken and Dumplings

∽

4 split, boneless chicken breasts

1 cup flour, seasoned with salt
   and pepper

2 tablespoons butter or
   margarine

1 tablespoon olive oil

8 large carrots, sliced

1 onion, chopped

1 small bay leaf

½ teaspoon thyme

2 14-ounce cans low-salt chicken
   broth

½ cup apple juice

1 bag frozen peas

DUMPLINGS:

1½ cups all-purpose flour   ½ teaspoon salt
½ cup cornmeal   1 cup milk
1 tablespoon baking powder

Rinse the chicken and pat dry. Roll the meat in the seasoned flour. In a large kettle, brown the chicken in melted butter and oil over medium-high heat, about 5 minutes per side. Remove the chicken and set aside on a plate.

Sauté the carrots and onion with the bay leaf and thyme in the same kettle used to brown the chicken, about three minutes. Add the broth, juice and chicken. Bring the liquid to a boil. Reduce heat, cover, and simmer until chicken is cooked through, about 10 to 15 minutes.

While chicken is cooking, prepare dumplings. Mix dry ingredients in a large bowl. Stir in the milk with a fork until a dough is attained.

Scoop dumplings out of dough with a large soup spoon and arrange them over the top of the cooking chicken mixture. Simmer chicken and dumplings, covered, for about 6 minutes. Add the peas and cook until dumplings and peas are done, about 6 additional minutes. (Dumplings are done when a wooden toothpick inserted in center comes out clean.) Discard bay leaf.

MAKES 4 TO 6 SERVINGS

When we tell stories, when we try to tell our experiences—verbalize them—then we take our paths toward understanding.

◁ **Edwidge Danticat**

Coq au Vin

At Jen's insistence, Maggie had begun joining them at dinner and once Maggie had even cooked, making coq au vin. "I don't think anybody makes this anymore," she admitted to all of them. "But in my day it was the classy dish, sort of like my mother's chicken à la king." Everybody ate the chicken happily, simply because it was something different. "I had to cheat, of course, with the wine," she said. "I suppose you can't call it coq au vin when you're using flat grape soda." She lowered her voice. "But I did add a little alcohol. Bryce smuggled it in to me. He injected some vodka into oranges that he brought me."

Olivia Goldsmith, *Pen Pals*

As you know, Hortense, I have always been interested in the culinary arts as a recreational pastime, but I have not yet offered my services in the "kitchen" such as it is (another excellent example of the inadequacies of language) nor indeed have I been asked to help with meal preparation. However, if I am to live here among these people I fully intend to take a turn at the stove . . . the fire . . . Perhaps I will make my tentmates a lovely little French dish, say a delightful Coq au Vin . . . Harry's favorite repast . . . though, of course, the first question that presents itself is where might I obtain a decent bottle of French burgundy wine? Or for that matter, any bottle of wine . . . Hah! . . . But now I allow myself to drift off again into thought of that old life, which can only make this new one so much more precarious and difficult, and . . . insupportable.

Jim Fergus, *One Thousand White Women*

A NOTE FROM JIM FERGUS: Given the unavailability of roosters in the markets, traditional coq au vin is difficult to find in America, and even in France. A large roasting chicken or capon can be substituted. If you happen to be a bird hunter, this recipe can also be used for cock grouse or rooster pheasants. (Note: It's important to use a good-quality red French Burgundy in this recipe.)

Nostalgic Coq au Vin
(Rooster in Red Wine)

1 large roasting chicken, capon,
   or rooster
2 yellow onions, chopped
4 shallots, chopped
2 carrots, chopped
4 garlic cloves, chopped
Bouquet garni (a bundle of
   selected herbs tied together,
   such as a few sprigs of
   parsley and thyme, bay leaf,
   and a couple short stalks of
   celery with leaves)

2 bottles good red French
   Burgundy
Salt and pepper to taste
2 to 4 tablespoons vegetable oil
2 tablespoons flour
¼ cup cognac
1 pint pearl onions
½ cup salt pork or bacon, diced
¾ pound cremini mushrooms or
   small white mushrooms
Toasted baguette slices, if desired

Cut up a large roasting chicken, capon, or rooster and place pieces in a large bowl with yellow onions, shallots, carrots, garlic cloves, and a *bouquet garni*. Add wine, mix all ingredients thoroughly, and marinate for 24 hours.

Remove chicken from marinade (reserve), pat dry with paper towel, season with salt and pepper, and brown in vegetable oil in a large, heavy skillet or casserole. Remove chicken pieces from pan and set aside. Add flour to pan and cook, stirring, until flour browns. Return chicken to pan, pour in cognac, and remove pan from heat. Light cognac with match or lighter. When flames extinguish, return pan to burner, add marinade, and bring to a boil. Reduce heat and simmer, partly covered, until chicken is tender, 1½ to 2 hours for a large chicken or capon, 3 hours or longer for an old rooster.

Remove chicken from pan, strain sauce, and return chicken and sauce to pan. Simmer uncovered over low heat until sauce is reduced by half.

Meanwhile, boil pearl onions for about 10 minutes and drain.

Sauté salt pork or bacon in a skillet until brown and crispy. Remove with slotted spoon and add to chicken. Sauté pearl onions and mushrooms in pork fat until lightly browned. Drain and add mushrooms and pearl onions to chicken. Serve with toasted slices of baguette.

—Recipe contributed by Jim Fergus

> When I don't write for a while, something feels wrong and missing.
>
>   Joanna Hershon

Chicken

ᴄᴠɔ

She had stayed for supper. Made supper, even. She had fussed a lot ("Is this what you call a chicken?" "How old is this rosemary?" "Have you no fresh garlic, for god sake?"), but he had thoroughly enjoyed it. He knew she was in a good mood when she bossed him around. ("Get me a sharp knife, no, a clean sharp knife, hand me a bunch of that flour, please, what? Is this all the flour? Don't tell me!") He had loved every minute of it. Fuss, flour on the floor, the smell of oil and butter smoking on the stove. The hiss and sizzle of delicious things hitting a hot frying pan. Ellie exclaiming on the sorry state of his kitchen floor (mopped that very morning) and refusing to touch the dish towels. He had stayed in the kitchen and watched her cook, his hands behind his back, while she frowned and measured and threw things together. Then they had eaten the chicken she had invented (using honey and soy sauce and an ancient bottle of horseradish) and it had been delicious. After supper they had watched a *Star Trek* rerun sitting on the red velvet sofa side by side (Walter holding his breath) and then she'd asked him some questions.

"Have you gone out at all in the last six months?"

"You mean out? As in with a woman?" He had shaken his head. "Why would I do that?" He had been genuinely bewildered.

◖ Abigail Thomas, "Walter's Book" from *Herb's Pajamas*

Worth-the-Fuss Grilled Lemon Chicken

∽

1 pound skinless, boneless chicken breasts

MARINADE:

2 tablespoons honey

1 tablespoon lemon juice

1 tablespoon soy sauce

1 teaspoon fresh, grated lemon
   zest

1 12-ounce can 7 UP

SAUCE:

½ cup water

1 tablespoon lemon juice

1 tablespoon honey

1 tablespoon cornstarch

½ teaspoon chicken bouillon
   granules

1 teaspoon fresh, grated lemon
   zest

Arrange the rinsed chicken in a lightly greased 8-inch square baking dish.

In a small bowl, combine the marinade ingredients. Pour the marinade over the chicken, cover, and marinate in refrigerator for 3 hours.

After the meat has been marinated, prepare a grill or broiler. Remove the chicken from the dish and discard the marinade. Slow-cook the chicken on a hot grill or under a broiler for about 25 minutes. If using a broiler, place pan on middle rack of oven, keeping meat away from the flame. Flip the chicken once while cooking for even baking.

While the chicken is cooking, combine the remaining ingredients for the sauce in a small saucepan. Cook the sauce over medium heat, stirring constantly, until thickened. Serve over hot grilled chicken.

MAKES 4 SERVINGS

In the meantime, Janey, blissfully unaware of Lupe's troubled heart, was reveling in her new-found treasure. She hardly knew where to start. . . . All she wanted was to be let alone for as long a time as possible to enjoy the feast. At last she decided on her book, and picking it up as reverently as she always did the willow plate, she backed over to a chair and began to read.

Doris Gates, *Blue Willow*

"I've lost some weight."

"Well, that's good," Ginelli said. "You were too big, William. I gotta say that, too big. How much you lose?"

"Twenty pounds."

"Hey! Congratulations! And your heart thanks you, too. Hard to lose weight, isn't it?" . . .

. . . "It actually wasn't hard at all."

"Well, you come on in to Brothers, William. I'm gonna fix you my own special. Chicken Neapolitan. It'll put all that weight back on in one meal."

"I might just take you up on that," Billy said, smiling a little. He could see himself in the mirror on his study wall, and there seemed to be too many teeth in his smile. Too many teeth, too close to the front of his mouth. He stopped smiling.

Stephen King (writing as Richard Bachman), *Thinner*

Non-Dieter's Delight
Chicken Neapolitan

1⅓ to 1½ pounds chicken breast tenders
Garlic powder
Ground black pepper
Dried basil
2 tablespoons olive oil
3 cups rinsed and peeled potatoes, cut into 1-inch cubes
1 red or green bell pepper, cut into strips
½ cup yellow onion, chopped

2 8-ounce cans tomato sauce
2 tablespoons fresh parsley, chopped
1 teaspoon fresh garlic, chopped
1 teaspoon salt
⅛ teaspoon ground seasoned black pepper
½ teaspoon dried basil
½ cup white cooking wine
1 cup chicken broth
¾ cup grated cheddar cheese

Clean chicken and pat dry. Sprinkle the meat with garlic powder, black pepper, and basil on both sides. In a large skillet, lightly brown the chicken in oil over medium-high heat, about 2 minutes per side. Reserve oil in the skillet.

Place the chicken in a large, heavy-bottomed pot. Add potatoes and bell pepper.

Sauté the onion in the reserved oil until soft, about 2 minutes.

In a medium bowl, combine the tomato sauce, onion, parsley, garlic, salt, black pepper, and basil. Stir well. Pour this mixture over the chicken, potatoes, and bell pepper in the pot. Add the wine and chicken broth. Bring to a boil, then reduce heat, partly cover, and simmer for about 1 hour. Serve topped with cheddar cheese.

MAKES 6 SERVINGS

It has occurred to me that the way a writer acquaints his readers with a character in his story should be no different from the way we come to know someone in ordinary life.

⊸ Jamie Langston Turner, *Some Wildflower in My Heart*

For the party I was making sweet-and-sour chicken, more or less on a dare, out of one of Lou Ann's magazines. The folks at Burger Derby should see me now, I thought. I had originally planned to make navy-bean soup, in celebration of Turtle's first word, but by the end of the week she had said so many new words I couldn't have fit them all in Hungarian goulash. She seemed to have a one-track vocabulary, like Lou Ann's hypochondriac mother-in-law, though fortunately Turtle's ran to vegetables instead of diseases.

⊸ Barbara Kingsolver, *The Bean Trees*

Any Beginner's Sweet-and-Sour Chicken

1 egg, beaten
3 tablespoons all-purpose flour
1 teaspoon salt
1 teaspoon dry sherry

1 pound chicken breast tenders,
    tendon removed and cut in
    half
1 tablespoon butter or margarine
2 tablespoons water, divided

SAUCE:

1 8-ounce can pineapple chunks   2 tablespoons soy sauce
   with juice   1 teaspoon Worcestershire sauce
3 tablespoons vinegar   2 tablespoons cornstarch mixed in
4 tablespoons sugar   2 tablespoons water

GARNISH:

⅓ cup yellow pepper, chopped   ⅓ cup maraschino cherries, stems
                                      removed

Mix the egg, flour, salt, and sherry together in a medium-sized bowl. Clean and cut the chicken tenders to size, add them to the bowl, and stir thoroughly to coat with the batter. Melt 1 tablespoon butter or margarine in a large frying pan. Add the chicken tenders with 1 tablespoon water to the pan, cover, and cook on medium-high heat for about 4 minutes, until chicken is golden brown on bottom side. Flip each piece of chicken to ensure even cooking. Add another tablespoon of water, cover and cook on medium-high heat for another 4 minutes, or until chicken is cooked through. Remove pan from heat, but keep chicken covered during preparation of the sauce.

Combine all the ingredients for the sauce in a saucepan. Bring to a boil and cook an additional 2 minutes, stirring continuously. Pour the sauce over the chicken and stir until chicken is thoroughly coated.

To serve, garnish with yellow pepper and maraschino cherries.

MAKES 4 SERVINGS

A book is a way of speculating about life. A way of asking yourself questions that you hope reverberate in the reader.
   Sue Miller

Beef Stroganoff

I open the refrigerator, pull out the steak. I'm making beef Stroganoff, David's favorite. *God, that's good!* he said, last time I made it. *You can cook, honey; that you can do.* I slice the meat thinly, look out the window at the tree branches swaying in the wind. It's supposed to storm tonight. *A power outage, and David stays to take care of us, how could he leave?*

Elizabeth Berg, *Open House*

Impressive Beef Stroganoff

1¼ pounds beef sirloin
2 tablespoons butter or
  margarine
1 yellow onion, chopped
½ teaspoon salt
½ teaspoon pepper
2 large portobello mushrooms,
  chopped
¼ cup dry white wine

¼ teaspoon basil
Pinch nutmeg
¾ cup milk
1 tablespoon all-purpose flour
1 cup sour cream
1 12-ounce package spinach
  fettuccine, cooked and
  drizzled with melted butter or
  margarine

Cut the beef across the grain into ¼-inch-thick slices. Then cut the slices into 1-inch-wide strips. Melt 1 tablespoon butter or margarine in a large frying pan and brown the meat on high heat for about 5 minutes, flipping once to cook evenly.

Reduce heat to medium-high, add the onion, salt, and pepper, and sauté an additional 2 minutes.

Remove the meat and onions from the pan, set aside in a bowl, and cover to keep warm. Add the mushrooms and remaining 1 tablespoon butter or margarine to the pan and sauté for 5 minutes, or until tender.

Return the meat and onion to the pan with the mushrooms. Add the white wine, basil, and nutmeg. Stir and heat for about 2 minutes over medium heat.

Remove the meat, mushrooms, and onions from the pan and set aside in covered bowl. Stir the milk and flour into the drippings left in the pan, heating over low heat until the sauce is somewhat thickened, for 1 to 2 minutes. Return the meat, mushrooms, and onions to the pan. Stir in the sour cream and warm the mixture over low heat for about 1 minute. Serve over buttered spinach fettuccine.

MAKES 4 TO 6 SERVINGS

But as the rest of the world grew stranger, one thing became increasingly clear. And that was the reason the two of us were here. Why others should suffer we were not shown. As for us, from morning until lights-out, whenever we were not in ranks for roll call, our Bible was the center of an ever-widening circle of help and hope. Like waifs clustered around a blazing fire, we gathered about it, holding out our hearts to its warmth and light. The blacker the night around us grew, the brighter and truer and more beautiful burned the word of God.

⟡ **Corrie ten Boom,** *The Hiding Place*

Pork

⟡⟢

I hadn't had a bite to eat since yesterday, so Jim he got out some corn-dodgers and buttermilk, and pork and cabbage and greens—there ain't nothing in the world so good when it's cooked right—and whilst I eat my supper we talked and had a good time.

⟡ **Mark Twain,** *The Adventures of Huckleberry Finn*

Pork Roast with Cabbage

1 2-pound boneless pork loin, center roast
6 small red potatoes, rinsed
⅛ teaspoon ground black pepper
¼ teaspoon garlic powder
¼ to ½ teaspoon paprika
½ teaspoon dried rosemary, chopped fine
½ onion, chopped fine
1 small head green cabbage, leaves peeled apart, rinsed and drained

Preheat oven to 325°. Rinse the pork loin and pat dry with paper towel. Place the meat in the center of a large casserole dish or roasting pan. Arrange the potatoes around the meat. Add ⅛ inch of water to the bottom of the pan. Sprinkle the meat with black pepper, garlic powder, paprika, rosemary, and onion.

Cover and bake for about 1½ hours or until internal temperature reaches 170°. Add the cabbage when 30 minutes remain in the baking time. Arrange the cabbage over the top of the meat and potatoes. Steam any remaining cabbage that does not fit in the pan separately on the stovetop. Serve with green salad.

MAKES 4 TO 6 SERVINGS

The role of the writer is not to say what all can say but what we are unable to say.

✎ Anaïs Nin

Veal

ᐕᐸ

Readers of John Grisham's *The Firm* will remember the extravagant meal Abby prepares for her husband, Mitch McDeere, thinking he will finally take an evening away from the tax firm and spend it with her. When Mitch fails to come home, she keeps her preparations in place and serves the dinner to him for breakfast. At first, Mitch is impressed by the lavish table setting, then confused when he finds veal piccata presented under a covered silver dish. Analyzing the situation for a moment, Mitch settles on the most appropriate response he can give and says, "Smells good."

"Good Life" Veal Piccata

ᐕᐸ

1 pound thin veal cutlets for
   scaloppini
⅓ cup all-purpose flour
1 teaspoon salt
¼ teaspoon ground black pepper
3 tablespoons vegetable oil
2 tablespoons chablis or other
   dry white wine

¼ cup lemon juice
½ cup mushrooms, cleaned and
   chopped
½ cup artichoke hearts, chopped
2 tablespoons butter or margarine
10 ounces linguine, cooked

Pound the veal with a flat-surfaced mallet between 2 pieces of waxed paper until they are about ¼ inch thick. Combine the flour, salt, and pepper in a bowl. Dip the veal in the flour mixture and coat thoroughly. Cook the veal over medium heat in a large frying pan with vegetable oil, about 3 minutes, then remove veal from the pan.

Add the wine and lemon juice to the pan with reserved drippings and bring to a boil. Stir the liquid with a wooden spoon until thickened. Return the veal to the pan along with the mushrooms, artichoke hearts, and butter or margarine. Cover and simmer for about 5 minutes.

Serve with cooked linguine.

MAKES 4 SERVINGS

—Recipe inspired by John Grisham

Imagination is more important than knowledge.

⟨ᴄ Albert Einstein

Saltimbocca

∾

Pausing, Michael took a deep swallow of wine. "So," he continued, "he buys into lawful enterprises, including whatever cash businesses he can get his hands on—caterers, limo services, vending machine operations, parking lots, bars, and restaurants. The illegal money gets siphoned into all these different fronts, which scrupulously report every dime, then fiddle the books to make proceeds of heroin look like they came from, say, a zillion plates of saltimbocca."

His eyes, Stella realized, sparkled with quiet laughter. Stiffly, she put down her wine. "*This* place."

Michael nodded. "Moro's. The food's good, by the way."

⟨ᴄ **Richard North Patterson,** *Dark Lady*

Law-Abiding Saltimbocca

1 pound thin veal cutlets for scaloppini (yields about eight cutlets), rinsed and patted dry
4 ounces sliced prosciutto
½ cup flour with ½ teaspoon salt and ½ teaspoon lemon pepper

8 thin slices (deli-style) provolone (about ¼ pound)
4 tablespoons butter or margarine
1 tablespoon vegetable oil
½ cup dry white wine
1 cup chicken broth
1 lemon, sliced into wedges for serving

Cover each piece of veal with a slice of prosciutto, trimmed to fit. The meat should stick together well without need for toothpicks to secure. Melt the butter or margarine with oil in a large skillet over medium heat. Dredge the veal-prosciutto patties in the flour mixture and sauté over medium heat, with the prosciutto side down first. Cook each side about 1 minute. Immediately transfer the meat to a heated dish and top each veal-prosciutto patty with a slice of provolone. After all the meat has been cooked, pour wine and broth into the skillet. Stir over high heat, scraping up leftover drippings from the bottom of the pan. Bring to a simmer, then remove pan from heat and pour the sauce over the veal. Serve at once with lemon wedges.

MAKES 4 SERVINGS

I live in gratitude to my parents for initiating me—and as early as I begged for it, without keeping me waiting—into knowledge, into the world, into reading.

    Eudora Welty, *One Writer's Beginnings*

Asian Food

ᴄⅳᴐ

After dinner one stiflingly hot day, 2 July 1943, we were planning next day's menu with Cook. Aunt Baba suggested we have Tianjin dumplings instead of rice. Freshly made with chives, ground pork, and spring onions, these dumplings were a great favorite among us children. We were all shouting out ridiculously high numbers as to how many we could eat. Grandmother developed a headache from all the commotion. She went to her room, lit a cigarette and lay down. Aunt Baba sat by her and narrated a story from *The Legend of the Monkey King*. Even though Grandmother knew many tales from the well-known Chinese classic, she found it relaxing to hear them told again and again by her daughter.

ᴄⅿᴐ   Adeline Yen Mah, *Falling Leaves: The True Story of an Unwanted Chinese Daughter*

Tianjin Dumplings

ᴄⅳᴐ

½ pound ground pork

⅛ pound uncooked shrimp,
　　shelled, deveined, and
　　chopped

½ teaspoon ground coriander

2 tablespoons green onions,
　　finely chopped

2 teaspoons chives, finely
　　chopped

2 teaspoons garlic, minced

½ teaspoon ground black pepper

2 teaspoons sugar

2 tablespoons soy sauce

¼ teaspoon ground ginger

2 tablespoons coconut milk

1 12-ounce package of square
　　wonton wrappers (about 50
　　individual wrappers)

Crisp, large green lettuce leaves
　　for steaming or parchment
　　paper lightly sprayed with oil

DIPPING SAUCE:

¼ cup soy sauce

3 tablespoons rice vinegar

2 tablespoons canola oil

1 teaspoon Oriental sesame oil

Pinch sugar

Mix the pork, shrimp, coriander, green onions, chives, garlic, black pepper, sugar, soy sauce, ginger, and coconut milk together in a bowl and then refrigerate for about 30 minutes to develop flavors. Place 1 teaspoon of filling in the center of each wonton wrapper. Fold the wrapper in half to make a triangle and crimp edges closed. Edges can be sealed by first folding one side two times toward filling. Flip wonton over and seal second side in same manner. Fold the two corners at each end of seam. (There are many ways to seal the wonton. Use a method that works well for you.)

Put as many wontons as room allows in steamer lined with lettuce leaves or parchment paper lightly coated with vegetable oil. Cooked wontons will stick together, so keep them separated. The leaves or paper will prevent the wontons from sticking to the steamer. Cover and steam for 15 minutes. Add water as needed to replenish what evaporates. A second layer of wontons can be placed on top of the first in the steamer by making a dividing layer with lettuce leaves or parchment paper to prevent wontons from sticking to one another.

To make dipping sauce whisk all ingredients together and serve warmed or cool with cooked wontons.

MAKES ABOUT 45 DUMPLINGS

W ords are, of course, the most powerful drug used by mankind.

 Rudyard Kipling

Pesto and Stuffed Sole

Lila had thought that if they had went through with it, she would feel absorbed by him, and perhaps absolved from her range of discomforts, which, as it happened, was not the case at all. Though Ben kept squeezing her shoulder, running his hand over her messy hair, she was still on her own, still her addled self, looking out the same borrowed car window, and thinking about Suzanne E. Wolfe, Suzanne Hannon, wife, art dealer, fan of orchids and lilies.

When they returned that Saturday night, Lila hadn't intended on staying at Ben's apartment, but they were both hungry and Ben had a full fridge and felt like cooking. After linguini and pesto, an enormous pot of broccoli, and a bottle of red wine, they started kissing on the couch, and by the time they acknowledged it was happening again, they were skidding, naked, from the living room to the bedroom.

Joanna Hershon, *Swimming*

Sun-Dried Tomato Pesto

⅓ cup sun-dried tomatoes

1 14-ounce can vegetable broth

1 cup basil leaves (not packed)

6 cloves garlic, peeled

½ cup pecans, chopped

¼ cup olive oil, divided

1 teaspoon lemon juice

Soak tomatoes in vegetable broth for 30 minutes. Drain broth and combine the tomatoes, basil, garlic, pecans, and ⅛ cup olive oil in a food processor and process until coarsely chopped. Add remaining olive oil, cheese, and lemon juice and process until smooth. To serve, mix a portion of the pesto into cooked pasta and stir to distribute, or serve with crackers.

Her Sole Stuffed with Shrimp

16 Dover sole fillets, long enough to roll around 2 tablespoons of
    stuffing, about 8 inches in length

STUFFING:

½ pound cooked shrimp, chopped

1 cup dried bread crumbs

2 tablespoons fresh parsley,
    chopped

1 tablespoon fresh chives,
    chopped

1 teaspoon fresh tarragon,
    chopped

2 teaspoons fresh garlic, chopped

½ teaspoon salt

¼ teaspoon ground black pepper

2 eggs, beaten

6 to 8 tablespoons butter or
    margarine, melted

TOPPING:

1 egg, beaten

½ teaspoon fresh grated lime zest

½ tablespoon lime juice

Bread crumbs for sprinkling

1 lime, cut into wedges

Rinse fillets and pat dry. Combine the shrimp, bread crumbs, herbs, garlic, salt, and pepper for stuffing in a bowl. Add the 2 beaten eggs and butter and mix well. Place about 2 to 3 tablespoons of stuffing near end of one fillet and roll up fillet around it. Place stuffed fish roll seam-side down in greased glass baking dish. Repeat for each fillet. Combine remaining beaten egg, lime zest, and lime juice, and whisk well. Brush the rolled fillets with the mixture; sprinkle with bread crumbs. Bake at 350° for about 30 minutes. Fish is done when it just starts to split. Serve with lime wedges.

MAKES ABOUT 6 SERVINGS

> A man will turn over half a library to make one book.
> ◁ **Samuel Johnson**

Crab and Slaw

ⱷⱾⱷ

"I don't have much time, and need something easy and light," I said.

A shadow passed over her face as she opened a jar of horseradish. "I'm afraid I can imagine what you've been doing," she said. "Been hearing it on the news." She shook her head. "You must be plumb worn out. I don't know how you sleep. Let me tell you what to do for yourself tonight."

She walked over to a case of chilled blue crabs. Without asking, she selected a pound of meat in a carton.

"Fresh from Tangier Island. Hand-picked it myself, and you tell me if you find even a trace of cartilage or shell. You're not eating alone, are you?" she said.

"No."

"That's good to hear."

She winked at me. I had brought Wesley in here before.

She picked out six jumbo shrimp, peeled and deveined, and wrapped them. Then she set a jar of her homemade cocktail sauce on the counter by the cash register.

"I got a little carried away with the horseradish," she said, "so it will make your eyes water, but it's good." She began ringing up my purchases. "You sauté the shrimp so quick their butts barely hit the pan, got it? Chill 'em, and have that as an appetizer. By the way, those and the sauce are on the house."

"You don't need to . . ."

She waved me off. "As for the crab, honey, listen up. One egg slightly beaten, one-half teaspoon dry mustard, a dash or two of Worcestershire sauce, four unsalted soda crackers, crushed. Chop up an onion, a Vidalia if you're still hoarding any from summer. One green pepper, chop that. A teaspoon or two of parsley, salt and pepper to taste."

"Sounds fabulous," I gratefully said. "Bev, what would I do without you?"

"Now gently mix all that together and shape it into patties." She made a motion with her hands. "Sauté in oil over medium heat until lightly browned. Maybe fix him a salad or get some of my slaw," she said. "And that's as much as I would fuss over any man."

Patricia Cornwell, *Unnatural Exposure*

Bev's No-Fuss Crab Cakes

1 pound crabmeat, fresh or
  canned
1 egg, slightly beaten
½ teaspoon dry mustard
Dash Worcestershire sauce
4 unsalted soda crackers, crushed

1 yellow onion, finely chopped
1 green pepper, finely chopped
1 to 2 teaspoons fresh parsley,
  finely chopped
Salt and pepper to taste
2 tablespoons olive oil

If using canned meat, drain well. Mix all the ingredients well in a large bowl, and shape meat mixture into patties. In a large frying pan, sauté the patties in olive oil over medium heat until each side is evenly cooked and lightly browned. Serve with sliced lemon and coleslaw.

MAKES 6 TO 8 SERVINGS

—Recipe inspired by Patricia Cornwell

Coleslaw

1 cup sour cream
¼ cup white vinegar
½ cup vegetable oil
3 tablespoons sugar
½ tablespoon celery seed

½ tablespoon salt
7 cups green cabbage, finely shredded
5 carrots, rinsed, peeled, and grated

Combine the sour cream, vinegar, oil, sugar, celery seed, and salt in a large bowl. Add the cabbage and carrots and toss until the cabbage is well coated. Chill for at least 1 to 2 hours before serving.

MAKES 10 TO 12 SERVINGS

A house without books is a room without a soul.

& Marcus Tullius Cicero

Shrimp

❧

I'm supposed to be a feminist. It's part of my identity, my persona, it goes with Irish, ag-nostic, lapsed Democrat. Old maid. I'm supposed to be *above* thinking that excessive shrimp-cleaning, apple-peeling, and snow pea string-pulling are only worth it if men are coming to dinner.

Ach, but I do love my gerruls. I was thinking in a Scottish brogue, because I'd just heard this guy interviewed on NPR, Lonnie McSomething. He wrote a profane Glaswegian coming-of-age novel, big deal, and now they're treating him like the Second Coming. No jealousy here, though, no siree. I flicked off the radio with the side of my wrist and started on another pile of shrimp.

Anyway, I go to at least as much trouble when it's my turn for the women's group as I do for dinner parties with couples. And a hell of a lot more trouble than I go to for indi-vidual guys, who are lucky to get a cup of coffee in the morning before I push them out the door. Politely—I'm always polite. And I enjoy cooking for my gerruls. Three of us are in an unspoken competition for second best chef (Isabel has a lock on first), and tonight's curried shrimp with snow peas and apples is a tough contender. Plus I have made a cake. Not from scratch—what am I? June Cleaver?—but I did add red food coloring to the white frosting and write in big letters, over an extremely artistic rendering of an hourglass, "Two Years & Counting—You Go Girl!" That's how long it's been, two years this month, since Isabel found the lump in her breast. They say you can't really start to relax until five years have passed, but this is still an anniversary, and by God, we're celebrating.

☙ **Patricia Gaffney,** *The Saving Graces*

Emma's Curried Shrimp with Snow Peas and Apples

1 pound shrimp, shelled,
   deveined, and rinsed
1 tablespoon curry powder
¼ teaspoon salt
2 large Granny Smith apples,
   pared, cored, and sliced
2 tablespoons sugar

4 tablespoons butter or margarine
2 8-ounce cans water chestnuts,
   drained
½ pound snow peas, stems and
   strings removed, rinsed
1 cup chicken broth

Sprinkle the shrimp with curry powder and salt. Set aside.

Sprinkle the apple slices with sugar and sauté them in butter in a large frying pan or wok for about 3 minutes. Remove the apple slices from the pan. Set aside and cover.

Sauté the water chestnuts and snow peas in the same pan used for apples, about 4 to 6 minutes. Add the chicken broth. Bring the broth to a boil, then stir in the shrimp. Cook until shrimp turn pink, about 2 to 4 minutes. Add the apple slices and cook an additional minute to warm through.

Serve with rice or rice noodles.

MAKES 6 GENEROUS SERVINGS

—Inspired by and created with Patricia Gaffney

Books, books, books! I had found the secret of a garret-room piled high with cases in my father's name; piled high, packed large,—where, creeping in and out among the giant fossils of my past, like some small nimble mouse between the ribs of a mastodon, I nibbled here and there at this or that box, pulling through the gap, in heats of terror, haste, victorious joy, the first book first. And how I felt it beat under my pillow, in the morning's dark. An hour before the sun would let me read! My books!

   Elizabeth Barrett Browning

Crab and Onions

"I've done it again," she said, sniffing. "I can never get it right. I sat down at my drawing table for just one minute. One minute! An hour later, I looked up, and the rice had boiled over and the roast had burned, and well, there you have it."

"Whatever your hand finds to do, do it with all your might!" he quoted cheerfully from Ecclesiastes. "You must have been doing something you liked."

She sighed. "I was drawing moles."

Moles again! That explains it, thought her caller. "Look here," he said, "if you don't mind, let me experiment with this." He made a broad gesture toward the ruined dinner.

"It will take a miracle," she said flatly.

"I'd be very open to a good miracle. Where's your carving knife?"

He drew the sharp knife across the end of the roast, and a thick slice peeled away neatly. "Well now! Just the way I like it. Overdone on the outside and rare in the middle." He carved a sliver and handed it to his hostess on the point of the blade. "See what you think."

Cynthia eyed it suspiciously, then did as he suggested. "Delicious!" she declared with feeling. "It is a miracle!"

He lifted the lid on the pot that had boiled over on the burner, and stirred the contents with a wooden spoon. "It's stuck on the bottom, but I think it's just right. Yes, indeed. Wild rice. A favorite!"

"You really are infernally kind," she said tartly.

"Not kind. Famished. I ran today and missed lunch entirely."

"Well," she said, the color coming back into her cheeks, "I did make a crab-meat casserole for the first course. That worked! And there are glazed onions with rosemary and honey that appear edible." She took two fragrant, steaming dishes out of the oven and set them on the counter.

"I hear you like a drop of sherry now and then," she said, and poured from a bottle with a distinguished label. She handed him a glass, and poured one for herself.

"You've prepared a grand feast!" exclaimed her guest.

"Cheers!" said his relieved hostess.

Jan Karon, *At Home in Mitford*

Glazed Onions with Rosemary and Honey

1 pint pearl onions, peeled
½ cup chicken broth
1½ teaspoons lemon juice
1 teaspoon fresh rosemary, chopped

Salt and pepper
1 tablespoon butter or margarine
1 tablespoon honey

Preheat oven to 375°. Place the onions in a small to medium-sized casserole dish. Combine the chicken broth and lemon juice. Pour the broth mixture over the onions. Add the rosemary and salt and pepper to taste. Cover and bake for 30 minutes, or until tender. Remove from oven and drain. Melt the butter in a skillet. Stir in the honey and baked onions. Cook over medium-high heat until lightly golden and caramelized.

MAKES 4 SERVINGS

Grand Feast Crabmeat Casserole

oⱱɔ

2 cups uncooked pasta shells	2 tablespoons butter or margarine
½ cup onion, finely chopped	½ cup dry white wine
1 cup mushrooms, chopped	Juice of ½ lemon
¼ cup celery, finely chopped,	1 bay leaf
including leaves	2 6-ounce cans crabmeat, drained
¼ pound shrimp, shelled and	1 cup frozen peas, thawed
deveined	

SAUCE:

1 cup milk	¼ cup grated Monterey Jack
1½ tablespoons flour	cheese

TOPPING:

¾ cup breadcrumbs	½ teaspoon ground black pepper
1 teaspoon fresh grated lemon	2 tablespoons butter or
zest	margarine, softened

Bring water to a boil in a pot, add pasta shells, and cook until just tender. Drain and set shells in a greased 2½-quart casserole dish.

Sauté the onion, mushrooms, celery, and shrimp in butter or margarine, wine, and lemon juice with the bay leaf in a large nonstick frying pan over medium-high heat until shrimp are pink and vegetables are tender, about 4 minutes. Remove the onion, mushrooms, and shrimp from the pan (leaving behind juices) and put them in the casserole dish. Stir the crabmeat and peas into the casserole dish. Discard bay leaf.

To make sauce, add milk and flour to the juices in the pan. Stir until flour is dissolved. Add cheese and cook over medium-high heat, stirring continuously, until thickened, about 2 minutes. Pour sauce over casserole and toss ingredients lightly to combine.

To make topping, mix all the ingredients together with a fork or fingers. Sprinkle topping over the casserole. Bake at 350° for about 25 minutes. Serve with glazed onions.

MAKES 8 SERVINGS

W̲hat is more important in a library than anything else—than everything else—is the fact that it exists.

   Archibald MacLeish

Fish

I ran the little fish through cornmeal and flour, and heated some oil in the skillet. The heads were off, the bodies slit and cleaned out, showing how elegantly simple their design was, the body a simple bag for the innards. You don't think of the human body as being designed in that way, but perhaps, I realized, it is. And what I think of as Lucille, the visible person, may be only a container—only a bag—for another girl. One nobody had ever seen, who maybe had a different name. "Ellicul," maybe.

   Josephine Humphreys, *Rich in Love*

His manner of proposing marriage struck my fancy also. One evening, two months following our meeting at the hardware store, he brought me a largemouth bass that he had caught. He filleted, breaded, and cooked it in a small deep fryer outside in my carport ("or else your house'd smell to high heaven," he said), and after we had eaten the fish along with the lima beans, corn on the cob, and fresh tomatoes he had brought from his garden, he looked me in the eye and said, "Barkis is willin'."

I was nonplused—not by the allusion, for I identified it instantly, but by the unprecedented phenomenon of Thomas' having made reference to a work of literature. Surely this distinctive quotation from *David Copperfield* was not the sort of thing one could utter accidentally.

He laughed heartily at my puzzled silence and said, "I sure hope it's not gonna take as long for you to answer me as it did for Peggotty to answer poor old Barkis." He went on to explain that his great-aunt Prissy, who had lived with his family for a time when he was a boy, had been a devoted admirer of Charles Dickens and over the course of several months had read aloud all sixty-four chapters of *David Copperfield* at the kitchen table after supper, regardless of whether anyone stayed to listen on a given evening. I believe it to be the only novel that Thomas is familiar with. If a person were limited to a single choice, however, he could do worse than to choose a work by Dickens, an author whom I deeply respect in spite of his penchant for sentimentality.

Jamie Langston Turner, *Some Wildflower in My Heart*

Willin' Fish Fillets

You, like Thomas, can strike the fancy of someone special by preparing this dish.—Jamie Langston Turner

1½ pounds bass fillets, or fish of choice

Dry white wine or water

Vegetable cooking spray or vegetable oil

COATING:

2 tablespoons butter or margarine, melted

3 tablespoons lemon juice

1 tablespoon Dijon mustard

TOPPING:

½ cup breadcrumbs

½ tablespoon paprika

½ tablespoon fresh dill, chopped

½ teaspoon salt

¼ teaspoon black pepper

Rinse and clean the fish, removing any bones. Combine the ingredients for coating and topping in separate bowls. The bowl for the topping should be wide enough to accommodate dipping the fillets. Brush fish fillets with the coating mixture, then dip in topping to cover fish with crumbs.

In lieu of cooking outside, place 1 to 2 tablespoons of vegetable oil in a nonstick skillet, or use cooking spray. Place the breaded fish fillets in the skillet. Cover and cook over medium-high heat until fish flakes easily with fork, for about 10 minutes, flipping once to cook each side. Add small amounts of dry white wine or water as necessary to skillet to prevent oil from burning in the pan. Serve with garden-fresh vegetables.

MAKES 4 SERVINGS

—Inspired by and created with Jamie Langston Turner

A NOTE FROM J. L. TURNER: I do have favorite books I'm always eager to talk about: The Habit of Being (Letters of Flannery O'Conner) *edited by Sally Fitzgerald;* Patchwork Planet *by Anne Tyler;* A Prayer for Owen Meany *by John Irving;* Cold Mountain *by Charles Frazier;* The Poisonwood Bible *by Barbara Kingsolver;* Kaaterskill Falls *by Allegra Goodman;* A Hundred White Daffodils *by Jane Kenyon;* Distinguished Guest *by Sue Miller;* Disobedience *by Jane Hamilton;* The Things They Carried *by Jim O'Brien;* We Were the Mulvaneys *by Joyce Carol Oates;* Stones from the River *by Ursula Hegi; and* Peace Like a River *by Leif Enger. These books carried me to new places and expanded my view of life. I came back to my own writing with renewed vigor and a vision of broader, greener fields to be explored.*

Persian Food

The gentleman from the San Mateo County Tax Office gave me a map for finding this home to be auctioned. He informed me to arrive by nine o'clock in the morning and be prepared to offer a ten-thousand-dollar deposit should I have a wish to purchase the property. He also to me said it was located upon a hill in Corona and if there were a widow's walk on the roof, you would see over the neighbor's homes to the Pacific Ocean below. I had not heard before this term "widow's walk," and so after traveling to the bank for a certified check of ten thousand dollars, I drove home to the high-rise and eventually last evening, after a dinner with Esmail and Naderah where I revealed nothing, a dinner of obgoosht and rice and yogurt with cucumber followed by tea, I dismissed my son from the sofreh upon the floor where we eat barefoot and I searched for "widow's walk" in our Persian-English dictionary. I found only "widow," a word in Farsi I know quite well enough, and I felt a sadness come to me because this did not seem a good sign for the purchase of a home.

Andre Dubus III, *House of Sand and Fog*

Naderah's Obgoosht
(Persian Eggplant-Lamb Casserole)

½ cup dried split green peas
1 medium eggplant, peeled and
    cubed
Olive oil
1 medium onion, chopped
1 pound lamb shoulder, cubed

⅛ teaspoon salt
⅛ teaspoon ground pepper
½ teaspoon ground turmeric
3 medium potatoes, peeled and
    cubed
1 16-ounce can stewed tomatoes

Rinse split peas. Soak for a few hours. Drain and rinse again.

In a large deep skillet, sauté the eggplant in 2 tablespoons of olive oil over low heat, stirring until all sides are cooked tender. Remove the eggplant with a slotted spoon and set aside. Sauté the onions in remaining olive oil for about 2 minutes until tender. Add the softened split peas. Stirring gently, continue to cook peas and onions for an additional 3 minutes. Add the meat and fry until meat is lightly browned on all sides. Add the salt, pepper, and turmeric. Add enough water to cover meat, place lid on skillet, and simmer for 30 minutes. Add the potatoes, eggplant, and tomatoes to stew mixture. Cover and simmer for another hour or until potatoes are tender, stirring occasionally and adding more water if needed. Serve hot with rice.

MAKES 6 SERVINGS

SERVING VARIATION: Strain broth from meat and vegetables and reserve. Fold wedges of pita bread around meat and vegetables and dip in broth.

Persian Cucumber and Yogurt

2 cups plain yogurt
2 medium cucumbers, seeds
   removed and grated
¼ cup walnuts, chopped

¼ cup raisins
Dash garlic salt (optional)
Fresh mint leaves, for garnish

Combine the yogurt, cucumbers, nuts, raisins, and garlic salt in a bowl. Chill well. Garnish with mint leaves and serve with wedges of pita bread.

A garden carried in a pocket.
  Chinese proverb

Tamales

Ⳟⲧ

She thrust at Nicholas the suitcase of clothes and an envelope bearing the address of the den where he might find Gertrudis, and she went back to her chores.

Soon she heard Pedro getting the carriage ready. Strange that he was doing that so early. But she saw from the sunlight that it was already late, that packing up some of Gertrudis' past along with her clothes, had taken longer than she imagined. It hadn't been easy to fit into the suitcase the day the three of them made their First Communion. The veil, the prayerbook, the photo taken outside the church all fit in pretty well, but not the taste of the tamales and atole Nacha had made, which they had eaten afterward with their friends and families. The little colored apricot pits had gone in, but not their laughter when they played with them in the schoolyard, nor Jovita their teacher, the swing, the smell of her bedroom or of freshly whipped chocolate. Luckily, Mama Elena's scoldings and spankings hadn't fit in either; Tita had slammed the suitcase shut before they could sneak in.

◖◗ Laura Esquivel, *Like Water for Chocolate*

Queen Nacha's Tamales

Ⳟⲧ

Dried corn husks (enough for 40 tamales)

MASA DOUGH:

4 cups corn masa (an instant corn
  flour used in Mexican
  cooking)
1 teaspoon baking powder
1 cup pork lard, whipped until
  fluffy

2 teaspoons salt
3 cups chicken broth
1 bunch fresh spinach, processed
  or blended smooth

CHILI SAUCE:

3 to 4 pounds Roma tomatoes,
seeds removed, chopped

1 large white onion, chopped

1 to 2 yellow chili peppers,
chopped

Fresh cilantro, to taste

Salt and black pepper, to taste

FILLING:

12 large eggs, hard-boiled and
mashed until crumbly

12 ounces roasted and salted
sunflower seeds, ground

2 cloves garlic, minced

Clean corn husks by removing silk and other debris. Cover them with warm water and let stand for at least 5 minutes until they are pliable. Drain and pat dry when ready to use.

Prepare masa dough by combining all the ingredients and mixing with hands until dough holds together. Set aside (keep at room temperature) and cover with plastic wrap.

Prepare sauce by combining tomatoes, onion, chili pepper, cilantro, garlic, salt, and pepper, and process until smooth in a blender or food processor.

For each tamale, lay a husk flat on a counter. Spread about 1 to 2 tablespoons of masa dough in center of husk, forming a rectangle that's flush with one edge of husk, an inch from opposite edge, an inch from bottom edge, and 3 inches from top edge. Spread a ribbon of sauce down center of masa. Sprinkle eggs over sauce and masa. Sprinkle ground sunflower seeds over top. Enclose tamale by rolling husk lengthwise around filling so masa edges meet (start with dough edge). Continue wrapping plain part of husk around outside of tamale. Fold both ends up toward center, then fold flat against tamale. Secure with heavy string if necessary.

Place closed tamales upright in a large steamer. Bring water to a boil, cover, and simmer over low heat for 90 minutes to 2 hours. Tamales are

done when masa does not stick to husk. To serve, peel off husk and pro-
vide salsa or chili sauce on the side.

MAKES 40 TAMALES

The return to the kitchen was not easy. I wanted my daughter to know her past, to
eat what I had eaten in my childhood; however, I quickly realized that I no longer remembered my family's recipes . . . I forced myself to try and remember a recipe on
my own. And that is how I discovered, as I had already known in my childhood, that
it was possible to hear voices in the kitchen.

   Laura Esquivel, *Between Two Fires*

Spinach

Spinach lasagna, King is making for me, a grand Sunday luncheon, and I'm bringing the
garlic bread. I spent the day attempting to make it from scratch, but now that it's out of the
oven, I regret the time I spent doing it. It looks awful. I break a piece off the end, taste it.
Well, if ever I think about baking bread for a living, I'll remember this. I dump the loaf into
the garbage and head for Franco's Market, home of Pepperidge Farm.

When I arrive at King's, he ushers me in with a flourish, bending low at the waist and
sweeping a dish towel through the air. He is wearing an apron and, when he stands up
straight again, I see that he has drawn on a thin mustache. I smile, reach out to touch it, but
he holds his hand up protectively. "Don't mess it up," he says. "It took me a long time to
get it so realistic-looking."

His kitchen table has been covered with a red-and-white-checked tablecloth; there are
bread sticks in a glass at the center of the table, an antipasto platter, a candle stuck into a
Chianti bottle. "Well, this is wonderful," I say, laughing.

"Thank you. Sit down. Would you like some wine?"

In the afternoon? Well, why not? I nod, pull my chair in close to the table, hold up my glass. He fills it halfway with red wine; then, when I don't put the glass down, he fills it to the top. This is my favorite restaurant.

Elizabeth Berg, *Open House*

Thanksgiving Spinach Casserole

Here is a recipe I love, and serve every Thanksgiving.—Elizabeth Berg

2 10-ounce packages frozen chopped spinach

3 3-ounce packages cream cheese with chives

Juice of 1 lemon

½ pound fresh mushrooms, sliced

Salt and pepper to taste

Preheat oven to 350°. Cook spinach just until tender, then drain. Blend in other ingredients. Place in a 1-quart casserole dish and bake for 30 minutes.

MAKES 6 TO 8 SERVINGS

—Contributed by Elizabeth Berg

In a curious way, the computer emphasizes the unique virtues of the book:

The book is small, lightweight and durable, and can be stuffed in a coat pocket, read in the waiting room, on the plane. What are planes but flying reading rooms?

E. Annie Proulx

Zucchini

The past isn't quaint while you're in it. Only at a safe distance, later, when you can see it as décor, not as the shape your life's been squeezed into.

They have Elvis Presley zucchini molds now: you clamp them around your zucchini while it's young, and as it grows it's deformed into the shape of Elvis Presley's head. Is this why he sang? To become a zucchini? Vegetarianism and reincarnation are in the air, but that's taking it too far. I'd rather come back as a sow bug, myself; or a stir-fried shrimp. Though I suppose the whole idea's more lenient than Hell.

✑ **Margaret Atwood,** *Cat's Eye*

Zucchini Lasagne

2 tablespoons olive oil
4 large zucchinis, thinly sliced
    lengthwise
4 large tomatoes, thinly sliced
2 Vidalia onions, thinly sliced
2 tablespoons fresh dill, chopped
1 tablespoon fresh thyme,
    chopped

Garlic powder, salt, and freshly
    ground pepper to taste
1 cup mozzarella and Parmesan
    cheese, grated and mixed
    together

Preheat oven to 400°. Spread olive oil on bottom of a large casserole baking dish. Arrange a layer of zucchini over bottom of dish. Add a layer of tomatoes. Add a layer of onions. Sprinkle half of the dill and thyme over onions. Sprinkle with garlic powder, salt, and pepper. Add half of the cheese. Repeat layers with the remaining ingredients.

Bake for about 30 minutes until zucchini is tender and cheese is melted.

MAKES 8 SERVINGS

I had forgotten about the warm way youngsters respond to books that touch them until I sat down and laughed and wept over every page of *Dear Laura*. It reminded me of the meaning books can bring to children's lives, how a special book may act as a rudder to steer them, fostering hope and understanding.

Mary Warren

Macaroni and Cheese

The neighborhood must have learned by now that Sarah had left him. People started telephoning on ordinary weeknights and inviting him to take "potluck" with them. Macon thought at first they meant one of those arrangements where everybody brings a different pot of something and if you're lucky you end up with a balanced meal. He arrived at Bob and Sue Carney's with a bowl of macaroni and cheese. Since Sue was serving spaghetti, he didn't feel he'd been all that lucky. She set his macaroni at one end of the table and no one ate it but Delilah, the three-year-old. She had several helpings, though.

Anne Tyler, *The Accidental Tourist*

I took out my knife, opened it, wiped off the blade and pared off the dirty outside surface of the cheese. Gavuzzi handed me the basin of macaroni.

"Start in to eat, Tenente."

"No," I said. "Put it on the floor. We'll all eat."

"There are no forks."

"What the hell," I said in English.

I cut the cheese into pieces and laid them on the macaroni.

"Sit down to it," I said. They sat down and waited. I put thumb and fingers into the macaroni and lifted. A mass loosened.

"Lift it high, Tenente."

I lifted it to arm's length and the strands cleared. I lowered it into the mouth, sucked and snapped in the ends, and chewed, then took a bite of cheese, chewed, and then a drink of the wine.

   Ernest Hemingway, *A Farewell to Arms*

Macaroni and Cheese

2 cups uncooked elbow macaroni

¼ cup butter or margarine

2 tablespoons all-purpose flour

2 cups milk

8 ounces cream cheese, softened

2 teaspoons Dijon mustard

½ teaspoon salt

½ teaspoon pepper

8 ounces mild or medium cheddar cheese, grated

Chives

Cook macaroni until just tender and drain. Melt the butter in a saucepan until it sizzles. Stir in flour. Continue cooking over medium heat for 1 minute. Add the milk, cream cheese, mustard, salt, and pepper. Continue cooking, stirring, until sauce is thickened, about 3 to 4 minutes. Remove from heat. Stir in the cooked macaroni and cheddar cheese.

To serve, top with snipped chives.

MAKES 6 TO 8 SERVINGS

If the communication is perfect, the words have life, and that is all there is to good writing, putting down on the paper words which dance and weep and make love and fight and kiss and perform miracles.

◖ Gertrude Stein

Soufflé

◌◌

"Hock or claret?" murmured Tressilian in a deferential whisper in Mrs. George's ear. Out of the tail of his eye he noted that Walter, the footman, was handing the vegetables before the gravy again—after all he had been told!

Tressilian went round with the soufflé. It struck him, now that his interest in the ladies' toilets and his misgivings over Walter's deficiencies were a thing of the past, that everyone was very silent to-night. At least, not exactly silent—Mr. Harry was talking enough for twenty—no, not Mr. Harry, the South African gentleman. And the others were talking too, but only, as it were, in spasms. There was something a little—queer about them.

◖ Agatha Christie, *A Holiday for Murder*

Alice Hammond's Laws of the Kitchen:

1. Soufflés rise and cream whips only for the family and for guests you didn't really want to invite anyway.

2. The rotten egg will be the one you break into the cake batter.

3. Any cooking utensil placed in the dishwasher will be needed immediately thereafter for something else; any measuring utensil used for liquid ingredients will be needed immediately thereafter for dry ingredients.

4. Time spent consuming a meal is in inverse proportion to time spent preparing it.

5. Whatever it is, somebody will have had it for lunch.

◖ Arthur Bloch, *The Complete Murphy's Law: A Definitive Collection*

Anticipation Cheese and Spinach Soufflé

5 tablespoons butter or
   margarine
¼ cup plus 1 tablespoon all-
   purpose flour
1 cup milk
4 egg yolks
½ tablespoon Dijon mustard
½ teaspoon salt
½ teaspoon ground black pepper

Pinch cayenne pepper
6 egg whites (about ¾ cup)
⅛ teaspoon salt
½ cup grated Parmesan cheese,
   plus 1 tablespoon for
   sprinkling
½ cup grated cheddar cheese
¾ cup frozen spinach, drained and
   chopped

Preheat oven to 400°. Grease a 2-quart soufflé dish with vegetable oil or cooking spray. Melt the butter or margarine in a medium-sized saucepan over medium heat. Whisk in the flour. Gradually whisk in the milk and continue cooking over low heat until the mixture thickens. Remove the pan from heat and whisk in the egg yolks one at a time. Stir in the mustard, ½ teaspoon salt, and peppers.

Beat the egg whites with ⅛ teaspoon salt until stiff, moist peaks form. Stir 1 cup of the beaten egg whites into the base mixture. Fold the remaining egg whites into the base mixture. Add the cheeses and spinach with a whisk. Do not overstir. Scoop the mixture into the prepared soufflé dish. Sprinkle the mixture with about 1 tablespoon Parmesan cheese.

Bake for about 30 to 35 minutes. Remove from oven and serve immediately.

MAKES 6 SERVINGS

> I think every fiction writer, to a certain extent, is a schizophrenic and able to have two or three or five voices in his or her body. We seek, through our profession, to get those voices onto paper.
>
> Ridley Pearson

Leeks

There is a white oval dish of braised leeks tossed in crème fraîche, spritzed with vodka, bubbling, golden under a crust of Emmenthaler and Parmesan. I don't know how to say "leek" in Italian, and so I have to get up to find my dictionary. "Ah, *porri*," he says. "I don't like *porri*." I quickly rifle the pages again, pretending to have made an error.

"No, they're not *porri*; these are *scalogni*," I lie to the stranger.

"I've never tasted them," he says, taking a bite. As it turns out, the stranger very much likes leeks, as long as they are called shallots.

Marlena de Blasi, *A Thousand Days in Venice*

A Gratin of Leeks

12 medium-to-large leeks
(approximately 3 pounds),
green parts trimmed off,
white part split, thoroughly
rinsed, and sliced thinly into
rounds (or 2 pounds of
onions or scallions—try a
mixture of sweet onions such
as Vidalia, Walla Walla, or
Texas Sweet with some big,
strongly flavored yellow
Spanish varieties)

2 cups mascarpone
1 teaspoon freshly grated nutmeg
1 teaspoon freshly cracked
   pepper
1½ teaspoons fine sea salt
½ cup grappa or vodka
⅔ cup grated Parmesan cheese
1 tablespoon unsalted butter

Place the prepped leeks into a large mixing bowl; in a smaller bowl combine all the remaining ingredients except the Parmesan and butter, and mix well. Scrape the mascarpone mixture into the bowl with the leeks and, using two forks, evenly coat the leeks with the mixture. Spoon the leeks into a buttered oval oven-safe dish 12 to 14 inches long, spreading the mixture evenly, or into six individual buttered oval dishes. Scatter the Parmesan over all, and bake at 400° for 30 minutes or until a deep golden crust forms (10 minutes less for smaller gratins).

YIELD: 6 SERVINGS

—**Recipe from Marlena de Blasi,** *A Thousand Days in Venice*

Novalee looked around her at a room filled with books. Books stacked in corners, standing on her dresser, crammed into her headboard, pushed into a bookcase. And in the library, Forney's library, there were more. More books ... more stories ... more poems. And suddenly, Novalee knew—knew what she hadn't known before. She wasn't who she had been. She would never again be who she was before.

≈ **Billie Letts,** *Where the Heart Is*

Rice

∽

And again the harvests were good and Wang Lung gathered silver from the selling of his produce and again he hid it in the wall. But the rice he reaped from the land of the Hwangs brought him twice as much as that from his own rice land. The earth of that piece was wet and rich and the rice grew on it as weeds grow where they are not wanted. And everyone knew now that Wang Lung owned this land and in his village there was talk of making him the head.

≈ **Pearl Buck,** *The Good Earth*

Fried Rice

¼ cup green onion, chopped

2 tablespoons green pepper, chopped

2 tablespoons vegetable oil

3 cups cooked rice

1 5-ounce can water chestnuts, drained and thinly sliced

1 3-ounce can sliced mushrooms, drained

4 tablespoons soy sauce

1 cup peas, blanched

¼ cup bean sprouts

1 cup cooked and diced ham, chicken, or crumbled bacon

3 eggs, cooked and scrambled

In a large frying pan, sauté the onion and green pepper in vegetable oil over medium-high heat until tender. Stir in the remaining ingredients, and continue cooking over medium-low heat until warmed through.

MAKES 6 TO 8 SERVINGS

Choose an author as you choose a friend.

  Wentworth Dillon

SHE EYED
HIS BEARD
AND SAID NO DICE
THE WEDDING'S OFF—
I'LL *COOK* THE RICE
BURMA-SHAVE

From Frank Rowsome Jr., *The Verse by the Side of the Road*

Wild Rice and Chicken Casserole

1 cup uncooked wild or brown
   rice
½ cup slivered almonds
½ cup onion, chopped
2 tablespoons butter or margarine
4 ounces shitake mushrooms,
   sliced

1 pound boneless chicken breast,
   cubed
¼ teaspoon salt
¼ teaspoon pepper
1 teaspoon fresh garlic, chopped
3 cups chicken broth

Preheat oven to 325°. Rinse rice. In a large frying pan, sauté the almonds and onions in butter or margarine, about 2 minutes. Add the mushrooms and sauté an additional minute. Place the almonds, onions, and mushrooms in a 3-quart casserole dish, reserving drippings in the pan. Add rice to the casserole dish. Lightly brown the chicken with garlic in same pan used for almonds and onions. Sprinkle with salt and pepper. Do not cook chicken through. Place the chicken and garlic in the casserole dish with rice, almonds, mushrooms, and onions. Add chicken broth. Stir all the ingredients together. Cover and bake for 1½ hours.

MAKES 8 SERVINGS

A good novel transports the reader to another world, showing that what seems immutable in his own society might only be a local custom.

ᐊᑉ **David Streitfeld**

Squash

ᴄᴧᴐ

Once upon a time a farmer planted a little seed in his garden, and after a while it sprouted and became a vine, and bore many squashes. One day in October, when they were ripe, he picked one and took it to market. A grocerman bought and put it in his shop. That same morning, a little girl, in a brown hat and blue dress, with round face and snub nose, went and bought it for her mother. She lugged it home, cut it up, and boiled it in the big pot; mashed some of it with salt and butter for dinner; and to the rest she added a pint of milk, two eggs, four spoons of sugar, nutmeg, and some crackers; put it in a deep dish, and baked it till it was brown and nice; and the next day it was eaten by a family named March.

ᴄᴧᴐ   Lousia May Alcott (as T. Tupman of "The Pickwick Portfolio,") *Little Women*

A Little Woman's Butternut Bevy

ᴄᴧᴐ

1 butternut squash, peeled and cubed	½ teaspoon salt
2 eggs, slightly beaten	¾ cup unsalted saltine crackers, crushed and mixed with
1 cup heavy cream or whole milk	2 tablespoons melted butter or margarine
1 tablespoon brown sugar	
¼ teaspoon nutmeg	

Cover the squash with water in a large, heavy-bottomed pot. Bring it to a boil over high heat, then reduce the heat to low, cover, and simmer until tender (about 25 minutes). Beat the eggs, cream, sugar, nutmeg, and salt together until well mixed. Drain the squash and place it in a large casserole dish coated with cooking spray. Add the creamed mixture. Sprinkle with crushed crackers. Cover and bake at 350° for about 30 minutes.

MAKES 6 TO 8 SERVINGS

—Recipe inspired by Louisa May Alcott

In Grandma's nest of flesh and flab and ancient sweat, I learned to read for myself, I now believe, or at least I imagine it as the locale where the black hieroglyphs on the page, meaningless scribbles until the mind's dimensions expand, finally opened like a flower, and the frivolous, seductive illustrations shrank into the background.

Shirley Abbott, *The Bookmaker's Daughter*

Potatoes

Could she actually eat the food from the plate? Only starvation made Addie brave enough to drop her hands from covering her eyes. Slowly and cautiously, she eased upward into a sitting position. She saw that the girl held a second dinner plate on her own lap and was chewing with enthusiasm. The girl swallowed as Addie watched.

"Brought you a fork," Hillary said, moments later. She held out napkin-wrapped silverware. Addie gingerly reached out, took the fork, spoon and knife. When she saw the girl look down, she eagerly grabbed a piece of meat with her fork. Her stomach growled as she lifted the fork to her lips. But then the meat touched her tongue. So delicious. Addie closed her eyes in ecstasy. When she opened them a moment later, the girl was staring at her.

"Good, isn't it?" the girl said. "Mom's a good cook."

Still staring into Hillary's brown eyes, Addie cautiously dipped her fork again. The meat was gone in three bites. The potatoes were soft, buttery and comforting. Her stomach felt gloriously full. But not too full for the carrots—sweet, buttery and delicious lumps. She fought to savor each one, but they were gone before she knew it. She was startled when the girl took her plate from her and placed it on top of her own.

ᘓ   Carolyn Campbell, *Reunited: True Stories of Long Lost Siblings Who Find Each Other Again*

Celebration Potatoes

We use this at all family gatherings. It's a real favorite. You may want to consider making one without onions.—Carolyn Campbell

1 32-ounce package frozen hash browns

2 10¾-ounce cans cream of chicken soup

1 8-ounce carton sour cream

⅓ cup green onions, chopped

1 cup grated cheese

2 tablespoons butter or margarine

TOPPING:

4 tablespoons butter or margarine

2 cups cornflakes, crushed

In a large bowl, mix together the hash browns, soup, sour cream, onions, and grated cheese. Melt 2 tablespoons butter or margarine in a large casserole dish. Add the mixture. To make topping, melt 4 tablespoons butter or margarine and combine with cornflake crumbs. Then place topping on top of mixture. Bake for 45 minutes at 350°.

MAKES 8 TO 10 SERVINGS

—Contributed by Carolyn Campbell

All of my books turn out differently than I thought they would. My characters take over and run away with them. In *Blood Lines*, I wrote 120 pages on one character—when I rewrote it, I discovered he was a minor character—so I cut him down to 20 pages. He fooled me completely.

Sidney Sheldon

Tomato Pie

ᴄᴠᴐ

Nick was never a picky eater but after suffering through so many of my culinary failures he was well within his rights when later that same day he poked at his food with his fork and asked tremulously, "What is it?"

"Tomato pie."

Lillian had given me the recipe and I followed it to a T. *Four to five tomatoes, blanched for easy removal of the skins. Three quarters of a cup a mayonnaise (feel free to use light but not fat-free). Pillsbury refrigerated pie crusts (bake the bottom crust for ten minutes in a moderate oven, otherwise you'll have a juicy mess). As much garlic as pleases you (Nick, as you must know by now, loves garlic). At least one and a quarter cup cheese (I use feta). Plus fresh basil. Put it all together and bake at three hundred and fifty degrees for about thirty minutes.*

I served it with a green salad and sweet tea. I watched out of the corner of my eye as Nick balanced a bite-sized morsel on his fork, lifted it to his lips, and discreetly sniffed. His face betrayed neither surprise nor disgust. Having gotten this far—even if the savory smell had offended him—he had little choice but to go ahead and eat. He popped it in his mouth and chewed tentatively but within a few seconds his eyes widened gratefully and his face relaxed in that way men have—you know, when they are suddenly and unexpectedly content (I have noticed that this phenomenon almost always revolves around food).

"This is really good!" he said.

"Thank you," I said, ignoring the note of amazement in his voice.

That night, he chewed heartily. He ate two more pieces and I wrapped up what was left and handed it to him as he walked out the door. As always, I followed him onto the porch to see him off and, also as always, he kissed me deeply. People accused us of still behaving like newlyweds. I considered that a compliment.

꧑   **Connie May Fowler,** *Remembering Blue*

Connie May's Tomato Pie

4 to 5 tomatoes
1 whole head of garlic
1 to 2 tablespoons olive oil
¾ cup mayonnaise
1¼ to 1½ cup cheese (4 ounces
    crumbled feta plus 4 ounces
    shredded mozzarella)

2 tablespoons fresh basil,
    chopped
3 to 4 tablespoons all-purpose
    flour
2 Pillsbury refrigerated pie crusts
Cream (optional)

To blanch tomatoes, bring water to boil in a large pot. Place tomatoes in boiling water for about 30 seconds. Remove and cool under cold tap water. Peel off skins.

To prepare roasted garlic, remove papery outer skin, but leave cloves intact on the garlic head. Slice off the tips of each clove, exposing pulp. Place in a small baker and drizzle with 1 to 2 tablespoons olive oil. Cover with lid or aluminum foil and bake at 475° for about 40 to 45 minutes. Remove and allow to cool slightly. Squeeze garlic head from base to extract roasted garlic pulp into large mixing bowl. Crush pulp slightly.

To prepare tomatoes for pie, remove core of each tomato, then slice off top of each tomato. Remove and discard the seeds and juice from each chamber in tomato. Chop tomatoes and place in the mixing bowl with garlic. Add remaining ingredients. Mix to combine. Place filling in a 9-inch pie dish lined with bottom pastry. Add top crust, crimp edges, and cut 5 one-inch slits in top for ventilation. Brush with cream, if desired.

Bake at 350° for about 55 minutes. Cool for 10 minutes and serve.

MAKES 6 TO 8 SERVINGS

—**Recipe inspired by and created with Connie May Fowler**

L̲ike any art form, writing is about communication.

ᴥ Leah Tribolo

Meat Pies

F̲or the next few years, on balmy spring days, blistering summer noons, and cold, wet, and wintery middays, Annie never disappointed her customers, who could count on seeing the tall, brown-skin woman bent over her brazier, carefully turning the meat pies. When she felt certain that the workers had become dependent on her, she built a stall between the two hives of industry and let the men run to her for their lunchtime provisions.

She had indeed stepped from the road which seemed to have been chosen for her and cut herself a brand-new path. In years that stall became a store where customers could buy cheese, meal, syrup, cookies, candy, writing tablets, pickles, canned goods, fresh fruit, soft drinks, coal, oil, and leather soles for worn-out shoes.

Each of us has the right and the responsibility to assess the roads which lie ahead, and those over which we have traveled, and if the future road looms ominous or unpromising, and the roads back uninviting, then we need to gather our resolve and, carrying only the necessary baggage, step off that road into another direction. If the new choice is also un-palatable, without embarrassment, we must be ready to change that as well.

Maya Angelou, "New Directions" from *Wouldn't Take Nothing for My Journey Now*

New Road Chicken Pies (a.k.a. Turnovers)

FILLING:

½ cup potatoes, diced

¼ cup carrots, diced

3 tablespoons celery, chopped

1 teaspoon onion, minced

1 tablespoon butter or margarine

3 tablespoons all-purpose flour

Salt and pepper to taste

1 cup chicken broth

⅓ cup milk

1 teaspoon fresh parsley, minced

¼ cup frozen peas, thawed

1½ cups chicken, cooked and
    diced

PASTRY DOUGH:

⅔ cup shortening or margarine

2 cups all-purpose flour

½ teaspoon salt

5 to 7 tablespoons water

1 egg white

1 teaspoon water

Boil the potatoes, carrots, celery, and onions until tender, about 6 to 8 minutes. Drain and set aside. In a separate saucepan, melt the butter or margarine over medium heat. Whisk in the flour, salt, and pepper. Gradually add the broth and milk, whisking continually to keep sauce smooth. Cook over medium heat until thickened. Stir in the cooked vegetables, parsley, peas, and chicken and continue cooking until warmed through.

Prepare pastry by mixing the shortening or margarine, flour, and salt in a bowl with a fork or pastry blender until the mixture is crumbly. Add water 1 tablespoon at a time until dough is pliable. Work dough into a ball with hands after last tablespoon of water is added.

With a rolling pin, roll the pastry dough out to a ¼-inch thickness on a lightly floured surface. Cut 4-inch or 5-inch-diameter circles from the dough. Put a spoonful of filling in center of each circle. Fold to a half-moon shape. Press edges together to make a seam. Crimp edges with a fork, dipping tines in flour as needed to keep from sticking to dough.

In a small bowl, whisk together egg white and 1 teaspoon water. Brush egg white mixture onto the tops of the turnovers with a pastry brush. Cut a small slit in the top of each turnover. Bake on ungreased cookie sheet at 375° for 15 to 20 minutes or until golden brown.

MAKES 8 TO 10 TURNOVERS

I n my rented St. Petersburg flat, all the bookshelves are empty . . . Of all the valuable possessions in her apartment, she hid her books.

Jeff Parker

Shepherd's Pie

c\v>

Sunday 19 March
124 lbs., alcohol units 3, cigarettes 10, calories 2465 (but mainly chocolate).

H urray. Whole new positive perspective on birthday. Have been talking to Jude about book she has been reading about festivals and rites of passage in primitive cultures and am feeling happy and serene.

Realize it is shallow and wrong to feel that flat is too small to entertain nineteen, and that cannot be arsed to spend birthday cooking and would rather dress up and be taken to posh restaurant by sex-god with enormous gold credit card. Instead am going to think of my friends as a huge, warm, African, or possibly Turkish family.

Our culture is too obsessed with outward appearance, age, and status. Love is what matters. These nineteen people are my friends; they want to be welcomed into my home to celebrate with affection and simple homey fare—not to judge. Am going to cook shepherd's pie for them all—British Home Cooking. It will be a marvelous, warm, Third-World-style ethnic family party.

◖ **Helen Fielding,** *Bridget Jones's Diary*

Sober Shepherd's Pie

2½ cups frozen vegetables (peas
    and carrots, corn, or mixed)
5 small to medium-sized potatoes
2 tablespoons butter or
    margarine
2 tablespoons milk
Salt and pepper

1 pound ground beef
½ cup onion, chopped
2 teaspoons garlic
2 tablespoons fresh parsley,
    chopped
2 cups beef or vegetable broth
3 tablespoons all-purpose flour

Place frozen vegetables in boiling water and cook for 2 minutes. Drain immediately. Set aside.

Peel and chop potatoes and place in boiling water. Cook until tender, about 30 minutes. Drain. Place the potatoes in a mixing bowl. Add about 2 tablespoons butter or margarine, 2 tablespoons milk, and salt and pepper to taste; beat well until smooth. Set aside.

Brown the ground beef in a large frying pan over high heat. When the meat is nearly browned, add the onion, garlic, parsley, and salt and pepper to taste; cover and cook for another 2 minutes. Add the broth and flour, bring the mixture to a boil while stirring continuously, and cook about 5 minutes until liquid is thickened. Transfer the meat mixture to a lightly oiled 9-inch pie dish or casserole dish. Top with the blanched vegetables. Then top the vegetable layer with the mashed potatoes, covering completely. Bake at 350° for about 30 minutes.

MAKES 6 TO 8 SERVINGS

The hard work of writing is not the initial setting down of words but the listening to them to hear what they are telling us about themselves.

৸৹   Helen Marie Casey

Empanadas

ত৸৹

Eliza organized a business in empanadas, delicious meat pies, which she sold at the price of gold, first to Chileans and then to North Americans, who quickly became addicted to them. She had begun making them with beef, when she was able to buy it from the Mexican ranchers who drove cattle from Sonora, but since that meat was often scarce she experimented with venison, hare, wild geese, turtle, salmon, and even bear. Her faithful customers gratefully ate them all, because the alternatives were canned beans and salt pork, the unvarying diet of the miners.

৸৹   Isabel Allende, *Daughter of Fortune*

Empanadas

I had [empanadas] in Daughter of Fortune *because they are typical from Chile. It would be unthinkable to celebrate Chile's Independence Day without them.—Isabel Allende*

1 pound ground beef
1 tablespoon olive oil
½ cup onion, chopped
½ cup mushrooms, chopped
2 teaspoons fresh garlic,
   chopped
2 teaspoons paprika

1 teaspoon dried parsley
¼ teaspoon salt
1 8-ounce can tomato sauce
2 to 3 tablespoons all-purpose
   flour
2 10-ounce packages refrigerated
   pizza crust

Brown ground beef in olive oil in a large frying pan over medium-high heat. Add onion, mushrooms, garlic, and spices, and sauté for an additional 3 minutes. Stir in tomato sauce. Stir in enough flour to thicken excess liquid. Place one pizza crust in bottom of a 9-inch pie dish. Trim dough to size. Pierce dough with fork to allow air holes in bottom of dish. Spoon meat mixture into crust. Top with second pizza crust, trim to size, and seal top and bottom crusts together. Cut about 5 1-inch slits in top crust. Bake at 350° for about 30 minutes, until crust is golden brown.

MAKES 6 TO 8 SERVINGS

Good writing does not come from fancy word processors or expensive typewriters or special pencils or hand-crafted quill pens. Good writing comes from good thinking.

   Ann Loring

Meatloaf

಄ಀ

Mom's café at the four-way stop in Salina, Utah, is high on my list of great places to eat. Mom's advertises THE BEST IN HOMEMADE PIES, SCONES, SOUP, AND MUCH, MUCH MORE! Mom's specializes in liver and onions, chicken-fried steak, deep-fried chicken, "real" french fries, and "real" mashed potatoes. But Mom's doesn't serve meatloaf. I called them long-distance to check my facts. The lady who answered the phone was a little surprised that I asked. "Don't you know nothing? Meatloaf is something you eat at home."

It's true. Meatloaf is mostly homemade. Mostly it's made by real moms, by hand. Constructed out of what's around. Some hamburger that may be going bad if it isn't used soon— sprouting potatoes, rubbery carrots, onions, salt, pepper, steak sauce, baking drippings, etcetera. I say "etcetera" because the list of what's possible is too long to print. Then there's the filler—meatloaf expander. Bread crumbs, corn flakes, Rice Krispies, oatmeal, or whatever—even dirt would work, I guess. And some egg to hold the whole thing together. Then it has to be mushed around by hand, kneaded into a loaf, and put into that family museum piece, the meatloaf pan. Into the oven to bake. Served hot with gravy, mashed potatoes, and Wonder bread. Yes. Yes!

But don't eat it all. Never eat all the meatloaf when it's fresh. Put about a third of it away in the back of the fridge and forget about it. This is the best part. The part you are going to eat about 2:00 A.M. some dark, rainy night when you need sustaining. No health department would allow such a thing to be served in a public restaurant. But nothing's better for you. It's a matter of mental health. I've never heard anybody say he was depressed by eating a cold meatloaf sandwich.

಄಄   **Robert Fulghum,** *Uh-Oh*

Ann Landers' (Infamous) Meatloaf

ᘓᕙᘒ

In 1970, Ann Landers received more than forty thousand letters about the meatloaf recipe she printed in her column, rating it from "great" to "mediocre." One reader assured her there was plenty left over for his dog. Ann responded with her characteristic humor and inquired after the dog's health. When the meatloaf episode subsided, Ann swore she would never print another recipe.

2 pounds ground round steak
    (or 2 pounds ground beef)
2 eggs
1½ cups breadcrumbs
¾ cup ketchup
1 teaspoon Accent seasoned salt

½ cup warm water
1 package Lipton's onion soup
    mix
1 8-ounce can Hunt's tomato
    sauce
2 strips bacon (optional)

Mix all ingredients together except tomato sauce and bacon. Put into loaf pan; cover with 2 strips bacon if you wish. Pour tomato sauce over all. Bake 1 hour at 350°.

MAKES 6 SERVINGS

Meatloaf-Stuffed Peppers

ᘓᕙᘒ

Cut a small slice off the top of 4 to 6 green or red peppers and hollow them out. Make sure the peppers can stand securely; if not, slice a small amount off the bottom, without penetrating the entire pepper. Fill the peppers with meatloaf mixture. With sharp knife, make three small slits about halfway to the top, penetrating the pepper, to allow drippings to escape while baking. Place the peppers in a glass baking dish, filled with ¼ inch of water, and bake at 375° for 45 minutes or until done.

MAKES 4 TO 6 SERVINGS

For a long time I was a reporter to a journal, of no very wide circulation, whose editor has never yet seen fit to print the bulk of my contributions, and, as is too common with writers, I got only my labor for my pains. However, in this case my pains were their own reward.

⟪ Henry David Thoreau, *Walden*

Meatballs

⟫⟪

We ate in the kitchen before we started. Aymo had a basin of spaghetti with onions and tinned meat chopped up in it. We sat around the table and drank two bottles of the wine that had been left in the cellar of the villa. It was dark outside and still raining. Piani sat at the table very sleepy.

"I like a retreat better than an advance," Bonello said. "On a retreat we drink barbera."

"We drink it now. To-morrow maybe we drink rainwater," Aymo said.

"To-morrow we'll be in Udine. We'll drink champagne. That's where the slackers live. Wake up, Piani! We'll drink champagne to-morrow in Udine!"

"I'm awake," Piani said. He filled his plate with the spaghetti and meat. "Couldn't you find tomato sauce, Barto?"

"There wasn't any," Aymo said.

⟪ **Ernest Hemingway**, *A Farewell to Arms*

Wished-For Spicy Tomato Sauce with Meatballs

1 large onion, chopped   1 tablespoon olive oil

MEATBALLS:

1 pound lean ground beef   ½ teaspoon dried oregano
1 teaspoon garlic, finely chopped   ⅓ cup crushed crackers
1 egg, beaten   Salt and pepper to taste

SAUCE:

2 14½-ounce cans diced tomatoes   ⅓ cup dry red wine
1 8-ounce can tomato sauce   1 teaspoon dried oregano
1 6-ounce can tomato paste   2 teaspoons dried parsley
1 teaspoon salt   ½ teaspoon crushed red pepper
2 teaspoons sugar   1 teaspoon fresh garlic, finely
1 bay leaf   chopped

In a wok or large heavy-bottomed saucepan, sauté the onion in olive oil until tender, about 2 minutes. Reserve ¼ cup of sautéed onion for meatballs; set aside the rest.

To prepare meatballs: Combine the ground beef, reserved ¼ cup of sautéed onion, garlic, egg, oregano, crackers, salt, and pepper. Form 1-inch-diameter meatballs and brown them in the same pan used for onion, over medium-high heat with pan covered, about 10 minutes. Stir occasionally for even cooking.

Add the remaining ingredients for sauce, including remaining sautéed onion, to the pan with the meatballs. Simmer over medium-low heat for about 20 minutes. Remove bay leaf.

Serve over pasta.

MAKES 8 SERVINGS

Give me books, fruit, French wine, and fine weather, and a little music out-of-doors, played by someone I do not know.

   John Keats

Pasta

She was cooking him the pasta dish she'd wanted to make that evening they'd all come for supper. The little pots of basil she'd bought in Butte were flourishing. As she chopped the leaves, he came up behind her and rested his hands lightly on her hips and kissed the side of her neck. The touch of his lips made her catch her breath.

"It smells good," he said.

"What, me or the basil?"

"Both."

"You know, in ancient times they used basil to embalm the dead."

"Mummies, you mean?"

"Daddies too. It prevents mortification of the flesh."

"I thought that was about banishing lust."

"It does that too, so don't eat too much."

   Nicholas Evans, *The Horse Whisperer*

Lusty Sun-Dried Tomato Sauce

ᴄᴧᴐ

1 14-ounce can vegetable broth
1 3-ounce package dried
  tomatoes, finely chopped
1 cup yellow onion, chopped
½ cup yellow or green pepper,
  chopped
2 tablespoons olive oil
1 teaspoon fresh garlic, chopped
½ teaspoon salt
¼ teaspoon ground black pepper
½ teaspoon rubbed sage

1 teaspoon sugar
1 to 2 tablespoons fresh parsley,
  chopped
1 tablespoon fresh basil, chopped
1 teaspoon dried oregano
2 teaspoons lemon juice
¼ cup dry red wine
1 cup mushrooms, sliced
1 pound penne pasta, cooked to
  taste
Grated mozzarella cheese

Boil the broth and combine it with the tomatoes in a medium bowl and set aside for about 15 minutes. In a large skillet, sauté the onion and yellow or green pepper in olive oil over medium heat until tender, for about 3 minutes. Drain tomatoes, reserving broth. Add the tomatoes with ½ cup broth to the skillet with onions and pepper. Stir in the remaining ingredients, except mushrooms. Bring the sauce to a boil, then reduce heat to low and simmer, uncovered, for about 30 minutes, stirring occasionally. Add broth in ¼ cup increments, as needed. Add mushrooms for last 10 minutes of cooking. Serve over cooked pasta. Sprinkle with mozzarella cheese.

MAKES ABOUT 6 SERVINGS

A simple conversation across the table with a wise man is better than ten years' study of books.

ᴄᴧᴐ **Henry Wadsworth Longfellow**

Noodles with Peppery Meat Sauce

"Now that you're safely here," Martin said, "let's all three have a beer before I take you out to dinner."

"Not me," Byron answered, "Chinese girls don't drink beer. What she needs is nice cup boiling water on cold night like this. Then big bowl noodles with lots of peppery meat sauce. I fix right this minute."

"Hot water?" Martin exclaimed, wrinkling his nose. "She's not an old lady from Chinatown like my mother! What she needs is an ice-cold beer. She doesn't want any noodles. I just told you we're going out to dinner."

Soon I had a cup of hot water and a cold beer placed in front of me, alternately sipping both.

Adeline Yen Mah, *Falling Leaves: The True Story of an Unwanted Chinese Daughter*

Uplifting Rice Noodles with Peppery Meat Sauce

1 pound Chinese sausage, cut
 into ½-inch pieces
2 tablespoons olive oil
½ cup yellow pepper, chopped
½ cup red pepper, chopped
1 teaspoon garlic, finely chopped
1 28-ounce can diced tomatoes

2 tablespoons fresh parsley, finely
 chopped
½ teaspoon salt
1 teaspoon sugar
½ teaspoon lemon pepper
12-ounce package rice noodles,
 cooked according to package
 directions

In a large frying pan, brown the sausage in olive oil over high heat, covered, for about 4 minutes, stirring occasionally to ensure even cooking.

Add the yellow and red pepper and cook another minute. Add the garlic, tomatoes, parsley, salt, and sugar and bring to a light simmer. Sprinkle with lemon pepper and cook an additional minute. Serve sausage sauce over cooked rice noodles.

MAKES 6 SERVINGS

A word is not a crystal, transparent and unchanged; it is the skin of a living thought, and may vary greatly in color and content according to the circumstances and the time in which it is used.

Oliver Wendell Holmes

Baked Potatoes

For supper they had Rose's pot roast, a salad with Macon's dressing, and baked potatoes. Baked potatoes had always been their favorite food. They had learned to fix them as children, and even after they were big enough to cook a balanced meal they used to exist solely on baked potatoes whenever Alicia left them to their own devices. There was something about the smell of a roasting Idaho that was cozy, and also, well, *conservative*, was the way Macon put it to himself. He thought back on years and years of winter evenings: the kitchen windows black outside, the corners furry with gathering darkness, the four of them seated at the chipped enamel table meticulously filling scooped out potato skins with butter. You let the butter melt in the skins while you mashed and seasoned the floury insides; the skins were saved till last. It was almost a ritual. He recalled once, during one of their mother's longer absences, her friend Eliza had served them what she called potato boats—restuffed, not a bit like the genuine article. The children, with pinched, fastidious expressions, had emptied the stuffing and proceeded as usual with the skins, pretending to overlook her mistake. The pepper should be freshly ground. Paprika was acceptable, but only if it was American. Hungarian paprika had too distinctive a taste. Personally, Macon could do without paprika altogether.

✎ **Anne Tyler,** *The Accidental Tourist*

Genuine Roasting Idaho Potato Boats, or Restuffed Potatoes

4 large baking potatoes
2 to 4 tablespoons butter or
   margarine
½ cup milk, or more to taste

Salt and freshly ground pepper, to
   taste
Paprika, if desired

Wash potatoes and pat dry. Pierce with fork to keep the skins from bursting. Do not rub with oil or margarine or wrap in foil, because the potato skin needs to be firm after baking. Bake for 1 hour, or until tender, at 400°. Remove potatoes from the oven and allow to cool until comfortable to the touch.

Cut a thin slice from the top of each potato. Remove the potato pulp with a spoon, being careful not to tear shells. Set the shells aside. Place the potato pulp in a bowl and whip until smooth with an electric mixer. Stir in the butter or margarine, milk, and seasonings. For eating potatoes and skins separately, place 1 tablespoon of butter or margarine in each potato shell, to melt. Slice shells into desired size. Sprinkle with paprika, salt, and freshly ground pepper to taste. Eat immediately. Serve with whipped potatoes.

To restuff potatoes, spoon the whipped pulp into the baked potato shells, pressing the mixture evenly with a rubber spatula or the back of a spoon. Return to oven and bake at 350° for 15 to 20 minutes, or until warmed through.

MAKES 4 SERVINGS

CHOICES FOR THE FILLING ARE ENDLESS: Additional seasonings, cooked meat (chicken, ground beef, ham, bacon), cooked vegetables, cooked eggs, grated cheese, sour cream, or cream cheese. Stir ingredients selected into the mashed potato pulp, or use as a garnish.

> My family can always tell when I'm well into a novel, because the meals get very crummy.
>
>   Anne Tyler

Corn

Smilow's next question drew Alex's attention back to him. Hammond exhaled without making it obvious that he'd been holding his breath.

"What time did you arrive at Hilton Head?"

"That was the beauty of the day. I had no plans. I wasn't on a schedule. I wasn't watching the clock, and I didn't take a direct route, so I don't remember what time it was when I actually got there."

"Approximately."

"Approximately . . . nine o'clock."

At approximately nine o'clock, they were eating corn on the cob that had left her lips greasy with melted butter. They laughed over how messy it was, and elected to forget their manners and shamelessly lick their fingers.

  Sandra Brown, *The Alibi*

Grilled Corn on the Cob

8 ears of corn, partially husked as described below

Melted butter or margarine

Salt and pepper

Prepare grill. Remove about half of the outer corn husk and discard. Peel back the remaining upper corn husks and remove cornsilk. Reposition remaining corn husks back over the cob, covering cob. Soak the cobs in cold water for about 30 minutes. Remove cobs from the water and drain excess water from cobs. Place the corn on the upper grill rack over a layer of aluminum foil, close grill cover, and cook about 20 minutes until kernels are tender, turning every 5 minutes. Remove cobs from grill. Cool slightly. Peel back husks against the lower stem, exposing entire cob. Wrap the lower stem and husks with a dry paper towel to make a comfortable handle for eating. Brush the corn with melted butter. Season to taste.

MAKES 8 SERVINGS

I realize the odds, and science, are against me. But science is not the total answer; this I know, this I have learned in my lifetime. And that leaves me with the belief that miracles, no matter how inexplicable or unbelievable, are real and can occur without regard to the natural order of things. So once again, just as I do every day, I begin to read the notebook aloud, so that she can hear it, in the hope that the miracle that has come to dominate my life will once again prevail.

And maybe, just maybe, it will.

Nicholas Sparks, *The Notebook*

Fried Green Tomatoes

⌒∿⌒

The Weems Weekly
(Whistle Stop, Alabama's Weekly Bulletin)
June 12, 1929

CAFÉ OPENS

The Whistle Stop Café opened up last week, right next door to me at the post office, and owners Idgie Threadgoode and Ruth Jamison said business has been good ever since. Idgie says that for people who know her not to worry about being poisoned, she is not cooking. All the cooking is being done by two colored women, Sipsey and Onzell, and the barbecue is being cooked by Big George, who is Onzell's husband.

If there is anybody that has not been there yet, Idgie says that the breakfast hours are from 5:30–7:30, and you can get eggs, grits, biscuits, bacon, sausage, ham and red-eye gravy, and coffee for 25¢.

For lunch and supper you can have: fried chicken; pork chops and gravy; catfish; chicken and dumplings; or a barbecue plate; and your choice of three vegetables, biscuits or corn bread, and your drink and dessert—for 35¢.

She said the vegetables are: creamed corn; fried green tomatoes; fried okra; collard or turnip greens; black-eyed peas; candied yams; butter beans or lima beans.

And pie for dessert.

My other half, Wilbur, and I ate there the other night, and it was so good he says he might never eat at home again. Ha. Ha. I wish this were true. I spend all my time cooking for the big lug, and still can't keep him filled up.

By the way, Idgie says that one of her hens laid an egg with a ten-dollar bill in it.

... Dot Weems ...

✒ Fannie Flagg, *Fried Green Tomatoes at the Whistle Stop Café*

Fried Green Tomatoes

⌇

1 medium green tomato
  (per person)
Salt and pepper

White cornmeal
Bacon drippings

Slice tomatoes about ¼ inch thick, season with salt and pepper, and then coat both sides with cornmeal. In a large skillet, heat enough bacon drippings to coat the bottom of the pan and fry tomatoes until lightly browned on both sides.

You'll think you died and gone to heaven!

Fried Green Tomatoes
with Milk Gravy

⌇

3 tablespoons bacon fat
4 firm green tomatoes, sliced
  ¼ inch thick
Beaten eggs

Dry breadcrumbs
Flour
Milk
Salt and pepper

Heat your bacon fat in a heavy frying pan. Dip tomatoes in eggs, then in breadcrumbs. Slowly fry them in the bacon fat until golden brown on both sides. Put your tomatoes on a plate. For each tablespoon of fat left in the pan, stir in 1 tablespoon of flour and blend well; then stir in 1 cup warm milk and cook until thickened, stirring constantly. Add salt and pepper till you like it. Pour over the tomatoes and serve hot.

The best there is.

—Recipes from Fannie Flagg, *Fried Green Tomatoes at the Whistle Stop Café*

> Why shouldn't truth be stranger than fiction? Fiction, after all, has to make sense.
> Mark Twain

Grilled Cheese Sandwiches

I stood at the long tiled kitchen counter, brushing olive oil on thick oatmeal bread; I spread the other side with honey mustard, layered on cheddar cheese, tomato slices, and sautéed Canadian bacon, placed a slice of oatmeal bread on top, put the two sandwiches in a cast-iron skillet sizzling with butter. Mrs. Gladstone leaned against the opposite wall, watching me. Never miss a good opportunity to shut up, Harry Bender had said. I kept quiet, flipped the sandwiches when they got perfectly browned on one side as Mrs. Gladstone cleared her old voice. We were standing there, as different as two human beings on this earth could be, and yet we were connected.

I put the sandwiches on two plates, cut them at an angle to show off, put them on the round glass kitchen table by the window that overlooked the rock garden. Our kitchen table at home overlooked the fire escape.

Mrs. Gladstone came to the table slowly. She'd been moving slower since Harry Bender died. We all had. Grieving sucks energy from a person's core. She took a bite of the sandwich; her face lit up.

"Superb."

I tried mine. It was, too.

 Joan Bauer, *Rules of the Road*

Lucky Day Grilled Cheese

Honey mustard

Dense bread, sliced for
    sandwiches

Cheddar cheese, sliced thin for
    sandwiches

Tomato slices

Canadian bacon, precooked

Extra-virgin olive oil

1 tablespoon butter or margarine

Spread honey mustard on 2 slices of bread. Layer the coated side of one slice with cheese, tomato slices, and Canadian bacon. Top with the second piece of bread, coated side down. Brush olive oil on outer sides of bread. Melt butter or margarine in a medium- to large-sized skillet. Once sizzling, place sandwich in skillet. Brown both sides to taste.

MAKES 1 SERVING

—**Recipe inspired by Joan Bauer**

I do think people want to be touched and moved and to identify and understand that the problems they have and things they have to face in their lives are also faced by others. That's what I try to do in all of my novels.

   Barbara Taylor Bradford

Corncakes

❧

Outside the door he squatted down and gathered the blanket ends about his knees. He saw the specks of Gulf clouds flame high in the air. And a goat came near and sniffed at him and stared with its cold yellow eyes. Behind him Juana's fire leaped into flame and threw spears of light through the chinks of the brush-house wall and threw a wavering square of light out the door. A late moth blustered in to find the fire. The Song of the Family came now from behind Kino. And the rhythm of the family song was the grinding stone where Juana worked the corn for the morning cakes.

The dawn came quickly now, a wash, a glow, a lightness, and then an explosion of fire as the sun arose out of the Gulf. Kino looked down to cover his eyes from the glare. He could hear the pat of the corncakes in the house and the rich smell of them on the cooking plate. . . .

Kino squatted by the fire pit and rolled a hot corncake and dipped it in sauce and ate it. And he drank a little pulque and that was breakfast. That was the only breakfast he had ever known outside of feast days and one incredible fiesta on cookies that had nearly killed him. When Kino had finished, Juana came back to the fire and ate her breakfast. They had spoken once, but there is not need for speech if it is only a habit anyway. Kino sighed with satisfaction—and that was conversation.

❧ John Steinbeck, *The Pearl*

Corn Tortillas

❧

3 cups corn masa (an instant corn flour used in Mexican cooking, available in specialty food sections)

1¾ to 2 cups water

In a bowl combine corn masa with enough water to form a smooth dough. Leave dough in the bowl, cover with a damp cloth, and let rest for 10 minutes. Divide dough into 18 1-inch balls. Cover balls with plastic wrap.

Cut wax paper into 36 7-inch squares. Put 1 square of wax paper on the bottom half of a tortilla press and arrange a dough ball on it, slightly off-center toward edge opposite handle. Flatten one dough ball slightly and cover with another square of wax paper. Lower top of press and push down firmly on lever. Remove the tortilla, keeping it between the wax paper squares. Cover the sheeted tortilla with a damp cloth and repeat procedure until all tortillas are pressed. Stack the tortillas as you go.

To make tortillas without a tortilla press: Place a 1-inch dough ball on a square of wax paper. Slightly flatten the dough ball, then cover it with a second square of wax paper. Roll the dough into a 6-inch circle with a rolling pin. Set aside tortilla, keeping it between the wax paper squares. Cover the sheeted tortilla with a damp cloth and repeat until all tortillas are rolled. Stack tortillas as you go.

Heat a griddle or cast-iron skillet over high heat. Carefully peel off top wax paper square from a tortilla and invert tortilla onto griddle. After 5 seconds, peel off remaining wax paper and cook the tortilla, turning, until dry and flecked with golden brown spots, 1 to 2 minutes. Wrap the tortillas in a kitchen towel as they are cooked. If not using tortillas immediately, wrap cooled tortillas in plastic wrap and chill. Tortillas store well in a plastic bag chilled 1 day or frozen 1 month.

MAKES 18 SIX-INCH TORTILLAS

No kind of writing lodges itself so deeply in our memory, echoing there for the rest of our lives, as the books we met in our childhood.

 William Zinsser

Mackerel

cv_o

"I am sixty-four years old, Madeline. I sleep badly. I drink rather too well. The machine begins to run down. I ask myself whether it was worthwhile, whether the making of money has made me happy. I ask myself these things more and more often." He glanced at the oven. The timer was on zero. "Madeline, I think your fish are cooked."

Using the gloves, he brought the mackerel out of the oven. He unwrapped them from the foil and poured the rest of the marinade over them. It smelled as I had imagined, sweet and hot and delicious. "I'll leave you to enjoy your dinner in peace, heh." He sighed theatrically. "I usually eat at my hotel, you know. I can choose any table I like, any dish from the menu. But my appetite—" He patted his stomach ruefully. "My appetite isn't what it once was. Perhaps the sight of all those empty tables—"

I still don't know why I asked him. Perhaps because no Devinnois ever refuses to offer hospitality. Perhaps because his words had struck a chord. "Why not eat with us?" I suggested impulsively. "There's enough to go around."

But Brismand laughed suddenly and hugely, his belly shaking with his giant mirth. I felt my cheeks redden, knowing I had been manipulated into showing sympathy where none was needed, and that my gesture had amused him.

"Thank you, Mado," he said at last, wiping tears from his eyes with the corner of his handkerchief. "What a kind invitation. But I must be on my way, heh? Today I have other fish to fry."

Joanne Harris, *Coastliners*

A NOTE FROM JOANNE HARRIS: When I was a child, I spent all my summer holidays at my Grandfather's house on the Islands of Noirmoutiers, off the coast of France. My uncle was a fisherman, and there was always fresh fish for the family. It was very easy to cook indoors or outdoors (guess which one was my favorite!).

Marinade for Other Fish to Fry

A second batch would make a delicious salad dressing.—Joanne Harris

4 mackerel fillets, about ½ pound
each
Juice and zest of one lemon
½ cup olive oil
¼ cup balsamic vinegar
2 tablespoons fresh rosemary,
minced

¼ teaspoon salt
¼ teaspoon fresh ground pepper
1 clove garlic, minced
1 lemon, cut in wedges
4 sprigs fresh dill

Whisk lemon juice, balsamic vinegar, and olive oil until just blended. Add lemon zest, garlic, and rosemary. Pour mixture over fish and marinate 1 to 2 hours in refrigerator in airtight container or zipper-lock plastic bag, turning twice.

To bake: Brush 4 pieces of foil with olive oil or spray with nonstick cooking spray. Sprinkle fillets with salt and pepper on each side and place on foil. Dribble a little olive oil on each fish fillet. Seal foil packets, leaving room at the top for steam. Put packets in roasting pan and bake at 350° for about 25 minutes or until fish flakes easily with a fork. Remove fillets from packages, arrange on serving dish and garnish with lemon wedges and dill.

To fry: Remove fish from marinade, discarding remaining marinade. Dip fillets in 1 beaten egg and then in a mixture of ⅔ cup cornmeal or fine dry breadcrumbs, ½ teaspoon salt, and a dash of pepper. Brown in ½ inch of hot oil until crisp and golden on each side. Drain on paper towels and serve with garnish of choice.

To grill: Remove fish and save remaining marinade. Grill over medium coals, turning once, and baste with marinade. Discard any remaining marinade. Remove to serving plate and garnish as desired.

To broil: Place fish on greased unheated rack of broiler pan. Broil for about 5 minutes, 4 inches from the heat. Turn fish over, using spatula. Brush with marinade. Broil about 5 minutes more or until fish flakes easily with a fork. Discard any remaining marinade. Using spatula, remove fish to serving plate and garnish as desired.

MAKES 4 TO 6 SERVINGS

Some books have to be reread right away . . . you love it so much that you don't want to leave it.

◁©   Susan Sontag

Pork

"This is great," I said about the pork chop, and I wasn't sucking up to her. It was the most tender, juicy, flavorful thing I could ever remember putting into my mouth.

"Thanks," she said, smiling.

She seemed to like the compliment about her cooking more than the one about her house.

"Jody loved them too. She ate two whole chops by herself."

The door banged open and all three kids came running in. Callie's kids were vanilla-skinned with big dark eyes; Esme with blue-black Snow White hair and Zack with a fawn-colored mop.

They skidded to a stop and stood beside each other. Esme leaned into Zack, and he gave her a two-handed shove. A pink tongue popped out of Esme's angel face, and Zack grinned like a soldier who's seen too many battles.

"You forgot to close the door," Callie told them.

"Can we have something to eat?" Esme asked.

"You just had dinner," Callie said. "Go close the door."

"We want dessert."

"We want dessert," Zack echoed.

"I haven't even cleaned up the dishes yet. Maybe later."

"Did you eat these pork chops?" I asked Jody.

"Yeah," she said. "I loved them."

"You hate pork chops."

"I hate your pork chops. They taste like napkins."

"It's probably just the marinade." Callie laughed. "It's a very simple one. Apple cider, lemon juice, honey, soy sauce. I could give you the recipe."

 Tawni O'Dell, *Back Roads*

Callie's Simple Pork Marinade

½ cup apple cider
2 tablespoons soy sauce
1 tablespoon honey

1 teaspoon lemon juice
Garlic salt to taste, if desired
1½ to 2 pounds pork

Mix ingredients together in a bowl. Place in a zipper-lock plastic bag with pork, and set in refrigerator. After ½ to 2 hours, discard marinade and cook meat as desired.

MAKES 4 TO 6 SERVINGS

Leafing through the books today, with messages from my parents written on title pages, reminds me of how special it is for a parent to give a book to a child. It also summons the sense of discovery I felt as I turned the pages—the delicious pleasure of reading late at night when the house was quiet, and I was supposed to be asleep.

〜 Elfrieda M. Abbe

SOUPS

Double, double, toil and trouble
Fire burn and cauldron bubble.

WILLIAM SHAKESPEARE, *MACBETH*

THE CANNIBALS
TOOK JUST ONE VIEW
AND SAID
HE LOOKS TOO NICE
TO STEW
BURMA-SHAVE

FROM FRANK ROWSOME JR., *THE VERSE BY THE SIDE OF THE ROAD*

Chili

One afternoon Eli came back from the lab for a few hours to eat—he had to return later to watch some experimental results. It was my night off, so I was in the kitchen, cooking. Eli helped me chop green peppers and celery and onions for chili. After only a few minutes, we were weeping from the pungent fumes. We began to invent reasons we would offer if someone came in and asked us what was wrong: we had discovered we were the wrong zodiacal signs for each other; we had discovered that worker bees could not have sex.

Sue Miller, *While I Was Gone*

Onions can make even Heirs and Widows weep.

Benjamin Franklin, *Poor Richard's Almanack, 1734*

Eli and Jo's Innocent Vegetarian Chili

Simmer for 1 hour while listening to Jefferson Airplane or the sound track to Hair.—Sue Miller

1 tablespoon olive oil
4 large yellow onions, diced
1 jalapeño pepper, diced
1 green pepper, diced
1 red pepper, diced
1 teaspoon mustard seed
1 tablespoon chili powder
¼ teaspoon cinnamon

1 teaspoon cumin
1 tablespoon oregano
1 6-ounce can tomato paste
3 15¼-ounce cans kidney beans
1 pound tomatoes, peeled and
   chopped
Salt to taste

In a large pot, sauté the onions and peppers in oil over medium heat until they are tender. Add the mustard seed and cook 1 minute. Add the remaining spices. Stir in the tomato paste. Add the beans (with liquid) and tomatoes. Stir. Cover, reduce heat to low, and simmer.

MAKES 8 TO 10 SERVINGS

—Recipe inspired by and created with Sue Miller

The library is inhabited by spirits that come out of the pages at night.

◖ **Isabel Allende**

Borscht

∽

"This is Russian cabbage-and-beet soup," she announced. "It's called borscht. It's the beets that turn it pink. You're supposed to put sour cream on top but that just seemed like calories up the kazoo. I got it out of *Ladies Home Journal*."

I could imagine her licking her index finger and paging through some magazine article called "Toasty Winter Family Pleasers," trying to find something to do with all that cabbage I kept bringing home from Mattie's. I fished out a pink potato and mushed it up in Turtle's bowl.

◖ **Barbara Kingsolver,** *The Bean Trees*

Lou Ann's Russian Borscht

1½ pounds lean stew beef

1 cup onion, chopped

1 bay leaf

1 teaspoon salt

6 to 8 peppercorns

6 cups water

4 to 5 beef bouillon cubes

3 cups beets, coarsely grated

1 cup carrots, coarsely grated

1 cup potatoes, diced

1 8-ounce can tomato paste

½ teaspoon salt

3 cups cabbage, shredded

Dried dill

Ground black pepper

Low-fat sour cream

In a large pot, sauté the onion and beef with olive oil over medium-high heat until the meat is browned and onion is tender. Drain fat, if necessary. Add all the ingredients except the cabbage, dill, sour cream, and ground black pepper. Cover and simmer over low heat for one hour.

Add the cabbage and simmer another ½ hour.

To serve, sprinkle with dill and ground black pepper and top with a dollop of low-fat sour cream.

MAKES ABOUT 8 SERVINGS

W riters of any significance have always played an oddly dual role. They have been voices and echoes at one and the same time.

&ea; **John Mason Brown**

Gazpacho

❧

They were having dinner with Rosemary. Tonight it was not a party, there were just the three of them. Ria knew what would be served: a chilled soup, grilled fish, and salad. Fruit and cheese afterward, served by the big picture window that looked out onto the large, well-lit garden.

❧ **Maeve Binchy,** *Tara Road*

Rosemary's Gazpacho

❧

2 large tomatoes, peeled, and
   seeds removed
1 large cucumber, peeled and
   halved, seeds removed
1 medium onion, peeled and
   halved
1 medium green bell pepper,
   quartered and seeded
1 2-ounce jar pimento, drained
2 12-ounce cans tomato juice
⅓ cup olive oil

⅓ cup red wine vinegar
¼ teaspoon Tabasco sauce
1½ teaspoons salt
⅛ teaspoon black pepper, coarsely
   ground
2 cloves garlic, peeled and
   minced
1 package seasoned croutons
   (herbed is preferred)
¼ cup chopped chives

Purée one tomato, half of the cucumber, half of the onion, half of the bell pepper, pimento, and half of the tomato juice in a blender or food processor. Finely chop the remaining vegetables. In a large bowl, mix the puréed and chopped vegetables with the remaining ingredients except croutons and chives. Chill in the refrigerator for at least 4 hours to develop flavors. To serve, top soup with croutons and chives.

MAKES 4 TO 6 SERVINGS

Books that make us feel, touch a nerve that goes deep into our own lives. Whether that nerve is warm and comforting, scared and anxious, happy or sad, it still reminds us to examine who we are.

✒ **Laura Backes**

Beef Stew

The beef stew was excellent, as Johanna's cooking always was, but Mr. McCauley found he could not swallow it. He disregarded the instruction about the lid and left the pot sitting open on the stove and did not even turn off the burner until the water in the bottom pot boiled away and he was alerted by a smell of smoking metal.

This was the smell of treachery.

✒ Alice Munro, "Hateship, Friendship, Courtship, Loveship, Marriage" in *Hateship, Friendship, Courtship, Loveship, Marriage*

Ma ladled stew into the tin plates, very little stew, and she laid the plates on the ground. "I can't send 'em away," she said. "I don't know what to do. Take your plates an' go inside. I'll let 'em have what's lef'. Here, take a plate into Rosasharn." She smiled up at the children. "Look," she said, "you little fellas go an' get you each a flat stick an' I'll put what's lef' for you. But they ain't to be no fightin'." The group broke up with a deadly, silent swiftness. Children ran to find sticks, they ran to their own tents and brought spoons. Before Ma had finished with the plates they were back, silent and wolfish. Ma shook her head. "I dunno what to do. I can't rob the fambly. I got to feed the fambly. Ruthie, Winfiel', Al," she cried fiercely. "Take your plates. Hurry up. Git in the tent quick." She looked apologetically at the waiting children. "There ain't enough," she said humbly. "I'm a-gonna set this here kettle out, an' you'll all get a little tas', but it ain't gonna do you no good." She faltered, "I can't he'p it. Can't keep it from you." She lifted the pot and set it down on the ground. "Now wait. It's too hot," she said, and she went into the tent quickly so she would not see.

◖ John Steinbeck, *The Grapes of Wrath*

Beef Stew

---

1 pound lean stew beef	2 teaspoons fresh garlic, minced
1¾ cups dry red wine or beef broth	4 peppercorns
	1 small bay leaf
¼ cup flour	½ teaspoon thyme
2 tablespoons butter or margarine	4 large carrots, sliced into rounds
1 onion, chopped	4 large red potatoes, peeled and cubed
½ cup water	

Rinse the meat under cold water and marinate it in 1 cup of red wine for at least 1 hour.

In a large pot, sauté the onion in butter until tender, about 2 minutes. Remove the onion from the pan and set aside.

Remove the meat from the wine and pat it with a paper towel to remove excess moisture. Roll the meat in the flour to coat. Brown meat over medium-high heat in the same pot used for the onion, adding an additional tablespoon or two of butter if needed. After meat is browned, add ¾ cup red wine and water as needed to cover the meat. Stir in the remaining spices and garlic and cooked onion. Bring the liquid to a boil over high heat. Reduce heat to low, cover, and simmer for 2½ hours. As sauce cooks away, periodically add water or red wine to taste in order to keep meat covered. Add carrots and potatoes for last hour of cooking.

MAKES ABOUT 6 SERVINGS

It is of some interest to me that much, perhaps most, of what I have learned about human interaction has come through books. While I believe that most people turn to fiction in order to confirm what they know of life, for most of my fifty-one years I have reversed the act— judging and validating life by the books I have read.

    Jamie Langston Turner, *Some Wildflower in My Heart*

Gruel

The evening arrived; the boys took their places. The master, in his cook's uniform, stationed himself at the copper; his pauper assistants ranged themselves behind him; the gruel was served out; and a long grace was said over the short commons. The gruel disappeared; the boys whispered to each other, and winked at Oliver; while his next neighbours nudged him. Child as he was, he was desperate with hunger, and reckless with misery. He rose from the table; and advancing to the master, basin and spoon in hand, said: somewhat alarmed at his own temerity: "Please, sir, I want some more."

The master was a fat, healthy man; but he turned very pale. He gazed in stupefied astonishment on the small rebel for some seconds, and then clung for support to the copper. The assistants were paralysed with wonder; the boys with fear.

"What!" said the master at length, in a faint voice.

"Please, sir," replied Oliver, "I want some more."

The master aimed a blow at Oliver's head with the ladle; pinioned him in his arms; and shrieked aloud for the beadle.

The board were sitting in solemn conclave, when Mr. Bumble rushed into the room in great excitement, and addressing the gentleman in the high chair, said,

"Mr. Limbkins, I beg your pardon, sir! Oliver Twist has asked for more!"

There was a general start. Horror was depicted on every countenance.

"For *more*!" said Mr. Limbkins. "Compose yourself, Bumble, and answer me distinctly. Do I understand that he asked for more, after he had eaten the supper allowed by the dietary?"

"He did, sir," replied Bumble.

"That boy will be hung," said the gentleman in the white waistcoat. "I know that boy will be hung."

Charles Dickens, *Oliver Twist*

Plentiful Dreamy Fish Stew
(a bit tastier than gruel)

1 to 1½ pounds haddock, or cod, or other white fish
¼ cup plus 2 tablespoons olive oil
2 cups yellow onion, chopped
¼ cup celery, chopped
2 to 3 garlic cloves, minced
¼ cup yellow pepper, diced
¼ cup fresh parsley, chopped
1 14½-ounce can diced tomatoes

1 8-ounce can tomato sauce
1½ cups dry red wine
¼ teaspoon ground black pepper
½ teaspoon dried basil
½ teaspoon paprika
1 teaspoon salt
1 pound small shrimp
1 pound small scallops

Line a broiler pan with aluminum foil and spray it with cooking oil spray. Rinse the fish, remove any bones, and broil it for 8 to 10 minutes to lightly precook fish before stewing.

In a large pot, sauté the onions, celery, garlic, and yellow pepper in ¼ cup olive oil over high heat until they are slightly tender. Add the parsley and sauté for another minute. Break the broiled fish into pieces and add it to the large pot with the tomatoes, tomato sauce, wine, and seasonings. Cover, reduce heat to low, and simmer for 1 hour.

Rinse, shell, and devein the shrimp. Rinse the scallops. Sauté the shrimp and scallops in a frying pan in 2 tablespoons of olive oil over medium-high heat for about 2 minutes. Add the shrimp and scallops to the large pot for the last 20 minutes of cooking for the stew. Add water to sauce as needed to keep fish covered.

MAKES ABOUT 8 SERVINGS

I have always come to life after coming to books.

≪ **Jorge Luis Borges**

Kartoffel Suppe

ᗧᗣ

She led me to a table near the side door and motioned for me to sit. She did not introduce me to anyone, and no one approached me. But I knew they were watching. I could feel their eyes. Their eyes were bullets.

In a few moments Nora Dowling returned with a bowl of soup. *"Kartoffel suppe,"* she said.

"Thank you."

She nodded once and left. Her voice boomed instructions across the kitchen. People ducked to their work.

I sipped the soup. It was delicious. I did not know what *kartoffel suppe* was and I wondered if my mother, who was a renowned cook in our community, would like it. I thought she would. I was hungry and I finished it quickly.

"So, was it good?" Nora Dowling demanded.

"Yes, ma'am," I answered politely. "What was it?"

She looked at me in amazement. "*Kartoffel suppe?* It's potato soup. That's what it means."

"Oh," I said. I did not know that people made soup from potatoes. In my family, we did not. We ate potatoes. "It's one of the best meals I've had in a long time."

Nora Dowling's sullen face flashed with amusement. A laugh bubbled from her abundant bosom. "*Ach du lieber Gott,*" she exclaimed. "Meal? That's not a meal. That's soup."

❦ Terry Kay, *Shadow Song*

Nearly-a-Meal Potato Soup

2 whole heads garlic, roasted	4 cups baking potatoes, peeled
2 tablespoons olive oil	and diced
4 cooked bacon slices	½ teaspoon salt
2 14-ounce cans vegetable broth	¼ teaspoon ground black pepper
1 cup onion, diced	1 bay leaf
1 cup carrot, diced	¾ cup milk

To roast garlic, remove papery skin and slice off tops of cloves to expose garlic. Place in a small baker, drizzle with 2 tablespoons olive oil, and bake at 425° for 40 to 45 minutes. Remove from oven and cool. Once cooled, remove roasted garlic cloves from their chambers with a knife or tines of fork. The base of the garlic head can also be squeezed to extract the garlic. Place garlic in a small bowl and mash into a paste.

After cooking bacon, trim any excess fat and chop meat.

In a large pot, combine the broth, bacon, onion, carrot, potatoes, roasted garlic paste, salt, pepper, and bay leaf and bring to a boil. Reduce heat to low and simmer for 20 to 30 minutes, or until potatoes are tender. Remove bay leaf and discard.

Remove 2 cups of the potato mixture to a blender or food processor. Purée until smooth. Return purée to pot. Stir in milk and cook over low heat until warmed through, stirring occasionally. Do not boil. Remove from heat and serve.

MAKES 6 TO 8 SERVINGS

Potato Soup with Cheese

6 potatoes, peeled and diced
1 large yellow onion, diced
6 cups chicken broth
½ cup butter or margarine
½ cup all-purpose flour
½ teaspoon salt

¼ teaspoon white pepper
3 cups milk
2 cups grated cheddar cheese
   (or cheese of choice)
Salt and white pepper to taste

Simmer potatoes and onions in the broth in a large pot. When the potatoes are nearly tender, melt butter or margarine in a separate saucepan on low heat. Whisk in flour, salt, and pepper. Add milk all at once. Cook on medium heat, stirring constantly, until mixture thickens and bubbles. Remove from heat. Add the cheese to the white sauce, return to low heat, and whisk until melted. With a ladle, dip two cups of the hot potato broth and stir into the cheese sauce until smooth. Remove the cheese sauce from heat and pour into the remaining potato/broth mixture in the large pot. Stir on low heat until blended (do not boil). Serve with salt and pepper to taste.

MAKES 8 TO 10 SERVINGS

It is wonderful how putting down on paper a clear statement of a case helps one to see, not perhaps the way out, but the way in.

A. C. Benson

Split Pea

"Look-a-here, pardner," he said, after a time. He regarded the corpse as he spoke. "He's up an' gone, ain't 'e, an' we might as well begin t' look out fer ol' number one. This here thing is all over. He's up an' gone, ain't 'e? An' he's all right here. Nobody won't bother 'im. An' I must say I ain't enjoying any great health m'self these days."

The youth, awakened by the soldier's tone, looked quickly up. He saw that he was swinging uncertainly on his legs and that his face had turned to a shade of blue.

"Good Lord!" he cried, "you ain't goin' t'—not you, too."

The tattered man waved his hand. "Nary die," he said. "All I want is some pea soup an' a good bed. Some pea soup," he repeated dreamfully.

Stephen Crane, *The Red Badge of Courage*

Veteran Split Pea Soup

2 cups dry split peas
1 cup onion, chopped
½ cup celery, chopped
1 cup carrots, chopped

1 cooked ham hock
1 bay leaf
1 teaspoon salt
6 whole peppercorns

Soak peas overnight in water. Drain and rinse. Combine all ingredients in slow cooker. Cover with water. Cook on low for 10 to 12 hours, or on high for 5 to 6 hours. Remove ham bone, bay leaf, and peppercorns.

MAKES 6 SERVINGS

Books are the carriers of civilization. Without books, history is silent, literature dumb, science crippled, thought and speculation at a standstill.

๕ Barbara W. Tuchman

Mixed Lentil

꒰ᐢ꒱

What's bowls, Mrs. Leibowitz?

Oh, Frankie. You don't know bowl? For the soup, darlink. You don' have a bowl? So get cups for the soup. I mix pea soup and lentil soup. No ham. Irish like the ham. No ham, Frankie. Drink, missus. Drink you soup.

She spoons the soup into my mother's mouth, wipes the dribble from her chin. Malachy and I sit on the floor drinking from mugs. We spoon the soup into the twins' mouths. It is lovely and hot and tasty. My mother never makes soup like this and I wonder if there's any chance Mrs. Leibowitz could ever be my mother. Freddie could be me and have my mother and father, too, and he could have Malachy and the twins for brothers.

꒰ᐢ **Frank McCourt,** *Angela's Ashes*

The idea of French luxury and elegance next had alarmed the Dean's daughters. The first day after Babette had entered their service they took her before them and explained to her that they were poor and that to them luxurious fare was sinful. Their own food must be as plain as possible; it was the soup-pails and baskets for their poor that signified. Babette nodded her head; as a girl, she informed her ladies, she had been cook to an old priest who was a saint. Upon this the sisters resolved to surpass the French priest in asceticism. And they soon found that from the day when Babette took over the housekeeping its cost was miraculously reduced, and the soup-pails and baskets acquired a new, mysterious power to stimulate and strengthen their poor and sick.

꒰ᐢ **Isak Dinesen,** *Babette's Feast*

Mrs. Leibowitz's Lentil-Vegetable Soup

6 cups water

3 large or 6 small vegetable
  bouillon cubes

1 tablespoon olive oil

1 small yellow onion, chopped

6 cloves garlic, finely chopped

2 cups celery, chopped with
  leaves

2 cups carrots, thinly sliced

1 cup broccoli (upper portions of
  stems, no heads), chopped

1 14½-ounce can whole kernel
  corn, drained

1 14½-ounce can diced tomatoes

1 8-ounce can tomato sauce
  (optional)

1 or 2 bay leaves (optional)

1½ tablespoons fresh parsley,
  finely chopped

1 teaspoon dried basil

½ teaspoon garlic powder

1 teaspoon dried thyme

Salt and pepper to taste

¾ cup lentils, rinsed

2 cups broccoli heads, divided
  into bite-sized portions

Fill a large pot with the water and add the bouillon cubes. Set water to boil. In a small frying pan, sauté the onion and garlic in olive oil over medium-high heat until tender, about 2 minutes. Add the onions, garlic, celery, carrots, tomatoes, and broccoli stems to the boiling water and cover. Boil for 30 minutes. Add the remaining ingredients except lentils and broccoli heads. Simmer over low heat for 3 hours, covered. Stir occasionally. Adjust seasonings to taste. Add lentils and broccoli heads and simmer another hour, covered. Remove bay leaf. Serve when lentils are tender.

Kino looked at his neighbors fiercely. "My son will go to school," he said, and the neighbors were hushed. Juana caught her breath sharply. Her eyes were bright as she watched him, and she looked quickly down at Coyotito in her arms to see whether this might be possible.

But Kino's face shone with prophecy. "My son will read and open the books, and my son will write and will know writing. And my son will make numbers, and these things will make us free because he will know—he will know and through him we will know." And in the pearl Kino saw himself and Juana squatting by the little fire in the brush hut while Coyotito read from a great book.

John Steinbeck, *The Pearl*

Tomato

A wave of gentle memories flowed through me as I leaned wearily against the door post and closed my eyes. When I opened them I saw Brandy coming round the corner of the street with Mrs. Westby. His nose was entirely obscured by a large red tomato soup can and he strained madly at the leash and whipped his tail when he saw me. . . .

. . . Tomato soup must have been one of his favorites because he was really deeply embedded and it took some time before I was able to slide the can from his face.

I fought off his slobbering attack. "He's back in the dustbins, I see."

James Herriot, "Brandy the Dustbin Dog" from *James Herriot's Favorite Dog Stories*

Brandy's Tomato-Beef Soup

1 pound lean ground beef
½ teaspoon salt, divided
½ cup celery, chopped
½ cup onion, chopped
½ cup green pepper, diced
   (optional)
4 cups tomato juice
1½ cups water
2 10¾-ounce cans cream of celery
   soup

½ cups carrots, rinsed, peeled,
   and grated
1 teaspoon sugar
½ teaspoon garlic salt
½ teaspoon ground black pepper
⅛ teaspoon ground marjoram
10 slices Swiss cheese (optional)

In a large frying pan, brown the beef and drain fat. Add ¼ teaspoon salt, celery, onion, and green pepper. Cover and simmer on low until vegetables are tender, about 10 minutes. In a large saucepan combine the tomato juice, water, cream of celery soup, grated carrots, sugar, garlic salt, the remaining ¼ teaspoon salt, black pepper, and marjoram. Add the beef mixture and bring to a boil. Simmer for 30 minutes.

   Place one slice of cheese in each bowl and ladle hot soup over it.

MAKES 8 TO 10 SERVINGS

I would say that last weekend was my lost weekend . . . and the culprit was a book . . .
   Therese Eiben

"I *wonder* if you have seen Bilks' *new* poem called *Table d'Hote*," said Eddie softly. "It's *so* wonderful. In the last Anthology. Have you got a copy? I'd *so* like to *show* it to you. It begins with an *incredibly* beautiful line: 'Why Must it Always be Tomato Soup?' "

"Yes," said Bertha. And she moved noiselessly to a table opposite the drawing-room door and Eddie glided noiselessly after her. She picked up the little book and gave it to him; they had not made a sound.

While he looked it up she turned her head towards the hall. And she saw . . . Harry with Miss Fulton's coat in his arms and Miss Fulton with her back turned to him and her head bent. He tossed the coat away, put his hands on her shoulders and turned her violently to him. His lips said, "I adore you," and Miss Fulton laid her moonbeam fingers on his cheeks and smiled her sleepy smile. Harry's nostrils quivered; his lips curled back in a hideous grin while he whispered: "Tomorrow," and with her eyelids Miss Fulton said: "Yes."

"Here it is," said Eddie. " 'Why Must it Always be Tomato Soup?' It's so *deeply* true, don't you feel? Tomato soup is so *dreadfully* eternal."

ᴖ **Katherine Mansfield, "Bliss" from *The Short Stories of Katherine Mansfield***

Eternal Cream of Tomato Soup

2 pounds tomatoes*
1 medium onion, chopped
3 large carrots, sliced
1 potato, diced
1 stalk fresh celery, chopped
1 6-ounce can tomato paste
2 tablespoons sugar
1 bay leaf

1 teaspoon lemon juice
¾ teaspoon salt
⅛ teaspoon white pepper
Lemon peel, cut as narrow strips
    from half of a lemon
4 cups chicken broth
2 dashes hot pepper sauce
    (optional)

4 tablespoons butter or
margarine, softened
4 tablespoons flour
1 cup half-and-half or milk

Garnish: orange or lemon zest,
sour cream, grated cheese,
chopped chives, toasted
croutons, or fresh snipped
parsley

Immerse tomatoes in boiling water for about 30 seconds; remove and cool. Peel skins from the fruit, then seed and chop the tomatoes. In a large kettle, combine all the ingredients except the butter, flour, and half-and-half or milk. Bring to a boil over moderately high heat. Cover, reduce heat to low, and simmer for 30 to 40 minutes, or until the vegetables are tender. Remove bay leaf and lemon peel and discard.

In a small bowl, mix the flour and butter together with a fork until the mixture resembles crumbs.

Transfer the tomato mixture to a blender and process until smooth. Return puréed mixture to kettle and continue cooking over low heat. Whisk in the flour-butter mixture and continue to stir until the soup boils and has a smooth, thick consistency.

Remove the soup from heat. Add the half-and-half or milk and stir well to blend. Return the soup to the heat and cook, stirring occasionally, until just steaming hot. Do not boil after half-and-half or milk is added. Add additional seasonings to taste, if desired. Garnish as desired.

To serve cold, do not return to heat after adding the milk; transfer to appropriate container and refrigerate until chilled.

MAKES 8 TO 10 SERVINGS

* Canned tomatoes may be substituted (two 14½-ounce cans, including juice). Reduce chicken broth to 3 cups.

Every human being is deeply involved with at least one story—his own.

  Elizabeth Spencer

Onion

In the meantime, Madame Magloire had served supper: soup, made with water, oil, bread, and salt; a little bacon, a bit of mutton, figs, a fresh cheese, and a large loaf of rye bread. She had, of her own accord, added to the Bishop's ordinary fare a bottle of his old Mauves wine.

Victor Hugo, *Les Misérables*

French Onion Soup

3 cups onions, sliced
¼ cup butter
6 cups beef broth
½ cup dry white wine
1 teaspoon salt

¼ teaspoon pepper
French baguette, sliced, toasted
    until crisp, and sprinkled with
    Parmesan cheese
1 slice Swiss cheese per serving

In a large, heavy-bottomed pot, sauté the onions in melted butter until golden brown. Add the broth, wine, salt, and pepper, and simmer for 30 minutes.

At serving, ladle the soup into individual bowls and top with a toasted baguette and a slice of Swiss cheese.

MAKES 6 SERVINGS

Either write something worth reading or do something worth writing.

Benjamin Franklin

White Bean

⌒⌒

Feeding herself was Ruby's to do as soon as she was old enough to be held accountable for it, which in Stobrod's opinion fell close after learning to walk. As an infant, Ruby foraged for food in the woods up and down the river at charitable farms. Her brightest childhood memory was of walking up the river trail for some of Sally Swanger's white bean soup and on the way home having her nightgown—for several years her usual attire, even in the daytime—get caught on a trailside blackthorn briar.

Charles Frazier, *Cold Mountain*

Swanger's Fulfilling White Bean Soup

⌒⌒

1 pound dried marrow, navy, or
    Great Northern beans
1½ pounds precooked ham or
    smoked pork butt

2 cups celery, diced
1 cup onion, chopped
1 8-ounce can tomato sauce
Salt and pepper to taste

Rinse beans and then soak them overnight in water. Drain the water. Combine all the ingredients in a slow cooker, along with any ham broth saved from the cooked ham. Cover with water. Cook at medium-low heat until beans are tender (about 10 hours).

MAKES 8 TO 10 SERVINGS

It is not the thing that dreams are made of, but writing is creating dreams for others.

G. Scott Wright Jr.

Bisque

०৩১৩

Novalee could hear kitchen sounds—a spoon scraping metal, the clink of glass against glass, but she could not imagine Forney managing ovens and burners or skillets and lids. She could see him dipping and swaying between a stove and a kitchen sink.

When he came back in, carrying a tray, he said, "Dinner is served," trying to speak with a French accent, the way he had practiced.

He set the tray on a cart beside the table, then placed a bowl in front of Novalee and one at his place. "Your soup, madam."

"I've never seen orange soup before."

"It's orange almond bisque," he said as he sat down.

Novalee took a taste, a wonderful nutty taste . . . tangy, velvety smooth—but cold. "Forney, it's just great."

She knew when he tasted it he would be embarrassed that it had gotten cold, but she couldn't imagine it would taste any better hot.

๛ Billie Letts, *Where the Heart Is*

Forney's Orange-Almond Bisque

०৩১৩

1 6-ounce can orange juice
  concentrate
6 ounces water
⅓ cup sugar
1 teaspoon lemon juice
2 tablespoons cornstarch
½ teaspoon almond paste
3 cups cantaloupe, peeled,
  seeded, and cut in ¾-inch
  cubes

3 6-ounce cartons Swiss-style
  French vanilla yogurt, or
  2½ cups half-and-half or heavy
  cream
1 11-ounce can mandarin orange
  sections, drained, for garnish
12 mint leaves, for garnish
½ cup sliced almonds, for garnish

In a small saucepan, combine the orange juice concentrate, water, sugar, lemon juice, and cornstarch. Over medium heat, whisk briskly until the mixture thickens and begins to bubble. Remove from heat and add the almond paste. Allow to cool to room temperature. In a blender or food processor, combine the orange mixture with the cantaloupe and yogurt or cream. Process until smooth. Refrigerate until chilled and serve. Garnish with mandarin orange sections arranged in a circle around mint leaves. Sprinkle with almonds.

MAKES 6 SERVINGS

> With good writing, I think, the most profound response is finally a sigh, or a gasp, or holy silence.
>
> ✒   Tim O'Brien

Chicken

I raced home to prepare a dish for Marla and Tony's evening meal out on the range. Or rather, by the trout-swollen brook. In the spirit of the taste testing I'd be doing later, and also because it could be such a comfort in rainy weather, I decided on homemade chicken soup. I chopped mountains of leeks, onions, carrots, and celery, then gently stirred them into a golden pool of olive oil along with the chicken breasts. If I hadn't been making the soup for cardiac patient Marla, of course, I would have used unsalted butter instead of oil. Small sacrifice.

I removed the chicken breasts when they were tender and milky white, then whisked in flour, white wine, and lowfat chicken broth. The homey scent of cooked vegetables wafted upward. My mind churned. As I sliced the chicken, I wondered how much of Tony's character Marla really knew. Or wanted to know. But then, as a former girlfriend, especially one who'd been jilted, Eileen Tobey was *not* the most reliable of sources. And besides, my own Tom had remembered *Albert* in connection with the goats and goat cheese, not Tony and Albert together. Maybe Eileen was indulging in some reputation-destroying back-stabbing, by exchanging the names and the players.

Diane Mott Davidson, *The Main Corpse*

Rainy Season Chicken Soup

2 dried porcini mushrooms

2 tablespoons butter

2 leeks, white part only, split, rinsed, and diced

1 medium-sized carrot, diced

1 medium-sized onion, diced

1 large celery rib, diced

2 boneless, skinless chicken breast halves

2 tablespoons all-purpose flour

2 tablespoons dry white wine

4 cups chicken stock, divided (see p. 146)

1 cup fat-free sour cream

1 cup fideo (fine-cut egg noodles)

Salt and pepper

Using a small pan, bring a cup of water to boiling and drop in the porcini mushrooms. Cook uncovered over medium-high heat for 10 minutes, then drain the mushrooms, pat them dry, and slice thinly. Set aside. In a sauté pan, melt the butter over low heat. Put in the leeks, carrot, onion, celery, and chicken, stir gently, and cover to cook over low heat for 5 minutes. Take off the cover, stir the vegetables, turn the chicken, and check for doneness. (The chicken should be about half done.) Cover and cook another 5 minutes, or until chicken is just done—not overdone. Remove the chicken from the pan and set aside to cool. Sprinkle the flour over the melted butter, vegetables, and pan juices, and stir to cook over low heat for 2 minutes. Slowly add the white wine and 2 cups of the chicken broth. Stir and cook until bubbly and thickened. Add the sour cream very slowly and allow to cook gently while you slice the chicken into thin, bite-sized pieces.

In a large frying pan, bring the remaining 2 cups of stock to boiling and add fideo. Cook 4 minutes, or until almost done. Do not drain. Slowly add the noodle mixture to the hot vegetables and sour cream mixture. Add the chicken and bring back to boiling. Serve immediately.

SERVES 4

—Recipe of Diane Mott Davidson from *The Main Corpse*

Chicken Stock

3 to 5 pounds chicken pieces
4 cups onions, chopped
2 cups carrots, peeled and
   chopped
1 cup celery with leaves,
   chopped
¼ cup fresh parsley
3 quarts water
1 tablespoon dried thyme
4 bay leaves
Vegetable oil

In a large, heavy-bottomed pot, brown the chicken in vegetable oil over medium-high heat. Add the onions, carrots, and celery, stirring often, and cook for 10 more minutes, or until vegetables are tender. Add the remaining ingredients and cover with water. Boil for 15 minutes and skim froth. Reduce heat to low, cover, and simmer for 2 hours. Skim every 30 minutes or as needed. Add more water as necessary to cover chicken and vegetables. Remove the pot from heat and cool slightly. Remove bay leaves.

Strain contents of pan, reserving liquid in a large bowl. Continue to extract juice from chicken and vegetables by pressing them with the back of a spoon. Discard remainder of chicken and vegetables.

Cover stock and refrigerate several hours or overnight. Remove any congealed fat that has formed on the top surface. Extra stock can be frozen for later use.

MAKES APPROXIMATELY 3 QUARTS

Where is human nature so weak as in the bookstore?

  Henry Ward Beecher

"Is any one else coming to dine besides Mr. Casaubon?"

"Not that I know of."

"I hope there is some one else. Then I shall not hear him eat his soup so."

"What is there remarkable about his soup-eating?"

"Really, Dodo, can't you hear how he scrapes his spoon? And he always blinks before he speaks. I don't know whether Locke blinked, but I'm sure I am sorry for those who sat opposite to him if he did."

"Celia," said Dorothea, with emphatic gravity, "pray don't make any more observations of that kind."

"Why not? They are quite true," returned Celia, who had her reasons for persevering, though she was beginning to be a little afraid.

"Many things are true which only the commonest minds observe."

"Then I think the commonest minds must be rather useful. I think it is a pity Mr. Casaubon's mother had not a commoner mind: she might have taught him better." Celia was inwardly frightened, and ready to run away, now she had hurled this light javelin.

Dorothea's feelings had gathered to an avalanche, and there could be no further preparation.

"It is right to tell you, Celia, that I am engaged to marry Mr. Casaubon."

Perhaps Celia had never turned so pale before. The paper man she was making would have had his leg injured, but for her habitual care of whatever she held in her hands. She laid the fragile figure down at once, and sat perfectly still for a few moments.

When she spoke there was a tear gathering.

"Oh, Dodo, I hope you will be happy." Her sisterly tenderness could not but surmount other feelings at this moment, and her fears were the fears of affection.

ᏍᎶ   **George Eliot,** *Middlemarch*

Mr. Casaubon's Chicken Noodle Soup

1 pound boneless, skinless
    chicken breast, cut into small
    pieces
2 tablespoons butter or
    margarine
1 yellow onion, chopped
3 14½-ounce cans fat-free chicken
    broth

2 cups carrots, chopped
1 cup frozen corn
1 teaspoon dried thyme
1 teaspoon dried parsley
¼ teaspoon ground pepper
½ teaspoon salt
4 ounces uncooked spaghetti,
    broken into smaller lengths

In a large pot, lightly brown the chicken on all sides in melted butter over medium-high heat, about 5 minutes. Add the onion and cook an additional 2 minutes until tender. Add the broth, carrots, corn, and seasonings, and bring to a boil. Reduce heat to low; cover and simmer for 3 hours. Add spaghetti and cook an additional 15 minutes.

MAKES 8 SERVINGS

Writing is nothing more than a guided dream.

    Jorge Luis Borges

Squash

I eyed her and shrugged my shoulders, wondering how on earth she thought this meal was good, but her wafer-thin body gave her away; not once in her life had she eaten good-tasting food. Closing my eyes, I imagined Matanni and Patanni spooning up soup at the kitchen table. During the winter, Matanni made different kinds of soup each week. This week, she would be fixing butternut squash and apple cider soup. The apple cider was made from the tart Winesaps that grew behind our house. She'd measure out three cups of home-made cider then two cups of Essie's whole cream. Then she'd add them to the bubbling, cooked squash. After which she'd plop on three dollops of butter. When the bowls were filled, Patanni would urgently bring his spoon toward him, dribbling soup down the front of his shirt. Matanni, on the other hand, would leisurely dip her spoon away from her. Her mama, she always said, had taught her manners. Sitting in front of this lump of gray meat clumped between two pieces of starchy white bread, I longed for my grandmother, for the steamy mist that clouded my face as I brought a spoonful of her soup to my mouth, for that warm heavy feeling in my stomach after I finished it.

    Gwyn Hyman Rubio, *Icy Sparks*

A NOTE FROM G. H. RUBIO: While working with me on my novel, my editor commented on the number of scenes which take place around the dinner table; she thought it was odd. I said, "But the setting is in Appalachia, and in the South most of our socializing happens around the preparing and sharing of food."

Matanni's Butternut Squash and Apple Cider Soup

4 cups butternut squash, peeled
    and cut into 1-inch cubes
    (other winter squash can be
    substituted)

3 cups apple cider
2 cups cream
1½ tablespoons butter
Dash of salt

Steam squash until tender. Drain and purée. Return to pan and turn heat to low. Add apple cider, cream, butter, and salt. Do not boil after cream is added. Stir until butter is melted. Serve immediately.

MAKES 6 TO 8 SERVINGS

—Recipe inspired by Gwyn Hyman Rubio, author of *Icy Sparks*

Fiction nurtures the imagination and gives the reader a creative vision of the diversity of life's possibilities. This is fiction's greatest power.

Kazumi Yumoto

SALADS

MY DEAR, HOW EVER DID YOU THINK UP THIS DELICIOUS SALAD?

This is a very sad ballad,
Because it's about the way too many people make a
    salad.
Generally they start with bananas,
And they might just as well use gila monsters or
    iguanas.
Pineapples are another popular ingredient,
Although there is one school that holds preserved pears
    or peaches more expedient,
And you occasionally meet your fate
In the form of a prune or a date.

Rarely you may chance to discover a soggy piece of
    tomato looking very forlorn and Cinderella-ry,
But for the most part you are confronted by apples and
    celery,
And it's not a bit of use at this point to turn pale or
    break out in a cold perspiration,
Because all this is only the foundation,
Because if you think the foundation sounds unenticing,
Just wait until we get to the dressing, or rather, the
    icing.
There are various methods of covering up the body,
    and to some, marshmallows are the pall supreme,
And others prefer whipped cream,
And then they deck the grave with ground-up peanuts
    and maraschinos
And you get the effect of a funeral like Valentino's,
And about the only thing that in this kind of salad is
    never seen
Is any kind of green,
And oil and vinegar and salt and pepper are at a mini-
    mum,
But there is a maximum of sugar and syrup and ginger
    and nutmeg and cinnamum,
And my thoughts about this kind of salad are just as
    unutterable
As parsnips are unbutterable,
And indeed I am surprised that the perpetrators haven't
    got around to putting buttered parsnips in these
    salmagundis,
And the salad course nowadays seems to be a month of
    sundaes.

OGDEN NASH, FROM *THE FACE IS FAMILIAR*

Fruit

Great mounds of fruit rose temptingly higher than their heads. Oranges, apples, grapes, and pears. And everything was shining and luscious.

Janey was lost in admiration of this abundance. Nowhere except in the pages of the Old Testament had she ever come upon such bounty. She felt as the men sent to spy out the Land of Canaan must have felt. Surely this San Joaquin Valley was a land flowing with milk and honey! If she had ever stopped to think about it, she wouldn't have supposed there could be so many different kinds of things to eat in all the world, and here they were spread out before her feasting eyes, within reach of her hand.

This fruit simply begged to be eaten, she thought. It didn't want to sit here uselessly gathering dust and growing overripe. Suppose she should put out her hand right now and seize that particularly tempting pear? Would its absence in the midst of so many be noticed? Yes, she was forced to admit to herself, it would. There would be a gaping hole in the neat and orderly display.

Doris Gates, *Blue Willow*

Summer Fruit Salad

1 11-ounce can mandarin oranges with juice

1 cup golden Delicious apples— peeled, cored, and chopped

1 cup green or red grapes, halved

1 cup pears, peeled and chopped

⅛ to ¼ cup 7 UP

Combine fruits in a bowl. Pour 7 UP over fruit and lightly toss to distribute. Chill for at least ½ hour before serving.

MAKES 6 SERVINGS

Fresh Fruit Dip

1 6-ounce can orange juice
   concentrate, thawed
¼ cup cold milk

1 package instant vanilla pudding
¼ cup sour cream

Combine the juice and milk in a bowl. Beat in the pudding mix at low speed for 2 minutes. Stir in the sour cream. Chill for about 2 hours before serving with fresh fruit.

MAKES ABOUT 1 CUP

Lemon Fruit Dip

8 ounces plain nonfat yogurt
3 tablespoons powdered sugar
1 teaspoon lemon juice

1 teaspoon finely grated lemon
   peel

Mix all the ingredients together in a bowl and chill for 24 hours before serving with fresh fruit.

MAKES 1 CUP

Books speak even when they stand unopened on the shelf. If you would know a man or woman, look at their books, not their software.

   E. Annie Proulx

Gelatin

∿

Nettie came into the kitchen, looking tired and sweaty and smelling like a sickroom. She was startled to see that so many of the Pickles were there. Tears came to her eyes as she smiled at each one of us and glanced at the food we'd set out. The perfection salad sat in the place of honor in the center, the celery and carrots sparkling like five-and-dime jewels, and when I moved aside, a beam of sunshine shot through the window, causing the clear gelatin to shimmer. It was so pretty that Nettie drew in her breath, then threw her arms around Mrs. Judd. "Oh, Septima, I never saw a thing as lovely as that."

☙ Sandra Dallas, *The Persian Pickle Club*

Perfection Salad

∿

1 3-ounce package lemon gelatin

1 cup boiling water

1 8-ounce can crushed pineapple, drained (reserve juice)

⅓ cup orange juice concentrate

1 11-ounce can mandarin oranges, drained

½ cup carrots, shredded

¼ cup celery, diced

In a large bowl, dissolve the gelatin in boiling water. Add enough water to the reserved pineapple juice to equal 1 cup; stir into gelatin. Add the orange juice concentrate. Chill until partially set. Fold in the pineapple, oranges, carrots, and celery. Pour into a mold and chill until set.

MAKES 6 SERVINGS

E-mail is conversation, and it may be replacing the sweet and endless talking we once sustained (and tucked away) within the informal letter. But we are all writers and readers as well as communicators, with the need at times to please and satisfy ourselves (as White put it) with the clear and almost perfect thought.

  Roger Angell

Carrots

"Stephen thinks Connie here will be very helpful," my mother said to her mother, and she gave my arm a small squeeze. *Don't you worry about Nonny*, that squeeze said: *You're going.*

"Helpful? Helpful how?"

"Connie will be a constant reminder for the jury that I'm not just some faceless defendant. I'm not just some midwife. I'm a mother. I have a daughter, a family."

Nonny had turned the last carrots from her vegetable garden into a salad with raisins and walnuts, and while the carrots were supposed to be shredded, the blender my grandmother used was older than I, and the salad still had a great many large orange chunks. I watched Nonny methodically chew one of those pieces while she thought about my mother's explanation, and noticed there was some dry dirt on the cuffs of her light-blue cardigan. From her garden, I thought. She'd probably harvested the carrots we were eating that very morning.

  Chris Bohjalian, *Midwives*

Carrot-Raisin-Pineapple Salad

4 cups carrots, grated
1 cup raisins
½ cup mayonnaise

1 20-ounce can crushed
  pineapple, drained
½ cup walnuts, chopped

Combine all the ingredients in a large salad bowl and chill for at least 2 hours before serving to blend flavors.

MAKES 10 TO 12 SERVINGS

Alternative Carrot-Raisin-Pineapple Salad

4 cups carrots, grated
1 cup raisins
1 20-ounce can crushed
  pineapple, drained

1 tablespoon lemon juice
1 teaspoon cinnamon

Combine all the ingredients in a large salad bowl and chill for at least 2 hours before serving to blend flavors.

MAKES 10 TO 12 SERVINGS

Good fiction should be beautiful, and powerful, but it should also work. It should have something in it that enlightens, something in it that opens the door and points the way.

 Toni Morrison

Potatoes

၈ა

T hat noon, Ruby said she wanted to walk up and check on the apple orchard, so Ada suggested they have their lunch there. They made a picnic of the leftover pieces of last night's fried chicken, a small bowl of potato salad for which Ruby had whipped up the mayonnaise, and some vinegared cucumber slices.

Charles Frazier, *Cold Mountain*

Ruby's Potato Salad

၈ა

8 potatoes	2 cups onions, diced
1 cup celery, diced	3 eggs, hard-boiled

DRESSING:

2 eggs, well beaten	½ teaspoon salt
1 cup sugar	¼ teaspoon pepper
1 cup vinegar	4 slices cooked bacon, diced
1 teaspoon mustard	

Boil the potatoes in their jackets over high heat until they are tender. Rinse the potatoes in cold water, then peel and chop them into small cubes. Place the chopped potatoes in a large bowl and add the celery, onion, and hard-boiled eggs. Toss to combine.

In a saucepan, combine the beaten eggs, sugar, spices, vinegar, and bacon. Cook over medium heat until the mixture thickens, stirring often. Pour the cooked dressing over the potato salad and toss lightly. Let the salad cool. Cover and refrigerate for several hours before serving to blend flavors. Best if made one day before eating.

MAKES 12 TO 15 SERVINGS

Summer Potato and Herb Salad

2 pounds red potatoes
6 tablespoons red vinegar
½ cup onion, chopped
1 tablespoon whole-grain
    powdered mustard
1 tablespoon fresh tarragon,
    chopped

1½ teaspoons fresh dill, chopped
1 teaspoon salt
1 teaspoon red and/or black
    pepper
6 tablespoons olive oil

Boil the potatoes in their jackets over high heat until they are tender. While the potatoes are cooking, prepare dressing by whisking together all the remaining ingredients in a medium bowl. When the potatoes have reached a desired tenderness, drain the hot water, and then rinse the potatoes in cold water. Chop the potatoes into 1-inch cubes. Place the chopped potatoes in a large bowl and cover them with the dressing. Toss gently. Serve warm or chilled.

MAKES 10 TO 15 SERVINGS

When I was little, the most thrilling words in the language were "once upon a time." When I heard those words, I snuggled up and waited, eager to be transported to castles with magic gardens, or deep, dark caves where giants dwelled.

   Mary Higgins Clark

Corn

c√ɔ

The noise was coming from there. She could see cornstalks jerking and moving. They dared not try to escape from this side. She watched, frozen, for Indians to emerge from the corn.

The first face poked out among the leathery stalks. But it was at knee-height. Then there was another. Mary suddenly went silly with mirth. She reached back and grabbed Ghetel's arm and pulled her down to the opening to show her the intruders.

The faces were looking toward the hut. They had comical black masks over their eyes, and busy little black noses. Then one of the raccoons rose on its hind legs, reached up with little hands and grasped an ear of corn. It shucked it skillfully and then started eating the tender kernels from the middle of the ear.

"Eh!" Ghetel cried. "It's *our* corn! GET!" She scrambled to her feet and ran toward the front door with her hickory lance, abandoning all caution. By the time she had plunged into the corn patch, flailing with her stick, the furry little bandits had vanished and Mary was almost helpless with laughter. It seemed the misery of ages dissolved and sloughed off with this release. She was wiping her eyes when Ghetel returned stooping, grumbling, through the door.

"Ah, Ghetel! You and your raccoons!"

  James Alexander Thom, *Follow the River*

A NOTE FROM JAMES ALEXANDER THOM: My favorite literary passages about food are not about gourmet feasts or delicate sauces, but about the simple, plain stuff we get when we're near starvation. I mean, food on the edge of life: for example, Hemingway's durable old fisherman sustaining himself on raw fish for the strength he needs to haul in the great marlin. Or that "movable feast," the Lewis and Clark Expedition. In the expedition journals, a masterpiece of American literature, they wrote constantly of food, because they were living off the land and nothing was guaranteed.

Worth-Fighting-For Corn Salad

10 ounces frozen sweet corn, thawed and rinsed

2 avocados, pit removed, peeled, and chopped

1 tomato, chopped

½ cup fresh basil, chopped

4 ounces cheddar-style, goat milk cheese, grated

DRESSING:

3 tablespoons fresh lime juice

2 tablespoons olive oil

1 tablespoon seasoned red wine vinegar

2 teaspoons sugar

½ teaspoon salt

¼ teaspoon pepper

1 teaspoon fresh garlic, chopped

Combine the corn, avocados, tomato, and basil in a medium bowl. Combine the dressing ingredients in a small bowl; stir well with a whisk. Pour the dressing over the salad, tossing gently to coat. Sprinkle with goat cheese.

MAKES 6 SERVINGS

There is more treasure in books than in all the pirate's loot on Treasure Island . . . and best of all, you can enjoy these riches every day of your life.

Walt Disney

Eggs

After we finished eating our egg salad sandwiches, cut in wedges with green olives and lettuce, and emptying our little bowls filled with melon balls, Aunt Sid brought out her three photo albums, each one filled with old pictures. She sat on the arm of my chair and told me about every picture. I couldn't look at them hard enough. I couldn't stop staring at the snapshots of May when she was a girl, squinting into the sunshine with her hand over her forehead. She was young and thin, with the entire world before her, or so she thought.

◆ Jane Hamilton, *The Book of Ruth*

Sunshine Egg Salad

It's always best to have eggs from your own chickens—they are so very yellow. Ruth certainly would have known that visual pleasure. —Jane Hamilton

6 eggs, hard-boiled, sliced
½ cup celery with leaves,
   chopped
½ cup Spanish olives stuffed with
   pimentos, sliced

¾ cup mayonnaise
¼ teaspoon lemon pepper
1 tablespoon fresh parsley,
   chopped

Combine all the ingredients in a bowl and mix well with a fork until creamy. Serve as filling for sandwiches.

MAKES 6 SERVINGS

—Inspired by and created with Jane Hamilton

Libraries are magical places. There's nothing quite like strolling the hushed aisles, letting your eye rove along dimly lit shelves. Each spine, each title, seems to beckon with a promise of incredible wonders, surprises, and adventures.

John Jakes

Strawberries

MILLIONS OF STRAWBERRIES

Marcia and I went over the curve,
Eating our way down
Jewels of strawberries we didn't deserve,
Eating our way down,
Till our hands were sticky, and our lips painted.
And over us the hot day fainted,
And we saw snakes,
And got scratched,
And a lust overcame us for the red unmatched
Small buds of berries,
Till we lay down—
Eating our way down—
And rolled in the berries like two little dogs,
Rolled
In the late gold.
And gnats hummed,
And it was cold,
And home we went, home without a berry,
Painted red and brown,
Eating our way down.

Genevieve Taggard

Strawberry-Spinach Salad

½ pint fresh strawberries, rinsed
   and halved
Fresh spinach leaves, stems
   removed, torn into bite-sized
   pieces
4 to 6 mushrooms, rinsed and
   chopped

½ red onion, chopped
¼ cup grated mozzarella or mild
   cheddar cheese
Brianna's Strawberry Vinegarette
   Salad Dressing

Combine the strawberries and vegetables in a large bowl. Top with cheese. Serve with dressing.

MAKES 4 SERVINGS

Alternative Strawberry-Spinach Salad

¼ cup sliced or slivered almonds
1 pound fresh spinach

1 pint fresh strawberries

DRESSING:

⅔ cup white vinegar
1½ cups sugar
2 cups vegetable oil
2 teaspoons salt

4 tablespoons poppy seeds
2 teaspoons powdered mustard
3 tablespoons minced onion

Place the almonds on a baking sheet and bake at 350° until golden. Let cool.

Rinse the spinach and remove stems. Tear the spinach into bite-sized pieces and place it in a large salad bowl. Slice and hull the strawberries. Add the strawberries to the spinach. Sprinkle with almonds.

To make the dressing, combine the vinegar, sugar, and oil in a saucepan and heat over medium heat for about 3 minutes, stirring occasionally, until the sugar dissolves. Pour the sugar mixture into a blender and add the remaining dressing ingredients. Blend well. Cool and pour over salad to taste.

MAKES 6 TO 8 SERVINGS

Some books leave us free, and some books make us free.

Ralph Waldo Emerson

Beans

Every day they all looked at that garden. It was rough and grassy because it was made in the prairie sod, but all the tiny plants were growing. Little crumpled leaves of peas came up, and tiny spears of onions. The beans themselves popped out of the ground. But it was a little yellow bean stem, coiled like a spring, that pushed them up. Then the bean was cracked open and dropped by two baby bean-leaves, and the leaves unfolded flat to the sunshine.

Pretty soon they would all begin to live like kings.

Laura Ingalls Wilder, *Little House on the Prairie*

A King's Bean Salad

2 cups fresh green beans, ends
   removed, cut into 1-inch
   pieces
1 16-ounce can garbanzo beans,
   drained and rinsed
1 16-ounce can kidney beans,
   drained and rinsed

½ cup yellow bell pepper,
   chopped
¼ cup red onion, chopped
2 tablespoons fresh parsley,
   chopped

DRESSING:

½ cup sugar
½ cup vinegar
¼ cup extra-virgin olive oil

½ teaspoon salt
½ teaspoon lemon pepper

In a large salad bowl, combine the beans, bell pepper, onion, and parsley. In small bowl combine all the ingredients for the dressing and stir well until the sugar dissolves. Pour the dressing over the salad. Cover and refrigerate overnight, stirring several times.

MAKES 10 TO 12 SERVINGS

I hate being in libraries, because I always feel there's something I'm missing.

Peter Carey

APPETIZERS, BREADS, AND OTHER FINGER FOODS

"Lounging and larking don't pay," observed Jo, shaking her head. "I'm so tired of it, and mean to go to work at something right off."

"Suppose you learn plain cooking; that's a useful accomplishment which no woman should be without," said Mrs. March, laughing inaudibly at the recollection of Jo's dinner party; for she had met Miss Crocker and heard her account of it.

LOUISA MAY ALCOTT, *LITTLE WOMEN*

There he got out the luncheon-basket and packed a simple meal, in which, re-membering the stranger's origin and preferences, he took care to include a yard of long French bread, a sausage out of which the garlic sang, some cheese which lay down and cried, and a long-necked straw-covered flask wherein lay bottled sunshine shed and garnered on far Southern slopes.

KENNETH GRAHAME, *THE WIND IN THE WILLOWS*

Bacon and Prunes

⌁

Because she was now such a near neighbor, Danny and Ria saw a lot more of Rosemary. She often called in around seven in the evening for an hour or so and they would all have a glass of wine mixed with soda in the front room. Ria made hot cheese savories, or bacon slices wrapped around almonds and prunes. It didn't matter that Rosemary waved them away; Danny would have a few, she and the children would eat the rest, and anyway it gave her a chance to bring out the Victorian china that she had bought at auctions.

◖ Maeve Binchy, *Tara Road*

Almond-Bacon Wraps

⌁

1 package fully cooked cottage
     or Canadian-style bacon
8 ounces prunes

30 small basil leaves
30 almond nuts

Heat oven to 425°. Spray a jelly roll pan, 15½ × 10 × 1 inch, with cooking spray.

Cut each bacon slice in half. Cut a slit in each prune; stuff it with an almond. Place a basil leaf on a bacon strip; wrap it around the stuffed prune. Place the wrapped prune seam side down on the pan.

Bake for 8 to 10 minutes, or until bacon is browned. Serve warm with toothpicks inserted through the seam for easy handling.

MAKES 30 APPETIZERS

—Recipe contributed by Maeve Binchy, as derived from Ria's culinary genius in
Tara Road

We read the verses of one of the great English poets, of Chaucer, of Marvell, of Dryden, with the most modern joy,—with a pleasure, I mean, which is in great part caused by the abstraction of all *time* from their verses. There is some awe mixed with the joy of our surprise, when this poet, who lived in some past world, two or three hundred years ago, says that which lies close to my own soul, that which I also had well nigh thought and said.

  Ralph Waldo Emerson

Mushrooms

That night, while grandmother was getting supper, we opened the package Mrs. Shimerda had given her. It was full of little brown chips that looked like the shavings of some root. They were as light as feathers, and the most noticeable thing about them was their penetrating, earthy odour. We could not determine whether they were animal or vegetable.

"They might be dried meat from some queer beast, Jim. They ain't dried fish, and they never grew on stalk or vine. I'm afraid of 'em. Anyhow, I shouldn't want to eat anything that had been shut up for months with old clothes and goose pillows."

She threw the package into the stove, but I bit off a corner of one of the chips I held in my hand, and chewed it tentatively. I never forgot the strange taste; though it was many years before I knew that those little brown shavings, which the Shimerdas had brought so far and treasured so jealously, were dried mushrooms. They had been gathered, probably, in some deep Bohemian forest.

✒ **Willa Cather,** *My Ántonia*

This time Alice waited patiently until it chose to speak again. In a minute or two the Caterpillar took the hookah out of its mouth and yawned once or twice, and shook itself. Then it got down off the mushroom, and drawled away into the grass, merely remarking as it went, "One side will make you grow taller, and the other side will make you grow shorter."

"One side of *what?* The other side of *what?*" thought Alice to herself.

"Of the mushroom," said the Caterpillar, just as if she had asked it aloud; and in another minute it was out of sight.

✒ **Lewis Carroll,** *Alice's Adventures in Wonderland*

Baked Stuffed Mushrooms

¼ pound shrimp, rinsed, shelled, and deveined
1 tablespoon olive oil
1 pound mushrooms
1 large celery stalk with leaves, chopped
½ cup onion, chopped

¼ teaspoon dried thyme
¼ teaspoon black pepper
1 teaspoon fresh garlic, chopped
¼ cup butter or margarine
¼ teaspoon salt
½ cup plain breadcrumbs

In a frying pan, sauté the shrimp in olive oil for about 2 minutes over medium-high heat. Remove the shrimp from the pan. Cool and finely chop. Set aside.

Remove stems from the mushroom caps. Chop the stems. Sauté the stems, celery, onion, thyme, pepper, and garlic in butter for about 3 minutes. Add salt. Remove from heat.

Combine the shrimp, sautéed vegetables, and breadcrumbs in a bowl. Mix well. Fill the mushroom caps with the stuffing. Place the mushroom caps on a broiler pan lined with aluminum foil in the center of the oven. Bake at 450° for 10 to 15 minutes until browned.

MAKES 8 SERVINGS

But the great Eudora Welty, who should have been writing that afternoon, insisted that I spend a couple of hours with her in her parlor in Jackson, Mississippi. She even opened a bottle of old bourbon so fine that it didn't have a label, only a number inscribed by pen in a fine hand, a gift, she said, from her friend Robert MacNeil of PBS. She talked about her Mississippi upbringing and her days in journalism, thoughtfully about the art of the short story, about good young writers she hoped to encourage, and when I left, walked me down her sidewalk to the curb and bestowed on me a parting smile that felt like a benediction. I knew about her genius from reading her books; that afternoon, I learned about Eudora Welty's generosity.

᠊ᘓ   **Charles Kuralt,** *A Life on the Road*

Shrimp

᠊ᘓ᠊

We were sitting around a pile of shrimp shells on a table covered with newspapers. I had overeaten. All the pink translucent shells, the juice soaking the papers, the four empty bottles next to my plate were evidence. Ordinarily I was not a big eater, but lately I found myself attracted to food. It wasn't an eating disorder; I wasn't binging and purging. But food had a new appeal to me, and I had that feeling in my abdomen that was similar to hunger, so it made sense to eat the food. Sometimes food made the feeling of hunger go away.

◄◖   **Josephine Humphreys,** *Rich in Love*

And if there is a finer place than Charleston in the spring, when azaleas bloom in every garden behind every wrought-iron gate on every street, I don't know it.

Unless, of course, it is Savannah (on the Savannah) in the spring, when the yellow forsythia gives way to the blue wisteria, which gives way to the dogwood, dazzling white. Then the citizens feel the urge to inhale April while strolling the cobblestones of the riverfront, which is crowded with shops and ships, now as ever; or to drive out to Desposito's across the Thunderbolt Bridge for a helping of hot, sweet, pink, miraculous shrimp, ordered by the pound, boiled in their shells, and served in a steaming pile.

◄◖   **Charles Kuralt,** *A Life on the Road*

River Town Cocktail Shrimp with Horseradish Sauce

2 teaspoons salt

1 medium-sized red onion,
   chopped

2 tablespoons celery seed

1 tablespoon prepared mustard

2 tablespoons powdered mustard

1 teaspoon peppercorns

2 cans beer

5 pounds uncooked large shrimp
   in the shell, rinsed

HORSERADISH SAUCE:

1 8-ounce package cream cheese

2 tablespoons mayonnaise

4 tablespoons horseradish

2 tablespoons Worcestershire
   sauce

2 tablespoons onion, minced

1 teaspoon salt

½ cup cream

Combine salt, onion, celery seed, mustards, peppercorns, and beer in a large saucepan and simmer for 15 minutes. Add the shrimp and cook an additional 15 minutes. Cool. Drain and shell the shrimp. Refrigerate the shrimp until ready to serve.

Combine all ingredients for horseradish sauce together in a bowl and beat well. Chill. Serve with shrimp.

MAKES ABOUT 20 SERVINGS

MAKES ABOUT 2 CUPS

S uch a sweet gift—a piece of handmade writing, in an envelope that is not a bill, sitting in our friend's path when she trudges home from a long day spent among wahoos and savages, a day our words will help repair. They don't need to be immortal, just sincere. She can read them twice and again tomorrow: *You're someone I care about, Corrine, and think of often and every time I do you make me smile.*

◄© Garrison Keillor, "How to Write a Letter" from *We Are Still Married*

Cheese

۵۵

T his answered my end, and in about a year and a half I had a flock of about twelve goats, kids and all; and in two years more I had three-and-forty, besides several that I took and killed for my food. After that, I enclosed several pieces of ground to feed them in, with little pens to drive them to take them as I wanted, and gates out of one piece of ground into another.

But this was not all; for now I not only had goat's flesh to feed on when I pleased, but milk too—a thing which, indeed, in the beginning, I did not so much as think of, and which, when it came into my thoughts, was really an agreeable surprise, for now I set up my dairy, and had sometimes a gallon or two of milk in a day.

And as Nature, who gives supplies of food to every creature, dictates even naturally how to make use of it, so I, that had never milked a cow, much less a goat, or seen butter or cheese made only when I was a boy, after a great many essays and miscarriages, made both butter and cheese at last, also salt (though I found it partly made to my hand by the heat of the sun upon some of the rocks of the sea), and never wanted it afterward.

How mercifully can our Creator treat His creatures, even in those conditions in which they seemed to be overwhelmed in destruction! How can He sweeten the bitterest providences, and give us cause to praise Him for dungeons and prisons! What a table was here spread for me in the wilderness, where I saw nothing at first but to perish for hunger!

◖ **Daniel Defoe**, *Robinson Crusoe*

W̲hat one relishes, nourishes.

◖ **Benjamin Franklin**, *Poor Richard's Almanack, 1734*

Baked Cheese Savories

2½ cups grated cheese (Colby jack, cheddar, or mozzarella)
½ cup butter or margarine, softened
½ teaspoon salt

1 cup all-purpose flour
1 cup puffed rice cereal (i.e., Rice Krispies)
¼ teaspoon garlic powder
½ teaspoon dried basil

Mix the cheese and butter together in a large bowl until creamy. Add the remaining ingredients and mix well until the batter is crumbly. Form the batter into small flat discs, about 1 to 1½ inches in diameter and ⅜ inch thick. For variation, form the dough into other flat shapes such as trian-gles, squares, and rectangles. Place the cheese shapes on an ungreased baking sheet. Bake at 375° for 10 to 12 minutes. Place on a paper towel to absorb excess fat. Serve with salsa.

MAKES ABOUT 24 APPETIZERS

The difference between the right word and the almost right word is the difference between lightning and a lightning bug.

✍ Mark Twain

Pâté

"I'm afraid we'll have to run if we want to make it. Or do we really care?" He was startled to hear her voice his own thoughts, and wasn't quite sure what the mischief in her eyes meant. It had been so long since he'd been out with anyone that he was afraid to misinter-pret and make the wrong move.

"Just exactly what are you thinking, Miss Townsend? Is the thought as outrageous as the look on your face?"

"Worse. I was thinking we could put together a picnic and go watch the boats on the East River." She looked like a little kid with a naughty idea. There they both were, dressed for dinner, he in a dark suit and she in a black silk dress, and she was proposing a picnic on the East River.

"It sounds terrific. Do you have any peanut butter?"

"Certainly not." She looked offended. "But I make my own pâté, Mr. Hillyard. And I have sourdough bread." She looked very proud of herself, and Michael was suitably im-pressed.

"My God. I was thinking more in the line of peanut butter and jelly, or hot dogs."

"Never." With a grin, she disappeared into the kitchen, where in ten minutes she concocted the perfect picnic for two. Some leftover ratatouille, the promised pâté, a loaf of sourdough bread, a healthy hunk of Brie, three very ripe pears, some grapes, and a small bottle of wine. "Does that seem like enough?" She looked worried, and he laughed.

  Danielle Steel, *The Promise*

Salmon Pâté

½ pound cooked salmon or one 7-ounce can salmon, drained
6 ounces reduced-fat cream cheese (⅓ less fat works well)
½ cup onion, finely chopped

1 teaspoon fresh garlic, minced
1 tablespoon lemon juice
1 teaspoon Dijon mustard
2 drops Tabasco sauce
Ground black pepper to taste

Place all ingredients in a food processor and process until smooth. Refrigerate for a couple of hours. Serve with crackers or bread.

When a writer sits down at her desk, she initiates a journey that will lead her to language and personal transformation. By turning to a clean sheet of paper and picking up a pen, she begins to give form to something nebulous within. It's an attempt to connect the invisible to the visible, to turn it into words.

  Patrice Vecchione, *Writing and the Spiritual Life*

Cucumber

When they had run and danced themselves dry, the girls quickly dressed and sat down to the fragrant tea. They sat on the northern side of the grove, in the yellow sunshine facing the slope of the grassy hill, alone in a little wild world of their own. The tea was hot and aromatic, there were delicious little sandwiches of cucumber and of caviare, and winy cakes.

"Are you happy, Prune?" cried Ursula in delight, looking at her sister.

"Ursula, I'm perfectly happy," replied Gudrun gravely, looking at the westering sun. "So am I."

 D. H. Lawrence, *Women in Love*

"Ruth, you'll never guess what we had for dinner—lunch, I mean,—cucumber sandwiches with the crusts cut off and iced tea with a sprig of mint in it. It tasted so fresh that way. Mrs. Owens says you must grow a patch of mint near your house for iced tea. And you know what she put on the plate—just for decoration, although you could eat them? Wild strawberries— you know those adorable tiny ones? Garnish makes the plate, that's what Mrs. Owens says."

 Christina Schwarz, *Drowning Ruth*

Summer's Day Cucumber-Tomato Sandwiches

One deli loaf of sourdough or French bread, sliced	3 tomatoes, sliced thin
Premium extra-virgin olive oil	Lemon pepper
2 cucumbers, peeled and sliced into ¼-inch-thick rounds	¼ pound Swiss cheese, sliced thin for sandwiches

Brush oil on a slice of bread. Next, layer one slice of cucumber, one slice of tomato sprinkled with lemon pepper, and one slice of Swiss cheese. Place the open sandwich on a broiler pan lined with aluminum foil. Repeat, making the desired number of sandwiches. Broil the sandwiches for a couple of minutes until cheese is melted.

All that mankind has done, thought, gained or been; it is lying as in magic preservation in the pages of books.

  Thomas Carlyle

Corn Bread

Mama liked to say, "Now you can do without a lot of things, but a family can't do without cornmeal. If you run out of meal you don't have any bread and you don't have any mush. And you don't have anything to fry fish in, or squirrels. When the meat runs out, and the taters runs out, the only thing that will keep you going is the corn bread. You can live a long time on bread and collard greens, if you have collard greens. And you can live a long time on bread alone if you have to, in spite of what the Bible says."

  Robert Morgan, *Gap Creek*

I stood at the open doorway, where, looking right, I could see along the broad road from Hudson, and, on the left, Father trudging down the lane from the house with our breakfast in a sack, hot corn bread, I hoped, and plum jam and boiled eggs. Father apparently had already been hard at work in the tannery, for, despite the morning coolness, he was not wearing his usual coat and shirt, only his red undershirt, with his trousers held up by wide suspenders.

He was fifty or sixty yards from the cabin, when I heard horses coming along the road and turned and saw a group of men approaching, three or four on horseback and several more in a light trap drawn by a pair of roans. One of the riders I recognized as the county sheriff, another as Mr. Chamberlain, the newly despised new owner of our farm.

ᐊᑦ **Russell Banks,** *Cloudsplitter*

Corn Bread

1 cup all-purpose flour	1 cup yellow cornmeal
½ teaspoon salt	1 egg, beaten
4 teaspoons baking powder	1 cup milk
2 tablespoons sugar	¼ cup shortening, melted

Stir the flour, salt, baking powder, and sugar together in a bowl. Add the cornmeal. Combine the egg, milk, and shortening together in a large bowl. Add the dry ingredients to the egg mixture and stir until smooth. Pour the batter into a greased 9-inch square pan and bake at 400° for about 20 minutes. For corn muffins, spoon the batter into greased muffin tins and bake for 10 to 12 minutes until lightly browned.

MAKES 8 SERVINGS

A tune is more lasting than the song of birds. And a word is more lasting than the wealth of the world.

ᐊᑦ **Irish saying**

Crackling Bread

ᴄᴠᴈ

They built a fire against the side of a great log twenty or thirty steps within the sombre depths of the forest, and then cooked some bacon in the frying-pan for supper, and used up half of the corn "pone" stock they had brought. It seemed glorious sport to be feasting in that wild, free way in the virgin forest of an unexplored and uninhabited island, far from the haunts of men, and they said they never would return to civilization. The climbing fire lit up their faces and threw its ruddy glare upon the pillared tree-trunks of their forest temple, and upon the varnished foliage and festooning vines.

When the last crisp slice of bacon was gone, and the last allowance of corn pone devoured, the boys stretched themselves out on the grass, filled with contentment. They could have found a cooler place, but they would not deny themselves such a romantic feature as the roasting campfire.

  Mark Twain, *The Adventures of Tom Sawyer*

Traditional Southern Crackling Corn Bread

ᴄᴠᴈ

1 pound country-style bacon or	½ teaspoon salt
pork rind, cut ⅓ inch thick	1¼ cups milk
1½ cups yellow cornmeal	2 large eggs, lightly beaten
1 cup all-purpose flour	4 tablespoons unsalted butter,
2 tablespoons sugar	melted
2 teaspoons baking powder	

Preheat the oven to 400°. In a 10-inch cast-iron skillet, cook the bacon or pork rind over moderate heat until crisp, about 7 minutes. Drain on paper towels; chop when cool. Reserve 2 tablespoons of the drippings.

Wipe out the skillet and set it over low heat. Add the drippings and swirl to coat the pan. In a medium bowl, combine the cornmeal with the flour, sugar, baking powder, and salt. In another bowl, combine the milk and eggs and add to the cornmeal mixture along with the butter; stir just until the cornmeal is moistened. Fold in the bacon and pour the batter into the warm skillet. Bake for about 20 minutes, or until golden and a toothpick inserted in the center comes out clean. Serve warm.

This corn bread can be refrigerated, well wrapped, for 2 days. Re-warm, wrapped in foil, in a 350° oven.

MAKES 6 TO 8 SERVINGS

Reading is the work of the alert mind, is demanding, and under ideal conditions produces finally a sort of ecstasy. This gives the experience of reading a sublimity and power unequaled by any other form of communication.

   E. B. White

Bagels and Soda Bread

⌒⌒⌒

"You miss that." Since it did smell seductive, she got down a mug for herself. "The delis, the hustle-bustle." She opened the refrigerator and got out her little carton of cream. "What else do you miss about New York?"

The toast popped. "Bagels."

"Bagels?" She got out butter and jam as well, then just stood holding them and staring at him. "A man of your resources, and what you miss about New York is coffee and bagels?"

"Right at the moment, I'd pay a hundred dollars for a fresh bagel. No offense to your Irish soda bread. But, really."

"Well, that's a wonder." . . .

. . . She got the kettle to fill as Trevor leaned back against the counter, spooning up soup where he stood. "I'll have some tea to keep you company. Since you're eating, you might want to have what's in the bag with your tinned soup."

"What is it?"

She only smiled and turned on the tap. Trevor set down his bowl, peeked in the bag. When his hand darted in, like an eager boy's into a pond after a prize frog, she laughed.

"Bagels?"

"Well, we couldn't have you pining, could we?" Delighted with his reaction, she carried the kettle to the stove. "Shawn made them, lest you think I've been baking—and believe me you're better off I haven't. He wasn't pleased with the first batch or you'd have had them a couple of days ago. But he's well satisfied with these, so I think you'll enjoy them."

Trevor only stood there, the plastic-wrapped bread in his hand, staring at her as she turned on the burner under the kettle. It was ridiculous, insane, but something was stirring inside him. Warm, fluid, lovely. In defense, he struggled with a joke.

"A full dozen, too. I guess I owe you twelve hundred dollars."

୶ **Nora Roberts,** *Heart of the Sea*

P a always said he did not ask [for] any other sweetening, when Ma put the prints of her hands on the loaves.

୶ **Laura Ingalls Wilder,** *Little House on the Prairie*

Irish Soda Bread

cᴠᴐ

3 cups all-purpose flour	1 cup sugar
1½ teaspoons baking powder	1½ cups golden raisins
1 teaspoon baking soda	1½ cups buttermilk
½ teaspoon cream of tartar	2 eggs, beaten
½ teaspoon salt	2 tablespoons butter, melted

Sift dry ingredients three times. Soak the raisins in hot water for 5 minutes, then drain well and add them to the dry ingredients. Mix the buttermilk, beaten eggs, and melted butter together and add to the dry ingredients. Stir just until moistened. Bake in a greased 2-quart casserole dish at 350° for 45 to 55 minutes. Cut into wedges when cool.

MAKES 8 TO 10 SERVINGS

> The culture I come from, we tell stories to survive. We tell stories to grace our lives with hope—not just to explain suffering, but to express and gratify our deepest desires.
>
> Debra Magpie Earling

Bagels

4 cups all-purpose flour

1½ teaspoons salt

1 package active dry yeast
  (or 3 teaspoons)

1 cup lukewarm potato water*

4 tablespoons honey

3 tablespoons oil

2 eggs, beaten

1 egg yolk, beaten

Desired toppings (poppy seeds,
  sesame seeds, coarse salt,
  onion flakes, cinnamon sugar
  mix)

Sift together the flour and salt in a large bowl. Mix the yeast in ⅓ cup of the potato water, then add this liquid to the flour. Add the honey, oil, and remaining potato water, mixing well. Add the eggs and mix well. Shape into a dough. On a lightly floured surface, knead the dough for 8 to 10 minutes until dough is soft, smooth, and elastic. Add more flour during kneading process if dough is sticky. Place the dough in a greased bowl, turning dough once so top is also greased. Cover it with a cloth and let rise at room temperature until doubled in bulk, 1 to 2 hours.

Divide the dough into 4 portions. Divide each portion into 6 pieces. (A long piece of string or dental floss works best. Place dough over middle of string on counter. Pick up each end of string in each hand, cross string ends, and pull through dough as if you were tying a half-knot.) Cover dough with plastic wrap and allow to rest for 20 minutes.

Pinch off dough and form into golf-ball-sized balls. Insert thumb in the center. Knead the dough to enlarge the center hole and shape bagel into a ring. Alternatively, knead the dough into a tubular shape, about ½ inch thick, and pinch ends together firmly, adding a drop or two of water if necessary. Seam must be secure so that circle will remain intact. Or bagels may be cut with a doughnut cutter. Place the bagels on a greased baking sheet, cover them with plastic wrap, and allow to rise for another 20 to 30 minutes.

Bring water to a full rolling boil in a large pot. Add 1 tablespoon of sugar. Drop bagels into the boiling water, a few at a time, allowing room for expansion. Boil the bagels for about 90 seconds and then flip them over, boiling another 90 seconds. Bagels should swell to nearly double their original size while boiling. Remove the bagels with a slotted spoon and drain them on a paper towel. Immediately dip the warm bagels in desired topping. If bagels are plain, brush them with egg white for a shinier surface.

Bake the bagels on a greased baking sheet at 375° for 25 to 30 minutes or until golden brown. For softer bagels, brush them with butter after removal from oven.

MAKES ABOUT 24 BAGELS

* Potato water is the liquid that remains after potatoes have been boiled. Save potatoes for other purposes.

Bread

∞

"Teddy!" she said at last.

"What?" he asked.

"I told you a lie," she said, humbly tragic.

His soul stirred uneasily.

"Oh aye?" he said casually.

She was not satisfied. He ought to be more moved.

"Yes," she said.

He cut a piece of bread.

"Was it a good one?" he asked.

She was piqued. Then she considered—*was* it a good one? Then she laughed.

"No," she said, "it wasn't up to much."

"Ah!" he said easily, but then with a steady strength of fondness for her in his tone. "Get it out then."

    D. H. Lawrence, *The White Stocking*

Hunger never saw bad bread.

    Benjamin Franklin, *Poor Richard's Almanack, 1733*

Upside down I may
take shape.
I may become resilient.
Kneaded, turned on end
I will become less
And somehow more
myself.

    Judith Ryan Hendricks, introduction to *Bread Alone*

Unbelievable Braided Bread

1 cup lukewarm water
3 tablespoons butter or
    margarine, chopped into
    smaller pieces
3 cups all-purpose flour

3½ tablespoons sugar
1 teaspoon salt
2 teaspoons active dry yeast
2 tablespoons butter or
    margarine, melted

Add the first 6 ingredients to a bowl in the order shown above. Mix with fork, pressing the flour into the butter and water. When the dough begins to take form, mix and knead dough with your hands. Knead the dough for about five minutes. Cover and let rise in a warm, draft-free place for about 30 minutes.

To braid bread: Divide the dough into three portions of equal size. (Using a clean string or dental floss works best. Place the dough over the string laid on the counter. Bring each end of the string up around dough, cross the strings, and pull them through the dough as if you were tying a half-knot.) Form each portion of dough into three snake-like strands by squeezing and kneading. Do not stretch the dough.

On a lightly oiled baking sheet, cross the strands on top of one another at their middles. Begin braiding from the middle of the loaf toward one end. Pinch the strands together at the end. Turn the pan and begin braiding toward the opposite end. Pinch the strands together at the end. Braiding from the middle of the bread keeps the loaf uniform in shape.

Cover the braided dough with a light, dry cloth and let it rise in a warm, draft-free place for about 45 minutes until dough is doubled in size.

Heat oven to 375°. Brush braided dough with melted butter. Bake for about 20 to 25 minutes until golden brown.

MAKES ONE LARGE LOAF

[I]t is imperative to read and to live with the same intensity . . . without flavor, life is not worth living . . . and . . . without the flavor of life, literature doesn't exist.

   Laura Esquivel, *Between Two Fires*

Loaf of Bread

ᴄᴡᴈ

Jean had no work. The family had no bread. No bread literally. Seven children!

One Sunday evening, Maubert Isabeau, the baker on the Church Square at Faverolles, was preparing to go to bed, when he heard a violent blow on the grated front of his shop. He arrived in time to see an arm passed through a hole made by a blow from a fist, through the grating and the glass. The arm seized a loaf of bread and carried it off. Isabeau ran out in haste; the robber fled at the full speed of his legs. Isabeau ran after him and stopped him. The thief had flung away the loaf, but his arm was still bleeding.

It was Jean Valjean . . .

. . . He admitted that he had committed an extreme and blameworthy act; that that loaf of bread would probably not have been refused to him had he asked for it; that, in any case, it would have been better to wait until he could get it through compassion or through work; that it is not an unanswerable argument to say, "Can one wait when one is hungry?"

   Victor Hugo, *Les Misérables*

Over fifty law enforcers dressed in desert fatigues stand guard.

We are standing in a prayer circle a few feet from the cattle guard that separates us from them. Step across that arbitrary line and you will be handcuffed and arrested.

A Maori woman begins to pray. Her voice is followed by Corbin Harney and Raymond Yowell, Shoshone elders. This is the Shoshone sunrise ceremony. They pray to the Four Directions. A hundred or so people have gathered together. It evolves into a circle of testimonies, stories of why people have come. A woman from the Marshall Islands speaks: "All living things are dying on my island."

A Dominican sister from England, dressed in her black and white habit, says, "I am here out of guilt, out of anger and grief. My country tests here."

A Japanese film crew from Hiroshima has traveled many miles. One man steps forward. "We are recording the present, which might prevent the past from reoccurring."

A loaf of bread is passed around the circle. Each of us breaks off a small piece and eats. I pass the loaf to my uncle. He is a spiritual man. He understands the idea of sacrament but did not anticipate this. Richard stands behind his aviator glasses, watching, his thumbs in the front pockets of his Levi's. He takes the bread, breaks it, and eats.

The bread continues around the circle, becoming smaller and smaller.

The rally begins.

   Terry Tempest Williams, *An Unspoken Hunger: Stories from the Field*

Multigrain Bread

1¼ cup warm water	4 teaspoons gluten flour*
1 teaspoon sugar	1 cup whole-wheat flour
1½ teaspoons yeast	1 cup white bread flour or all-
1 teaspoon salt	purpose flour
1 tablespoon honey	1 teaspoon dough enhancer*
2 tablespoons oil	1 cup 7-grain cereal*

Dissolve the yeast and sugar in the warm water and set aside. In a large bowl, mix the salt, honey, and oil. Gradually stir in the flours, enhancer, and cereal. Gradually add the yeast mixture and mix well. As the dough forms, knead it into a ball with your hands, then place it on a lightly floured board and continue kneading it until the gluten is properly developed (the dough will be firm and elastic), about 10 to 18 minutes. Place the dough in an oiled bowl about twice its size. Turn the dough over so that the top is oiled. Cover it with a towel and allow it to rise in a warm place until it is doubled in size. Punch the dough down, roll it out with a rolling pin, and then roll the dough tightly into a loaf, sealing the edges. Put the loaf seam side down in a greased loaf pan, cover, and allow it to rise until doubled in size.

Bake at 350° for 35 to 40 minutes, or until loaf sounds hollow when tapped lightly with your finger. Remove the bread from the pan and brush the top with melted butter.

MAKES ONE LARGE LOAF

Available at health food stores, supermarkets, or kitchen specialty stores.

Without writers there would be no need for librarians or libraries, publishers or bookstores.

   Maia Wojciechowska

Yeast

Leaven, which some deem the soul of bread, the *spiritus* which fills its cellular tissue, which is religiously preserved like the vestal fire,—some precious bottleful, I suppose, first brought over in the Mayflower, did the business for America, and its influence is still rising, swelling, spreading, in cerealian billows over the land,—this seed I regularly and faithfully procured from the village, till at length one morning I forgot the rules, and scalded my yeast; by which accident I discovered that even this was not indispensable,—for my discoveries were not by the synthetic or analytic process,—and I have gladly omitted it since, though most housewives earnestly assured me that safe and wholesome bread without yeast might not be, and elderly people prophesied a speedy decay of the vital forces. Yet I find it not to be an essential ingredient, and after going without it for a year am still in the land of the living; and I am glad to escape the trivialness of carrying a bottleful in my pocket, which would sometimes pop and discharge its contents to my discomfiture. It is simpler and more respectable to omit it.

Henry David Thoreau, *Walden*

Safe and Wholesome Refrigerator Rolls

2 cups milk	4 eggs, beaten
½ cup butter or margarine	½ cup sugar
2 tablespoons dry yeast	½ teaspoon salt
1 tablespoon sugar	7 to 8 cups all-purpose flour
1 cup lukewarm water	

Scald the milk with the butter in a saucepan; cool to lukewarm. In a small bowl, stir the yeast and 1 tablespoon of sugar into 1 cup of warm water. In a large bowl, combine the dissolved yeast, eggs, and cooled milk mixture. Stir in the remaining sugar and salt. Add 3 cups of the flour and beat well. Add 3 more cups of the flour and beat well. Gradually add the remaining flour until the dough is pliable and smooth and can be formed into a ball.

Place the dough in a large, greased bowl and allow it to rise in a warm place until it doubles in size (about 2 hours). Shape the dough and bake according to a selected recipe below. Since this recipe makes 4 dozen rolls or 2 pull-apart loaves, place any dough not needed, prior to rising, in a greased, air-tight container and refrigerate for up to 3 days until needed again. At that time, remove the dough from the refrigerator and allow it to rise in a warm place until it doubles in size and proceed with a recipe below.

Variations:

Dinner rolls: Form the dough into walnut-sized balls and place them with sides touching on a 9 × 13-inch greased baking sheet. Cover and allow to rise until almost doubled and bake for 12 to 15 minutes at 350°.

Cloverleaf rolls: Form the dough into 1-inch balls. Place them in greased muffin tins, 3 balls per section. Cover and allow to rise until almost doubled. Bake for 12 to 15 minutes at 350°.

Knots: Roll the dough into a ¼-inch-thick rectangle on a lightly floured surface. Cut it into strips that are ½ inch wide and 5 inches long. Tie each strip loosely into a single knot. Place them in greased muffin tins, knot side down. Cover and allow to rise until almost doubled. Bake for 12 to 15 minutes at 350°.

Parker House rolls: Roll the dough out to a ¼-inch thickness on a lightly floured surface. Cut the dough with a round 2½-inch-diameter cookie cutter. Make a crease across each circle, slightly off center, using table knife. Fold the short side onto the long side and press the edges together. Place the rolls with edges touching on a greased baking sheet. Cover and allow to rise until almost doubled. Bake for 12 to 15 minutes at 350°.

Onion rolls: Add 2 single-serving packages of dry onion soup mix to the dough. Shape the dough into balls. Place them on a 9 × 13-inch greased baking sheet and brush them with melted butter. Cover and allow to rise until almost doubled. Bake for 12 to 15 minutes at 350°.

Cheese rolls: Roll the dough out to ¾-inch thickness on a lightly floured surface and cut with a round, 2½-inch-diameter cutter. Place the dough circles with sides touching on a greased baking sheet. Brush them with melted butter or margarine and sprinkle with grated Parmesan cheese or grated cheddar cheese. Cover and allow to rise until almost doubled. Bake for 12 to 15 minutes at 350°.

Cinnamon rolls: Roll the dough out on a lightly floured surface into an 8 × 12-inch rectangle, ¼ inch thick. Brush it with melted butter or margarine and sprinkle generously with cinnamon and sugar. Starting with the 8-inch side, roll the dough tightly into a log shape and pinch the seams together to seal. Place the roll seam side down on a flat surface and cut it into 1-inch round slices. Place the slices with sides touching in a greased 9 × 12-inch pan. Cover and allow them to rise until almost doubled. Bake for 12 to 15 minutes at 350°. Frost while warm. Variation of cinnamon filling: Sprinkle 1 cup chopped nuts and 1 cup raisins over cinnamon-sugar mixture before shaping into roll.

Cinnamon pull-apart loaf: Shape the dough into 36 1-inch balls. Dip each ball in melted butter and roll it in cinnamon and sugar. Then layer the balls in a greased loaf pan. Bake at 350° for 30 to 35 minutes. Frost while warm and still in the pan, allowing frosting to drip down sides of the loaf (see cinnamon roll variation). When cooled, turn the pan over and tap gently until the loaf slides out of the pan. Turn upright and serve.

Orange rolls: Prepare as directed for cinnamon rolls, substituting the following filling: ½ cup sugar, ¼ cup melted butter or margarine, and 1 tablespoon grated orange zest. Cover and allow to rise until almost doubled and bake for 12 to 15 minutes at 350°. Frost when warm. For frosting, combine up to ¼ cup orange juice with 2 cups powdered sugar.

I believe that the job of the novelist is to be out there on the fringes and speaking for an experience that has not really been spoken for.

⊷ **Donna Tartt**

Sourdough

ᐉᐁᐉ

On the first night out of Fort Sumner, Nacho prepared a chicken stew with potatoes and gravy, which Mr. Skimmerhorn pronounced one of the best he'd ever eaten, but Canby, Gompert and Savage refused it. "We don't want no Mexican grub," they complained. "We want real food," so Nacho took down a Dutch oven, cut off six big steaks, two per man, put the oven in the fire, piled coals on the lids, and when the chewy meat was nearly black, served it to the grumblers.

"That's decent food," Canby said, as he chewed the tough meat.

The same thing happened next night when Nacho served a kind of chili, hot and meaty and very tasty. Again Mr. Skimmerhorn complimented the Mexican, and again Canby and his colleagues complained that they didn't come on no cattle trail to eat Mexican grub, and where were the steaks? Sad-eyed, Nacho decided to give them an extra ration of biscuits. He was especially good with biscuits, for which he kept a large crock of sourdough fermenting in the back of his wagon. He had started this crock working back in Jacksborough: flour, water, some sugar, a little vinegar, some clean wood ash and some salt. When it was well fermented he threw away about two-thirds—"To keep the crock happy"—and refilled it with flour and water.

Sourdough wouldn't breed unless the temperature was just right, so on very cold nights Nacho took the crock to bed with him; on unusually hot days he kept it in the wagon wrapped in a wet cloth.

To make his biscuits he took from the crock a good helping of sourdough, mixed it with flour, water and salt, and pinched off nubbins, which he placed around the bottom of a Dutch oven, maybe forty biscuits to one baking.

Nacho's biscuits were the best the men had ever eaten, and he told them his secret: "More coals on top than on the bottom." He achieved this by placing his oven in dying embers and heaping upon the lid the liveliest coals he could find. In this way the biscuits came out brown and crisp on top, well done on the bottom and just about perfect inside. It was not unusual for him to bake eighty for a meal, so that each rider could have six or seven, but this night he outdid himself.

Knowing that the treat he had for them would be appreciated, he baked up three ovenfuls of biscuits, many more than a hundred, and told the men, "For that young bull Mr. Poteet traded, look what we got!" And he opened four jars of the finest sagebrush honey, dark and aromatic and tasty.

The men ate ravenously, and Canby said, "For a lousy Mexican, you are one great cook." The chili and the chicken stew were forgiven. Men broke open the crusty biscuits, drenched the feather-light insides with honey and ate them like Christmas candy.

◖ **James A. Michener,** *Centennial*

Rocky Mountain Sourdough Starter

2 cups all-purpose flour

2 tablespoons sugar

2½ teaspoons yeast

1 teaspoon salt

2 cups warm water (about 100° to 105°)

In a large bowl mix the flour, sugar, yeast, and salt. Gradually stir in the water; mix or whisk until smooth. Cover with a towel; set in a warm (80° to 85°), draft-free place. Stir 2 or 3 times a day for about 3 days until starter is bubbly and produces a yeasty aroma. Transfer this mixture to a larger bowl, jar, or plastic container. Cover with snug lid; punch holes in lid to allow ventilation. Makes about 1½ to 2 cups starter, depending on thickness. It can be creamy or as thick as dough because of room conditions, age and other variables.

A few tips: Never mix your starter in a metal container or use a metal spoon—use a plastic or glass container and a wooden spoon. Stir once a day. If liquid separates on top, stir it back in if it's orange-colored. If green, throw out and start again. Every time the starter is used, replenish it with an equal quantity of flour and water. Use weekly if kept in the refrigerator. If starter is not used on a weekly basis, stir it every 5 days or so and add a small amount of flour and water to maintain it. Starter can be frozen for 3 to 5 months. Allow 24 hours for thawing and stir well before using. Refrigerate when not in use.

Rocky Mountain Sourdough Biscuits

1 cup all-purpose flour
1 tablespoon baking powder
½ teaspoon salt
½ teaspoon soda
½ teaspoon sugar

¼ cup shortening
1 cup sourdough starter
2 tablespoons melted butter or
  margarine

Stir the dry ingredients together in a bowl. Cut in the shortening with a pastry blender or fork until mixture is crumbly. Stir in the starter until a soft dough forms. Gather the dough into a ball and knead for about 30 seconds. Roll the dough out to ½-inch thickness on a lightly floured surface. Cut the dough with a biscuit cutter. Place the biscuits on an ungreased baking sheet. Brush the tops with melted butter and let rest for 15 minutes. Bake at 425° for about 12 minutes.

MAKES 16 BISCUITS

I aim to bring the reader into an imaginary world that will stay so real that toward the end there will be an enormous sense of loss. That involves the creation of a total atmosphere.

  James A. Michener

Bowl of Punch

❧

"I will go to Meryton," said she, "as soon as I am dressed and tell the good, good news to my sister Philips. And as I come back, I can call on Lady Lucas and Mrs. Long. Kitty, run down and order the carriage. An airing would do me a great deal of good, I am sure. Girls, can I do anything for you in Meryton? Oh! Here comes Hill. My dear Hill, have you heard the good news? Miss Lydia is going to be married; and you shall all have a bowl of punch, to make merry at her wedding."

❧ Jane Austen, *Pride and Prejudice*

Merry Punch

❧

1 12-fluid-ounce can frozen grape juice concentrate, thawed
1 2-liter bottle of 7-UP, chilled

Ice
Sliced limes

Mix the juice concentrate and 7-UP together in a large punch bowl. Add ice and arrange sliced limes to float on top.

MAKES ABOUT 12 (6-OUNCE) SERVINGS

We read books to find out who we are. What other people, real or imaginary, do and think or feel is an essential guide to our understanding of what we ourselves are and may become.

❧ Ursula K. Le Guin

DESSERTS

With her fingernail she writes on his chest, Milk, Butter, Eggs, Sugar. The invisible ink of her finger rises up like a welt. In the shower it becomes perfectly clear—dermatographism. For the moment he is a walking grocery list—it will fade within the hour.

A. M. HOMES, "THE WEATHER OUTSIDE IS SUNNY AND BRIGHT," IN *THINGS YOU SHOULD KNOW*

SIMPLE SIMON

Simple Simon met a pieman
Going to the fair;
Says Simple Simon to the pieman,
"Let me taste your ware."
Says the pieman to Simple Simon,
"Show me first your penny";
Says Simple Simon to the pieman,
"Indeed I have not any."

TRADITIONAL CHILDREN'S POEM

Pie Crust

Grandma Welty, with each work day in the week set firmly aside for a single task, was not very expectant of conversation either. Of course I remember Friday best—baking day. Her pies, enough for a week, were set to cool when done on the kitchen windowsills, side by side like so many cheeky faces telling us "One at a time!"

 Eudora Welty, *One Writer's Beginnings*

Marie took the pie out of the oven and the crust was so perfect that Nora got to her feet.
   She stood next to Marie at the stove and watched the steam rise from the golden pastry.
   "How do you do that?" Nora said, awed.
   "The secret of a pie is in the crust," Marie confided. Her daughter-in-law to be, Rosemary, was such a good baker that it gave Marie the greatest pleasure to have Nora admire her pie.
   "I can bake everything except pie crust," Nora said. "Mine are always white. They look like glue."
   "You use butter," Marie guessed.
   "Butter and sugar," Nora said.
   "Never," Marie told her. "Use Crisco instead."
   "Ah." Nora nodded.
   Nora and Marie looked at each other and smiled.
   "Prick the top with a fork seven times after you flute the edges," Marie said.
   Nora put her arms around Marie and thanked her.
   "What's a pie crust?" Marie shrugged.
   "You know what I mean," Nora said.

 Alice Hoffman, *Seventh Heaven*

Lower-Fat Sweet Pie Pastry

FOR ONE 2-CRUST, 9-INCH PIE:

7 tablespoons shortening or
   margarine
3 tablespoons applesauce
2 tablespoons sugar

2 cups all-purpose flour
½ teaspoon salt
5 to 7 tablespoons water

FOR ONE 1-CRUST, 9-INCH PIE, OR ONE 2-CRUST 8-INCH PIE:

6½ tablespoons shortening or
   margarine
1½ tablespoons applesauce
1 tablespoon sugar

1½ cups all-purpose flour
¼ teaspoon salt
4 to 5 tablespoons water

Mix the shortening, applesauce, sugar, flour, and salt in a bowl with a fork
or pastry blender until the mixture is crumbly. Add water 1 tablespoon at
a time until dough is pliable. Work dough into a ball with hands after last
tablespoon of water is added.

Traditional Pie Pastry

FOR ONE 2-CRUST, 9-INCH PIE:

⅔ cup shortening or margarine
2 tablespoons sugar (optional)
2 cups all-purpose flour

½ teaspoon salt
5 to 7 tablespoons water

FOR ONE 1-CRUST, 9-INCH PIE, OR ONE 2-CRUST, 8-INCH PIE:

½ cup shortening or margarine   ¼ teaspoon salt
1 tablespoon sugar (optional)   4 to 5 tablespoons water
1½ cups all-purpose flour

Mix the shortening, sugar, flour, and salt in a bowl with a fork or pastry blender until the mixture is crumbly. Add water 1 tablespoon at a time until dough is pliable. Work dough into a ball with hands after last tablespoon of water is added.

Libraries are the custodians of civilization.

&   Barbara Cooney

Blueberry

Everybody was watching Violet Beauregarde as she stood there chewing this extraordinary gum. Little Charlie Bucket was staring at her absolutely spellbound, watching her huge rubbery lips as they pressed and unpressed with the chewing, and Grandpa Joe stood beside him, gaping at the girl. Mr. Wonka was wringing his hands and saying, "No, no, no, no, no! It isn't ready for eating! It isn't right! You mustn't do it!"

"Blueberry pie and cream!" shouted Violet. "Here it comes! Oh my, it's perfect! It's beautiful! It's . . . it's exactly as though I'm swallowing it! It's as though I'm chewing and swallowing great big spoonfuls of the most marvelous blueberry pie in the world!"

"Good heavens, girl!" shrieked Mrs. Beauregarde suddenly, staring at Violet. "What's happening to your nose!"

"Oh, be quiet, mother, and let me finish!" said Violet.

"It's turning blue!" screamed Mrs. Beauregarde. "Your nose is turning blue as a blueberry!"

&   Roald Dahl, *Charlie and the Chocolate Factory*

Not Violet, but Blueberry Pie

Pastry for one 2-crust 9-inch pie

4 cups blueberries, fresh or
  frozen (if frozen, do not thaw)

1 tablespoon lemon juice

½ teaspoon fresh grated lemon
  zest

⅓ cup all-purpose flour

¾ cup sugar

4 teaspoons cornstarch

Pinch of salt

Place berries in a bowl. Drizzle them with lemon juice. Add the remaining ingredients and toss to distribute. Pour the berries into a 9-inch pie pan layered with a bottom crust rolled ⅜ inch thick. Position top crust, crimp edges together, and trim. Bake at 400° for about 50 minutes. (Frozen berries require longer baking time.) Cool and serve with vanilla ice cream or whipped cream.

Handle them carefully, for words have more power than atom bombs.

◁ℚ **Pearl Strachan Hurd**

Rhubarb

❧

As they cut their pie, the men discussed corn. Tom asked Grover how many bushels he figured he'd get from an acre, but instead of answering, Grover put up his finger to tell Tom to hold off a minute. He put a big bite of pie into his mouth before he said, "The way I see it—" He swallowed, stared at his pie a minute, then gave me a questioning look.

Tom tried his pie, and got the very same expression on his face. He didn't swallow, however. Instead, he pinched in his cheeks, keeping the pie in the middle of his mouth. "Queenie . . ." Tom said, moving the food in his mouth from side to side.

"What's wrong?"

"What kind of pie is this, anyway?" Grover asked.

"Rhubarb," I said. "Don't you know rhubarb pie? I thought it was your favorite."

"It doesn't taste like rhubarb," Tom said. He finally swallowed what was in his mouth and made a face.

"I picked it today, on the north side of the barn," I said. Then I cut my own piece, but I couldn't bring myself to eat it.

Rita tasted hers and spit it out onto her plate.

Grover studied what was left of his pie, moving the crust aside, then picking at the filling. "This is not rhubarb, Queenie." Grover grinned at me. "It's Swiss chard! You made a rhubarb pie out of red Swiss chard!"

⋐ Sandra Dallas, *The Persian Pickle Club*

Somewhere during that first month at Rivercrest, Ray made a couple of friends: Stony, a retired roofer who'd once fought Willie Pep in the Golden Gloves, and Norman, who'd fought in World War II at Bataan. Back in the old days, Norman claimed—when he was a kid working at his father's horse-drawn lunch wagon in downtown Three Rivers—he had served Mae West a piece of rhubarb pie. Free of charge. She was passing through town in vaudeville. There was a lot of kidding back and forth about that. What else had he served her? What had *she* served *him?* Maybe that new one—what'd she call herself? Madonna? Maybe *she* liked a little of Norman's rhubarb pie, too.

⋐ Wally Lamb, *I Know This Much Is True*

Extra-Special Rhubarb Pie

Pastry for one 2-crust, 9-inch pie

3½ to 4 cups rhubarb, sliced into
  ¼-inch-thick pieces

1 cup sugar

¼ cup all-purpose flour

3 teaspoons cornstarch

¾ teaspoon nutmeg

½ teaspoon cinnamon

½ teaspoon fresh grated orange
  zest

½ teaspoon sugar

Preheat oven to 350°. Mix all the ingredients together in a large bowl until well combined and let sit for about ½ hour. Line a 9-inch pie plate with the pastry rolled ⅜ inch thick. Place the filling in the pie shell. Position the top crust and crimp and seal the edges together. Cut slits in the top crust to allow steam to escape. Sprinkle the top crust with ½ teaspoon sugar. Bake at 350° for about 45 to 50 minutes. Cool.

VARIATION: Substitute 2 cups sliced strawberries for 2 cups rhubarb.

E very theme, every story, every tragedy that exists in literature takes place in my little community. *Hamlet* takes place on my reservation daily. *King Lear* takes place on my reservation daily. It's a powerful place. I'm never going to run out of stories.

   Sherman Alexie

Pecan

ᴄᴧᴐ

"Snip, snip, snip," says Jess, coming in the front door. "When are you guys going to quit fighting?" Ryan is behind her, carrying a pie plate. Her mother eyes it with phony delight masking her alarm.

"We're not fighting, for heaven's sake. Now, what's that you've got, Ryan Dougherty? You're a guest here. I hope you didn't think you had to bring your own food to Thanksgiving dinner!"

"Small contribution," he says with a smile. "Made it myself. Chocolate pecan pie. My mother's recipe."

"Why, how lovely!"

Jess takes the pan from Ryan, carrying it out to the kitchen, while Annie follows her.

"Oh, you are a devil, sister."

"What?" Jess gives her an innocent look, but they both know: holiday menus never vary—it's turkey on Thanksgiving, shepherd's pie at Christmas, ham for Easter. Likewise, with the side dishes and desserts. They've never thought to challenge it.

"Did he really make it himself?"

"He did. He's a great cook."

ᴌᴏ **Judith Guest, *Errands***

Mother's Chocolate Pecan Pie

Pastry for one 1-crust 9-inch pie

4 ounces milk chocolate chips
(about ½ to ⅔ cup)

1 cup light corn syrup

1 cup dark brown sugar, packed

3 large eggs

2 tablespoons unsalted butter,
melted and slightly cooled

1½ teaspoons vanilla

¼ teaspoon salt

1 cup pecans, chopped

WHIPPED CREAM:

1 cup whipping cream

¼ cup powdered sugar

2 to 4 tablespoons brandy

Roll the pastry to a ⅜-inch thickness, position it in a pie pan, trim edges, and chill for 30 minutes. Arrange the chocolate chips in the bottom of the chilled pie shell. In a large bowl, mix all the remaining ingredients, except pecans, until well combined. Add the pecans and whisk together. Slowly pour the batter over the chocolate chip layer. Bake on top of a cookie sheet at 350° for 55 to 60 minutes, or until puffed and golden brown. Cool completely. Prepare whipped cream by beating whipping cream and sugar together into soft peaks. Drizzle with brandy, to taste.

—Recipe contributed by Judith Guest

I've never thought of writing as the mere arrangement of words on the page but as the attempted embodiment of a vision: a complex of emotions, raw experience.

Joyce Carol Oates

Strawberry

When they got back, they were surprised to see Cotton's car in front. The house was dark and they cautiously opened the door, unsure of what they would find. The lights flew up as Louisa and Eugene took the black cloths from around the lanterns and they and Cotton called out "Happy Birthday," in a most excited tone. And it was their birthday, both of them, for Lou and Oz had been born on the same day, five years apart, as Amanda had informed Louisa in one of her letters. Lou was officially a teenager now, and Oz had survived to the ripe old age of eight.

A wild-strawberry pie was on the table, along with cups of hot cider. Two small candles were in the pie and Oz and Lou together blew them out. Louisa pulled out the presents she had been working on all this time, on her Singer sewing machine: a Chop bag dress for Lou that was a pretty floral pattern of red and green, and a smart jacket, trousers, and white shirt for Oz that had been created from clothes Cotton had given her.

⌒ **David Baldacci,** *Wish You Well*

Wild Strawberry Pie

Pastry for one 1-crust 8-inch pie
3 pints fresh strawberries, rinsed,
    halved, and sprinkled with
    ¼ cup sugar
½ cup sugar

½ cup water
3 tablespoons orange juice mixed
    with 2 tablespoons cornstarch,
    dissolved
Red food coloring

Roll the pie dough to a ⅜-inch thickness. Position it in an 8-inch pie pan and trim outer edge. Prick holes in bottom crust to allow air ventilation during baking. Bake at 400° for 10 to 12 minutes. Remove from oven and cool.

Let the strawberries and sugar stand for 1 to 2 hours to create a light syrupy juice. Then pour the juice and 1 cup of the strawberries into a saucepan. Add ½ cup sugar and water to the pan. Cook over medium-high heat until berries are tender, 3 to 5 minutes. Remove the berries from the pan and set aside in a bowl to cool, leaving the syrupy juice in the pan. Add the orange juice and cornstarch mixture to the syrupy juice in the pan and a couple of drops of red food coloring, if needed, to produce a dark red color. Cook over medium-low heat, stirring constantly, until thickened, about 1 to 2 minutes.

Transfer both the cooked and uncooked strawberries to the baked and cooled pie crust. Cover the strawberries with the thickened sauce, working the sauce down into the berries. Smooth surface with back of spoon. Refrigerate to chill until set.

> Books are what connect the generations of humans over thousands of years.
>
> Alan Lightman

Apple

At midday, while Ginelli was still sleeping deeply in the other room, Billy had another episode of arrhythmia. Shortly after, he dozed off himself and had a dream. It was short and totally mundane, but it filled him with a queer mixture of terror and hateful pleasure. In this dream he and Heidi were sitting in the breakfast nook of the Fairview house. Between them was a pie. "This will fatten you up," she said. "I don't want to be fat," he replied. "I've decided I like being thin. You eat it." He gave her the piece of pie, stretching an arm no thicker than a bone across the table. She took it. He sat watching as she ate every bite, and with every bite she took, his feeling of terror and dirty joy grew.

Stephen King (writing as Richard Bachman), *Thinner*

One fall day I went to the kitchen and got out a bag of flour and made the first apple pie I made in my life. Made it from scratch, mixing butter with flour to make a great crust, and loaded it with sour apples and brown sugar and nutmeg, baked it to a T, and of course it was delicious. My guests for dinner were a couple who seemed to be coasting from a bad fight. We ate the pie and sat in a daze of pleasure afterward, during which the wife said that it reminded her of pies she ate when she was a little Norwegian Lutheran girl in Normania Township on the western Minnesota prairie. "We had love, good health, and faith in God, all things that money can't buy," she said, glancing at her husband, apropos of something. "This time of year, we were always broke, but somehow we made it. We'd fix equipment, feed the animals, and sleep. My mother made apple pie. One year she made thirty in one day. My dad was sick and thirty of our neighbors came in with fourteen combines and harvested his three hundred acres of soybeans. It took them half a day to do it, a time when they were racing to get their own soybeans in, but out there, if your car broke down in the country, the next car by would stop. My mother baked thirty pies and gave one to everybody who helped us." Naturally, I was pleased, until later, when it occurred to me that I would never bake another one as surprisingly good, having hit a home run on my first try. (They are still married, by the way.)

∝ **Garrison Keillor**, "Lutheran Pie" from *We Are Still Married*

Pure Pleasure Apple Pie

∿

Pastry for one 2-crust 9-inch pie

5 tart apples, pared, cored, and sliced (great combinations include Granny Smith and Macintosh, Granny Smith and golden Delicious, Macintosh and Jonathan)

1 cup sugar

3 tablespoons all-purpose flour

1 teaspoon cinnamon

¼ teaspoon nutmeg

2 tablespoons butter or margarine, melted

⅛ cup sugar

¼ teaspoon cinnamon

Pinch of nutmeg

Combine the apples, 1 cup sugar, flour, 1 teaspoon cinnamon, and ¼ teaspoon nutmeg in a large bowl. Stir well, coating the apples thoroughly. Line a 9-inch pie plate with pastry rolled ⅜ inch thick. Fill the pie pan with the apple mixture. Drizzle the melted butter over the apple filling. Position the top crust, crimp edges together, and trim. Cut slits in the top crust to allow steam to escape. Mix ⅛ cup sugar with ¼ teaspoon cinnamon and pinch of nutmeg. Sprinkle over top crust (save any extra cinnamon sugar for use in other recipes). Bake at 400° for about 45 minutes.

VARIATION: For a golden brown, crispy crust, brush top crust with melted butter before sprinkling with cinnamon sugar.

W ords have the power to convey every nuance of emotion, every tactile sense and mental sensibility. Words are the writer's pigment.

 Garrison Keillor, "How to Write a Letter" from *We Are Still Married*

Mincemeat

"My first aim will be to *clean down* (do you comprehend the full force of the expression?) to *clean down* Moor House from chamber to cellar; my next to rub it up with beeswax, oil, and an indefinite number of cloths, till it glitters again; my third, to arrange every chair, table, bed, carpet, with mathematical precision; afterwards I shall go near to ruin you in coals and peat to keep up good fires in every room; and lastly, the two days preceding that on which your sisters are expected, will be devoted by Hannah and me to such a beating of eggs, sorting of currants, grating of spices, compounding of Christmas cakes, chopping up of materials for mince-pies, and solemnizing of other culinary rites, as words can convey but an inadequate notion of to the uninitiated like you. My purpose, in short, is to have all things in an absolutely perfect state of readiness for Diana and Mary, before next Thursday; and my ambition is to give them a beau-ideal of a welcome when they come."

ᴸᴳ   Charlotte Brontë, *Jane Eyre*

"Look on the branch above your head," said the Gnat, "and there you'll find a Snap-Dragon-fly. Its body is made of plum-pudding, its wings of holly-leaves, and its head is a raisin burning in brandy."

"And what does it live on?" Alice asked, as before.

"Frumenty and mince-pie," the Gnat replied, "and it makes its nest in a Christmas-box."

ᴸᴳ   Lewis Carroll, *Through the Looking-Glass*

Festive Mini Mincemeat Pies

Preparation of traditional mincemeat filling involves an extensive canning and aging process. Fortunately, good commercial mincemeat is available in most supermarkets.

Pastry for one 2-crust 9-inch pie	½ cup dried cherries
1 29-ounce jar mincemeat,	¼ cup butter or margarine, melted
flavored with rum or brandy	⅛ cup sugar mixed with
1 golden Delicious apple, diced	¼ teaspoon cinnamon

Combine mincemeat filling, apple, and cherries in a large bowl. Let sit for about 30 minutes to develop flavors. Roll out pie dough ¼ inch thick. Cut dough with a round cookie cutter, about 3 inches in diameter. Place 1½ to 2 tablespoons of mince filling on half of the dough circles. Cover each with a second circle. Crimp edges. Brush top crust with melted butter. Sprinkle with cinnamon sugar. Prick top crust with fork and set pies on an ungreased baking sheet. Bake at 400° for about 20 minutes.

> A country's literature is a crystal ball into which its people may look to find some foretaste of their future.
>
>   **Robertson Davies**

Blueberries

T en minutes later he emerged from the woods into a meadow where trees had given way to tangles of grass, thistles, burdock, and scrub. *Wild blueberries, not packaged in plastic,* he reminded himself, and obviously hidden by overgrowth and needing a keen eye to find. He stepped carefully through the tall grass, peering down and into it for a glimpse of blue concealed among the shadows. There was dew still on the grass and a faint movement of air, not yet a breeze; the grass resisted his passage, and he began stamping it down to create a path. *At least I'm creating something, if only a path,* he thought, *why must there always be this hunger to create with words?* Leaning over to inspect what lay in the shadows of a tall bush he found a site rich with blue and sat down, heedless of damp grass. Stretching out a hand he began to cull the berries from their stems, dropping them into a bowl.

The sun was warm, and the unbroken silence was no longer menacing to him now but soothing. Seated here on the ground, half concealed among the tall grasses, he felt a very real pleasure in his connection with the earth, and crammed a handful of berries into his mouth. They tasted of fresh air, cool and moist and delicious.

  Dorothy Gilman, *Thale's Folly*

Blueberry Crisp

∽

TOPPING:

½ cup all-purpose flour

⅓ cup sugar

½ teaspoon ground cinnamon

4½ tablespoons unsalted butter or margarine

BERRIES:

2½ cups blueberries, fresh or frozen (if frozen, do not thaw)

2 teaspoons lemon juice

¼ cup sugar

2 teaspoons cornstarch

Combine the flour, ⅓ cup sugar, and cinnamon in a bowl. Cut the butter into the flour mixture and blend with a fork or your fingers until the mixture is crumbly. Set aside.

Sprinkle the lemon juice over the berries and lightly toss to distribute. Combine the ¼ cup sugar and cornstarch, then sprinkle over berries and lightly toss to coat.

Place the berries in an 8-inch pie pan or cake pan coated with cooking spray. Sprinkle the crumb mixture over them. Bake for 30 to 40 minutes at 350°, or until juices are bubbling. (Frozen berries require a longer baking time.)

Serve warm with whipped cream or vanilla ice cream.

I write about personal questions and issues and situations, but writing creates a fictional safety net that allows me to take greater risks and come a lot closer to the truth.

≪ Amy Tan

Peaches and Sweet Bread

❧

"**W**hat'd she die from?"

"Essie's pie."

"Don't say?"

"Uh-huh. She was doing fine. I saw her the very day before. Said she wanted me to bring her some black thread to patch some things for her boy. I should have known just from her wanting black thread that was a sign."

"Sure was."

"Just like Emma. 'Member? She kept asking for thread. Dropped dead that very evening."

"Yeah. Well, she was determined to have it. Kept on reminding me. I told her I had some at home, but naw, she wanted it new. So I sent Li'l June to get some that very morning when she was laying dead. I was just fixing to bring it over, 'long with a piece of sweet bread. You know how she craved my sweet bread."

"Sure did. Always bragged on it. She was a good friend to you."

"I believe it. Well, I had not more got my clothes on when Sally bust in the door hollering about how Cholly here had been over to Miss Alice saying she was dead. You could have knocked me over, I tell you."

"Guess Essie feels mighty bad."

"Oh Lord, yes. But I told her the Lord giveth and the Lord taketh away. Wasn't her fault none. She makes good peach pies. But she bound to believe it was the pie did it, and I 'spect she right."

"Well, she shouldn't worry herself none 'bout that. She was just doing what we all would of done."

"Yeah. 'Cause I was sure wrapping up that sweet bread, and that could have done it too."

"I doubts that. Sweet bread is pure. But a pie is the worse thing to give anybody ailing. I'm surprised Jimmy didn't know better."

"If she did, she wouldn't let on. She would have tried to please. You know how she was. So good."

❧   Toni Morrison, *The Bluest Eye*

To-Die-For Peach Pie

Pastry for one 2-crust 9-inch pie
1 cup sugar
3 tablespoons all-purpose flour
¼ teaspoon nutmeg
Dash of salt

5 cups fresh peaches, peeled,
    sliced
2 tablespoons butter or
    margarine, melted

Preheat oven to 400°. Line a 9-inch pie pan with pastry rolled ⅛ inch thick, and cover it with a towel or plastic wrap while the filling is prepared.

Combine the dry ingredients in a large bowl and add the peaches. Mix thoroughly. Spoon the filling into the pie pastry. Drizzle the melted butter over the filling. Secure the top crust, lattice-style. Seal and crimp the edges. Bake for 45 to 50 minutes, or until done. Serve with whipped cream or vanilla ice cream.

Innocent Sweet Bread

5½ to 5¾ cups sifted all-purpose
    flour
½ teaspoon ground cardamom
½ teaspoon ground nutmeg
2 cups milk
4 tablespoons butter or
    margarine

¾ cup sugar
1 teaspoon salt
2 packages active dry yeast
    (or 5 teaspoons)
2 tablespoons butter or
    margarine, melted

In a large mixing bowl, mix together 2½ cups of the flour, the cardamom, and the nutmeg. In a saucepan, heat the milk, butter, sugar, and salt until just warm over low heat to melt the butter; stir constantly. Do not boil. Let cool to lukewarm, continuing to stir often. After the milk mixture is cooled, add the yeast and let sit for 5 minutes. Add the milk mixture to the dry ingredients and beat for about 30 seconds on low speed, scraping bowl constantly. Beat for 3 minutes at high speed. By hand, mix in enough of the remaining flour to make a moderately stiff dough. Place the dough on a lightly floured surface and knead until smooth and elastic. Place the dough in a large bowl coated with cooking spray. Turn the dough over once. Cover and let rise in warm, draft-free place until it is doubled in size, about 1 to 1½ hours.

Remove the dough from the bowl, put it on a floured surface, divide it into three parts, and let rest for 10 minutes. Shape each portion into a long, snakelike roll, then form it into a tight figure-eight shape. Or divide each portion into three equal parts, shape into long rolls, and braid. Place the dough on a large greased baking sheet, cover with a warm cloth, and let rise again until doubled in size, about 45 minutes. Bake at 375° for about 25 minutes or until golden brown. Remove the bread from the oven and brush with melted butter.

Stories are discoveries. Our ordinary lives are going on around us, but as we read stories, the ordinary drops away and, for a moment, the veil is pierced.

✎ **Elizabeth Evans**

Green Tomatoes

༨Ͻ

The first killing frost of winter came on Valentine's Day. Mattie's purple bean vines hung from the fence like long strips of beef jerky drying in the sun. It broke my heart to see that colorful jungle turned to black slime, especially on this of all days when people everywhere were sending each other flowers, but it didn't faze Mattie. "That's the cycle of life, Taylor," she said. "The old has to pass on before the new can come around." She said frost improved the flavor of the cabbage and Brussels sprouts. But I think she was gloating. The night before, she'd listened to the forecast and picked a mop bucket full of hard little marbles off the tomato vines, and this morning she had green-tomato pies baking upstairs. I know this sounds like something you'd no more want to eat than a mud-and-Junebug pie some kid would whip up, but it honestly smelled delicious.

Barbara Kingsolver, *The Bean Trees*

First Frost Green-Tomato Pie

ༀͻ

The night before the first frost: harvest, halve, and slice green toma-toes . . . I'll warn you that I've never convinced my family this is edible. [But] I like green-tomato pie! Green tomatoes also make a terrific chut-ney.—Barbara Kingsolver

Pastry for one 2-crust 9-inch pie
3 cups green tomatoes, sliced
   over a bowl to catch juice
   and placed in that same bowl

1 teaspoon ground ginger
1½ cups sugar (brown or white), or
   more to taste
4 teaspoons cornstarch

Dissolve cornstarch in collected tomato juice. In a large saucepan, combine tomatoes with ginger and sugar, and juice with cornstarch. Simmer until thickened. Roll pie dough to a ⅛-inch thickness. Position it in a 9-inch pie pan. Place the filling in the lined pie pan. Cover the filling with the top pastry and crimp and seal edges. Cut slits in top pastry crust to allow steam to escape during baking. Bake at 425° for 15 minutes, then reduce temperature to 375° and continue baking for another 30 minutes.

—Recipe contributed by Barbara Kingsolver

"Yes," he thinks. "I should never have let myself get out of the habit of prayer." He turns from the window. One wall of the study is lined with books. He pauses before them, seeking, until he finds the one which he wants. It is Tennyson. It is dogeared. He has had it ever since the seminary. He sits beneath the lamp and opens it. It does not take long. Soon the fine galloping language, the gutless swooning full of sapless trees and dehydrated lusts begins to swim smooth and swift and peaceful. It is better than praying without having to bother to think aloud. It is like listening in a cathedral to a eunuch chanting in a language which he does not even need to not understand.

   William Faulkner, *Light in August*

Tarts

Bessie had been down in the kitchen, and she brought up with her a tart on a certain brightly painted china plate, whose bird of paradise, nestling in a wreath of convolvuli and rosebuds, had been wont to stir in me a most enthusiastic sense of admiration; and which plate I petitioned to be allowed to take in my hand in order to examine it more closely, but had always hitherto been deemed unworthy of such a privilege.

   Charlotte Brontë, *Jane Eyre*

A tiny boy with a head like a raisin and a chocolate body came round with a tray of pastries—row upon row of little freaks, little inspirations, little melting dreams. He offered them to her. "Oh, I'm not at all hungry. Take them away."

He offered them to Hennie. Hennie gave me a swift look—it must have been satisfactory—for he took a chocolate cream, a coffee éclair, a meringue stuffed with chestnut and a tiny horn filled with fresh strawberries. She could hardly bear to watch him. But just as the boy swerved away she held up her plate.

"Oh, well, give me one," said she.

The silver tongs dropped one, two, three—and a cherry tartlet. "I don't know why you're giving me all these," she said, and nearly smiled. "I shan't eat them; I couldn't!"

   Katherine Mansfield, "Mr. and Mrs. Dove," from *The Complete Short Stories of Katherine Mansfield*

Privileged Tart

PASTRY:

1¼ cups all-purpose flour

¼ cup sugar

¼ teaspoon salt

5 tablespoons butter or
    margarine, softened

1 large egg yolk

1 tablespoon lemon juice

1½ tablespoons water

TOPPING:

3 teaspoons cornstarch

⅓ cup orange juice

2 cups raspberries or
    strawberries, fresh or frozen

¾ cup sugar

Combine the flour, sugar, and salt in a large bowl. Add the butter and mix together with a fork or fingers until the texture is crumbly. In a separate bowl, mix the egg yolk with the lemon juice. Stir the yolk mixture and water into the crumbly flour. Use your hands to form the dough into a ball, then divide the dough into four portions. Press the dough into four 4-inch tart pans to about a ⅜-inch thickness. Refrigerate these pastries while making the topping.

For topping, dissolve the cornstarch in orange juice. Combine all the ingredients in a medium saucepan and cook over low heat, stirring continually until very thick. Spoon the topping onto each tart pastry, leaving an uncovered ¼-inch margin at the edge.

Bake at 400° for 10 minutes. Reduce heat to 350° and bake for another 15 minutes. Cool. Remove tarts from pans and slice as desired for serving.

I haven't told why I wrote the book [*Charlotte's Web*], but I haven't told why I sneeze either. A book is a sneeze.

   E. B. White

Cherry Tart

"Mrs. Dowdel, we cannot pussyfoot anymore over these cherry tarts." Mrs. Weidenbach grappled with her giant purse and came up with the *Piatt County Call* newspaper. "I need a commitment. My land, it's in the paper now, where it has inspired two lines of bad verse."

Grandma didn't read the paper, so Mrs. Weidenbach shook it open and read,

> *The high school will have its big red hearts*
> *But where will the DAR get its cherry tarts?*

"Doesn't that just turn your stomach?" she demanded. "I don't call it reporting, and I don't call it poetry. It's snooping, and possibly by a foreign power. The dignity of the DAR is on the line."

Grandma picked a loose thread from her apron front.

"Mrs. Dowdel, I need your answer before we get any more publicity of this sort."

"Oh well." Grandma turned over a large hand on oilcloth. "If it's my patriotic duty, I'll bake up a mess of tarts."

◖ **Richard Peck,** *A Year Down Yonder*

A Small Mess of Cherry Tarts

PASTRY:

2½ cups all-purpose flour

½ cup sugar

½ teaspoon salt

½ cup plus 2 tablespoons butter
  or margarine, softened

2 large egg yolks

2 tablespoons lemon juice

3 tablespoons water

TOPPING:

4 tablespoons flour

1 cup sugar

1 cup sour cream

2 teaspoons orange juice

2 cups pitted and sliced sour
  cherries

To make pastry, combine the flour, sugar, and salt in a large bowl. Add the butter and mix together with a fork or fingers until the texture is crumbly. In a separate bowl, mix the egg yolks with the lemon juice. Stir the yolk mixture and water into the crumbly flour. Use your hands to form the dough into a ball. If more moisture is required, Grandma Dowdel says to add about a mouthful. Press the dough into the bottom only of two 9-inch pie pans or two 9-inch springform pans to about a ⅜-inch thickness. Refrigerate the crusts for about 15 minutes.

For the topping, combine all the ingredients, except cherries, in a medium bowl and mix well. Fold in cherries. Spread the mixture to about a ½-inch thickness on top of the chilled crust, leaving a ¼-inch margin uncovered at the edge.

Bake at 425° for 15 minutes. Reduce heat to 350° and bake for about another 40 to 45 minutes. Cool. Slice as desired for serving.

—Recipe inspired by and created with Richard Peck, who improved the instructions

For in addition to following the cycles of life, I chronicle it. While there is not a typewriter, telephone, dictionary, or cool glass of lemonade by my hand, I have learned that wherever I am, I must tender that other life, the one of observation, play, imprint and desire that walks with me across the rolling hills beneath the shadows of the clouds. Like the young shoots that thrive in our alkaline soil, the words of my mind must be planted, hoed, watered, thinned and weeded to yield a bumper crop.

❧ **Wanda Rosseland**

Cobbler

ᴔ

I drove around to the other side of the hill once more, and saw with relief that the vacant lot next door to 122 Alamo Street had been left untouched, undeveloped, unimproved, unscathed. Uncanny what survives and what doesn't: the same pines, the same underbrush, the same blackberry brambles, even the same faint smell of resin. In that primeval landscape the curly-haired child, protesting in vain that the briars scratched and poisonous snakes surely lurked underfoot, had picked the making of berry cobblers and thrifty jars of jam. The same cardinals sang "sweet sweet cheer" in the same rich contralto. I have never believed that birds die. If they died, you'd see their bodies all around, but you never see them. They live forever. These selfsame birds had sung to the blackberry picker forty years ago, had awakened her on a summer morning, like the nightingale serenading Ruth, who stood in tears amid the alien corn.

ᴔ   **Shirley Abbott,** *The Bookmaker's Daughter*

Blackberry Cobbler

ᴔ

⅓ cup sugar mixed with 1
   teaspoon cornstarch
16 ounces frozen blackberries
   (do not thaw) or 3 cups fresh

2 tablespoons butter or
   margarine, melted

TOPPING:

1 cup sugar

2 tablespoons butter or
  margarine, cut up

1 cup all-purpose flour

1 teaspoon baking powder

½ teaspoon salt

1 egg, beaten

½ cup milk

1 tablespoon lemon juice

Combine ⅓ cup sugar and the cornstarch. Stir the sugar-cornstarch mixture into the blackberries and gently toss to cover berries. Spread 2 tablespoons melted butter over a 2-quart casserole dish, coating well. Add the blackberries to the dish and set aside.

To prepare the topping, mix 1 cup sugar and 2 tablespoons butter in a large bowl until blended. Combine the dry ingredients and add them to the sugar-butter mixture. Mix in the egg, milk, and lemon juice until blended. Spoon the batter over the blackberries. Bake at 350° for about 55 minutes. (Frozen berries require longer baking time.) Serve with whipped cream or vanilla ice cream.

The thing I love about language is that when you do it well, you have the ability as a writer to seduce readers—but sometimes you also have the ability to seduce yourself. The pleasure of the language, the ability to put words together in what strikes you as just the right fashion—I love it.

   Richard Russo

Strawberry Shortcake

✧

Rooster rushed into the chicken coop. "It has to be here," he said. He looked high and low, and there it was at last, hidden under a nest—her cookbook. *The Joy of Cooking Alone* by L. R. Hen.

Rooster carefully turned the pages. "So many recipes—and I thought she just baked bread! Look at the strawberry shortcake!"

"That's it! I'll make the most wonderful, magnificent strawberry shortcake in the whole wide world. No more chicken feed for me!"

✎   Janet Stevens and Susan Stevens Crummel, *Cook-a-Doodle-Doo!*

Great-Granny Hen's Magnificent Strawberry Shortcake

✧

2 cups all-purpose flour, sifted
2 tablespoons sugar
1 tablespoon baking powder
½ teaspoon salt
½ cup butter

1 egg, beaten
⅔ cup milk
3 to 4 cups strawberries, washed
    and sliced
1 cup whipping cream, whipped

Preheat oven to 450°. Sift flour, then sift together with the remaining dry ingredients. Cut in butter until mixture resembles coarse crumbs. Add egg and milk, stirring by hand just enough to moisten. Spread dough in greased 8-inch round pan, building up edges slightly. Bake for 15 to 18 minutes. Remove cake from pan; cool on cooling rack for 5 minutes. Split into two layers with a long knife; lift top off carefully. Alternate layers of cake, whipped cream, and strawberries, ending with strawberries on top.

—**Recipe from Janet Stevens and Susan Stevens Crummel, *Cook-a-Doodle-Doo!***

I learned from the age of two or three that any room in our house, at any time of day, was there to read in, or to be read to. My mother read to me. She'd read to me in the big bedroom in the mornings, when we were in her rocker together, which ticked in rhythm as we rocked, as though we had a cricket accompanying the story. She'd read to me in the dining room on winter afternoons in front of the coal fire, with our cuckoo clock ending the story with "Cuckoo," and at night when I'd got in my own bed. I must have given her no peace. Sometimes she read to me in the kitchen while she sat churning, and the churning sobbed along with *any* story. It was my ambition to have her read to me while *I* churned; once she granted my wish, but she read off my story before I brought her butter. She was an expressive reader. When she was reading "Puss in Boots," for instance, it was impossible not to know that she distrusted *all* cats.

It had been startling and disappointing to me to find out that story books had been written by *people*, that books were not natural wonders, coming up of themselves like grass. Yet regardless of where they came from, I cannot remember a time when I was not in love with them—with the books themselves, cover and binding and the paper they were printed on, with their smell and their weight and with their possession in my arms, captured and carried off to myself. Still illiterate, I was ready for them, committed to all the reading I could give them.

Eudora Welty, *One Writer's Beginnings*

Lane Cake

Readers will remember when Miss Maudie's house burns down in Harper Lee's *To Kill a Mockingbird* and she's more concerned about the commotion it caused, the danger to other homes, and the well-being of old Mr. Avery, who's overexerted himself. She plans to bake him a Lane cake, but only when Miss Stephanie isn't around to snoop at her recipe; Miss Stephanie's been after it for thirty years. Scout's had a glimpse of Miss Maudie's recipe and doesn't think Miss Stephanie could follow it anyway. Among other ingredients, Scout remembers it called for one cup of sugar.

Miss Maudie's Lane Cake

The Lane cake's origin is traced to the Alabama State Fair prize-winning entry of Emma Rylander Lane, who first published the recipe under the name "Prize Cake" in her cookbook, Some Good Things to Eat, in 1898. Many variations by others followed. Ours is based on the "one cup of sugar" mentioned by Scout, who's had a glimpse at Miss Maudie's precious recipe.

½ cup plus 6 tablespoons butter, at room temperature
1 cup plus ¾ cup sugar
1 teaspoon vanilla extract, divided
1½ cups plus 2 tablespoons all-purpose flour
1¾ teaspoons baking powder
¼ teaspoon salt

1 cup milk
4 eggs, separated (reserve yolks for filling)
½ teaspoon brandy or rum
½ cup raisins
¼ cup shredded or flaked coconut
¼ cup dried cherries
¼ cup finely chopped pecans
Fresh grated zest of ½ lemon

Beat egg whites until stiff, but not dry. Combine ½ cup butter, 1 cup sugar, and ½ teaspoon vanilla and beat well. Sift together flour, baking powder, and salt. Add them to the butter mixture, alternating with milk. Gradually fold in egg whites.

Pour batter into two 9-inch round cake pans, greased and floured. Bake at 375° for 20 to 25 minutes, or until a toothpick inserted in center comes out clean. Remove from oven and let stand for 5 minutes. Invert cakes on a cooling rack. Cool completely.

To prepare filling, beat egg yolks with ¾ cup sugar until light and fluffy. In top pan of a double boiler, melt 6 tablespoons butter. Beat in eggs and sugar and continue to stir over medium-high heat for about 5 minutes. Remove pan from heat and add ½ teaspoon vanilla and brandy. Stir in remaining ingredients. Let cool slightly, then spread on top of one cake, leaving a ¼-inch margin at edge. Position second cake on top of first.

FROSTING:

1⅓ cups ultrafine sugar
⅓ cup water
2 egg whites
2 teaspoons light corn syrup

1 teaspoon vanilla extract
2 tablespoons sweetened, flaked coconut or chopped pecans

In top pan of a double boiler, combine sugar, water, egg whites, and corn syrup. Beat with a mixer on low speed while cooking over medium-high heat for about 5 minutes. Remove from heat and add vanilla. Beat an additional 2 to 3 minutes, until frosting forms soft peaks. Spread over cake. Sprinkle coconut or pecans over frosting.

The secret of the back burner is the power to transform a disaster into a miracle, whether it be to pare an unwieldy poem down to its best lines or to find the right voice for telling a tale that has haunted you for years.

Nancy Willard

Tea Cake

༄

And really it was a wonderful tea. There was a nice brown egg, lightly boiled, for each of them, and then sardines on toast, and then buttered toast, and then toast with honey, and then a sugar-topped cake. And when Lucy was tired of eating the Faun began to talk. He had wonderful tales to tell of life in the forest.

☞   C. S. Lewis, *The Lion, the Witch and the Wardrobe*

Sugar-Topped Tea Cake

༄

½ cup applesauce

1 cup sugar

1 cup sour cream

2 egg whites

2 cups all-purpose flour

1 teaspoon baking soda

1 teaspoon baking powder

½ teaspoon salt

1 teaspoon vanilla

2 tablespoons butter or
    margarine, melted

2 teaspoons cinnamon

1 large apple, diced

2 tablespoons sugar

½ cup walnuts, chopped

Cream the applesauce, sugar, sour cream, and egg whites together in a bowl. Add the flour, baking soda, baking powder, salt, and vanilla, and mix well. Set batter aside. In a separate bowl, combine butter or margarine, cinnamon, apple, sugar, and nuts, and stir well.

Spoon half of the batter into a greased and floured tube pan. Spread half of the apple mixture over the batter in the pan. Pour the remaining batter into the tube pan. Spread the remaining filling on top.

Bake at 350° for approximately 50 to 55 minutes.

Outside of a dog, a book is a man's best friend.
Inside a dog, it's too dark to read.

  Groucho Marx

Liniment Cake

Mrs. Allan took a mouthful of hers and a most peculiar expression crossed her face; not a word did she say, however, but steadily ate away at it. Marilla saw the expression and hastened to taste the cake.

"Anne Shirley!" she exclaimed, "what on earth did you put into that cake?"

"Nothing but what the recipe said, Marilla," cried Anne with a look of anguish. "Oh, isn't it all right?"

"All right! It's simply horrible. Mrs. Allan, don't try to eat it. Anne, taste it yourself. What flavoring did you use?"

"Vanilla," said Anne, her face scarlet with mortification after tasting the cake. "Only vanilla. Oh Marilla, it must have been the baking powder. I had my suspicions that the bak—"

"Baking-powder fiddlesticks! Go and bring me back the bottle of vanilla you used."

Anne fled to the pantry and returned with a small bottle partially filled with a brown liquid and labeled yellowy, "Best Vanilla."

Marilla took it, uncorked it, smelled it.

"Mercy on us, Anne, you've flavored that cake with *anodyne liniment*. I broke the liniment bottle last week and poured what was left into an old empty vanilla bottle. I suppose it's partly my fault—I should have warned you—but for pity's sake why couldn't you have smelled it?"

  Lucy Maud Montgomery, *Anne of Green Gables*

Anne's Anodyne Liniment Cake
(Without the Anodyne Liniment)

The author of this recipe, Kate MacDonald, is the granddaughter of Lucy Maud Montgomery.

2 cups all-purpose flour
1 tablespoon baking powder
Pinch of salt
1¼ cups sugar

½ cup butter, melted
1 cup milk
3 eggs
2 teaspoons vanilla

Preheat oven to 350°. Combine the dry ingredients and stir well. Add the butter and milk and mix well, beating for about 1 minute. Add the eggs and vanilla and beat for an additional 3 minutes. Pour the batter into two greased and floured 9-inch cake pans. Bake for about 25 to 30 minutes. Test cakes with a wooden toothpick. Cool for 10 minutes before removing from pans. After cakes have completely cooled, frost with creamy butter frosting.

Creamy Butter Frosting

¼ cup butter, melted
⅓ cup cream

1 teaspoon vanilla
3 cups powdered sugar

Combine all ingredients in a large bowl and beat well until frosting is thick and creamy.

—Derived from *The Anne of Green Gables Cookbook,* **by Kate MacDonald, illustrated by Barbara Di Lella**

[The success of the Harry Potter books] says that in an age when technology is king and the future of publishing often seems uncertain, words printed on pages bound together with glue and thread still have the power to thrill and delight readers.

James Cross Giblin

Chocolate Swirl Cake

Pig was lonely, but baking raised his spirits.
He baked a lot.
One day Pig baked his favorite chocolate swirl fudge cake.
He set it on the windowsill to cool.
Crow came and perched next to the cake.
"I will give you magic seeds for that cake," said Crow. He placed a lumpy bundle on the windowsill.
"I do not believe in magic," said Pig.
"These seeds take away loneliness, especially from lonely pigs," said Crow, cocking his head.
Everyone knew how sly Crow was.

Kay Chorao, *Pig and Crow*

Pig's Chocolate Swirl Fudge Cake

Pig, being an old-fashioned country pig, prefers to use butter rather than margarine in his cooking—not only for the taste, but to serve food with fewer chemicals to little eaters.—Kay Chorao

1½ cups sugar
½ cup plus 1 tablespoon butter
2 eggs
½ cup applesauce
1 teaspoon vanilla
2 cups all-purpose flour
1½ teaspoons baking soda

½ teaspoon salt
1 cup milk with 1 teaspoon
  vinegar
½ cup cocoa
¾ cup boiling water
½ cup semisweet chocolate chips

Mix the sugar, ½ cup butter, and eggs in a large bowl until creamed. Mix in the applesauce, vanilla, flour, baking soda, salt, milk with vinegar, cocoa, and ½ cup of boiling water. Stir well. Reserve ½ cup of the batter. Pour the remaining cake batter into two prepared 9-inch round cake pans or one 11-inch tube pan.

Melt the chocolate chips in a double boiler with butter and water, stirring continuously. Once melted, remove from heat and immediately add the reserved ½ cup cake batter. Stir well. Drizzle this chocolate mixture over the cake batter in pans. Drag a butter knife back and forth through the batter to make swirls. Do not overmix.

For 9-inch pans, bake the cakes at 350° for 35 to 40 minutes. For a tube pan, bake the cake at 350° for about 55 minutes. Swirled topping may retain a pudding-like or moist consistency on the interior while baking. Cake is done when edge pulls slightly away from pan and toothpick inserted near edge (out of swirled area) comes out clean. When cooled, drizzle with chocolate icing, if desired. Serve with vanilla ice cream.

CHOCOLATE ICING:

⅔ cup semisweet chocolate chips   1½ cups powdered sugar
3 tablespoons butter   3 tablespoons hot water

Melt the chocolate and butter in a double boiler, stirring continuously. Remove and stir in powdered sugar and hot water until smooth. Drizzle over cake.

—Recipe inspired by and created with Kay Chorao

I write in some sense not to be alone.
🙶 **Adam Haslett**

Chocolate Cake

I had bacon, sausages, and eggs all lined up when my four-year-old arrived, looking so adorable with her cute face and little braids.

"Morning, Daddy," she said.

"Okay," I said, "what do you want for breakfast?"

"Chocolate cake," she replied.

"Chocolate *cake?* For *breakfast?* That's ridiculous."

Then, however, I thought about the ingredients in chocolate cake: milk and eggs and wheat, all part of good nutrition.

"You want chocolate cake, honey?" I said, cutting a piece for her. "Well, here it is. But you also need something to drink."

And I gave her a glass of grapefruit juice.

When the other four children came downstairs and saw the four-year-old eating chocolate cake, they wanted the same, of course; and since I wanted good nutrition for them, too, I gave each of them a piece.

So there my five children sat, merrily eating chocolate cake for breakfast, occasionally stopping to sing:

> *Dad is the greatest dad you can make!*
> *For breakfast he gives us chocolate cake!*

The party lasted until my wife appeared, staggered slightly, and said, "Chocolate cake for *breakfast?* Where did you all get that?"

"*He* gave it to us! *He* made us eat it!" said my five adorable ingrates in one voice; and then my eight-year-old added, "*We* wanted eggs and cereal."

ᗕ   **Bill Cosby,** *Fatherhood*

Daddy's Rich Chocolate Cake

2 cups sugar
¼ cup margarine
½ cup applesauce
1½ cups boiling water
2½ cups all-purpose flour

½ cup cocoa
1 teaspoon baking soda
2 large egg whites
1 teaspoon vanilla

Preheat oven to 350°. In a large bowl, beat the sugar and margarine until creamed. Stir in the applesauce. Add the boiling water and mix. Combine the dry ingredients and add with egg whites to the mixture. Add the vanilla and beat well. Pour the batter into a greased and floured 13 × 9-inch cake pan. Bake for about 35 minutes. Frost when cooled.

Vanilla Frosting

2½ cups confectioners sugar
2 tablespoons butter or
   margarine, at room
   temperature

1 teaspoon vanilla
¼ teaspoon cream of tartar
3 tablespoons rice milk or water

Combine the sugar, margarine, vanilla, and cream of tartar. Add 2 tablespoons rice milk or water and stir well. Add third tablespoon of liquid 1 teaspoon at a time, stirring until smooth and creamy.

If you love the language, the greatest thing you can do to ensure its survival is not to complain about bad usage but to pass your enthusiasm to a child. Find a child and read to it often the things you admire, not being afraid to read the classics.

Exposing children to the words of the classics will do them no more harm than articulate adults do in conversation. Not to be exposed is not to have the chance of learning.

Robert MacNeil, *Wordstruck: A Memoir*

Fruitcake

And then, just when I had decided that this time I had really been forgotten, the wholesaler would look up, catch sight of me as though for the first time, and strike his forehead with the heel of his hand.

"A guest! A guest in my gates and I have offered her no refreshment!" And springing up he would rummage under shelves and into cupboards and before long I would be holding on my lap a plate of the most delicious treats in the world—honey cakes and date cakes and a kind of confection of nuts, fruits, and sugar. Desserts were rare in the Bje, sticky delights like these unknown.

Corrie ten Boom, *The Hiding Place*

Delicious Fruitcake

2 cups raisins
2 cups hot water
2 cups sugar
1 cup shortening
½ teaspoon ginger
1 teaspoon allspice
1 teaspoon nutmeg

½ teaspoon ground cloves
  (optional)
1 teaspoon cinnamon
4¼ cups all-purpose flour
½ teaspoon salt
2 teaspoons soda
1 cup chopped nuts
2 cups (1 pound) candied fruit mix

Combine the raisins, water, sugar, shortening, and spices in a saucepan. Simmer together for 15 minutes. When cooled, transfer the raisin mixture to a large bowl and add 4 cups flour, baking soda, and salt, mixing well. Dredge the nuts and fruit (so they will not all rise to the top during baking) by putting them in a plastic bag with ¼ cup flour and shaking gently to coat them. Add the floured fruit and nuts to the cake mixture and mix gently. Pour the batter into two loaf pans, greased and lined with parchment paper. Bake at 300° for two hours.

I know literature helps. I'm not one of those artists who feels this is just an exercise in self-indulgence. Literature changes things; it's a force.

   Sapphire

Coconut Cake

᠅

Well, this man kissing Miss Love, he didn't just kiss her. He kept on kissing her. A string of kisses a mile long melted together as his lips brushed her ears, her neck, her arms, her hair, and then got back to her mouth again. And Miss Love was kissing him back, no doubt about it. I didn't know what to do. I stood on one foot, then the other, and if I'd had a third foot, I'd of shifted to it. For sure I was in the way and I ought to slip on out. But I was pinned to the sight.

Oh, gosh, what if Grandpa walked in! Like it was me that was guilty, I glanced through the open door, half-expecting to see him. Who I saw instead was Miss Effie Belle Tate from next door hurrying up the walk with a frosted coconut cake!

I first thought she was bringing it to Miss Love as a welcome-to-the-bride present. But in her hurry to get over there, Miss Effie Belle had forgot to change out of her bedroom shoes, so I knew right off she hadn't planned a social call. What happened, I guessed, was that Miss Effie Belle saw the tall stranger walk into Grandpa's house with the saddle and, as an excuse to get a good look at him, had grabbed up the cake she just frosted.

Bursting out onto the veranda, I met her at the top step. "Sure is a hot day, ain't it, Miss Effie Belle?" I talked as loud as I could. She wasn't deaf or anything, like her brother, but I was hoping if Miss Love had any ears left, she would hear me and run sit down prim and proper in the parlor. If the stranger sat clear over on the other side of the room, they could make like they'd just been talking.

As Miss Effie Belle marched toward the doorway, I kind of stepped in front of her and yelled, "Did you see that tall feller that's come callin', Miss Effie Belle? Ain't he a buster! Uh, I think he's her lawyer or somebody." I had my voice aimed halfway at the coconut cake and halfway into the hall. "Miss Love would have more time to set a spell if you'd come back later, Miss Effie Belle."

"Oh, shut up, Will," she said. But she stopped at the door, chewed on her bottom lip like she was thinking, and then seemed to change her mind about barging in. The way the big pink wart on her lip quivered, I couldn't tell if she had seen them kissing or just lost her nerve. At any rate, she turned on her heel, nearly losing a bedroom slipper, and without a word and without so much as handing me the coconut cake—though I reached for it—she marched down the steps and took her cake back home.

ᐊᑯ   Olive Ann Burns, *Cold Sassy Tree*

Effie Belle's Coconut Cake

⌀⌀⌀

½ cup butter

1 cup sugar

2 eggs

1¾ cups flour

½ teaspoon salt

1 teaspoon baking powder

½ teaspoon vanilla extract

¾ cup milk

½ cup sweetened, flaked coconut,
   plus additional for garnish

In a large bowl, beat butter and sugar together until fluffy. Add eggs and beat until light and creamy. Mix the dry ingredients together and add to batter along with vanilla, alternating with milk. Mix well. Stir in coconut. Pour batter into greased and floured 9 × 11-inch pan. Bake at 350° for 35 to 40 minutes. Cool, then frost with butter frosting and garnish with flaked coconut.

Effie Belle's Butter Frosting

3 tablespoons butter, at room
    temperature
1½ cups powdered sugar

½ teaspoon vanilla
3 tablespoons (approximately)
    milk or cream

Combine butter, powdered sugar, vanilla, and 2 tablespoons of the milk in a large bowl. Mix together until creamy, adding remaining milk as needed. Spread on cooled cake. Garnish with flaked coconut.

> In the case of good books, the point is not to see how many of them you can get through, but rather how many can get through to you.
>
> Mortimer Jerome Adler

Spice Cake

But, to return to our friends, whom we left wiping their eyes, and recovering themselves from too great and sudden a joy. They are now seated around the social board, and are getting decidedly companionable; only that Cassy, who keeps little Eliza on her lap, occasionally squeezes the little thing, in a manner that rather astonishes her, and obstinately refuses to have her mouth stuffed with cake to the extent the little one desires,—alleging, what the child rather wonders at, that she has got something better than cake, and doesn't want it.

Harriet Beecher Stowe, *Uncle Tom's Cabin*

She went to her room, knelt before a big black-walnut chest and hunted through its contents until she found an old-fashioned cook book. She tended the fire as she read and presently was in action. She first sawed an end from a fragrant, juicy, sugar-cured ham and put it to cook. Then she set a couple of eggs boiling, and after long hesitation began creaming butter and sugar in a crock.

An hour later the odour of the ham, mingled with some of the richest spices of "happy Araby," in a combination that could mean nothing save spice cake, crept up to Elnora so strongly that she lifted her head and sniffed amazedly. She would have given all her precious money to have gone down and thrown her arms around her mother's neck, but she did not dare move.

⸂⸃ **Gene Stratton Porter,** *Girl of the Limberlost*

Sugar-'n'-Spice Cake

½ cup applesauce
2 cups brown sugar
2 egg whites
2 cups flour
½ teaspoon salt

1 teaspoon cinnamon
1 teaspoon allspice
1 teaspoon baking soda
1 cup milk or rice milk with 1
     teaspoon vinegar

Mix the applesauce, brown sugar, and egg whites together in a large bowl. Stir in the dry ingredients. Gradually add milk mixture and beat well. Pour the batter into two greased and floured 9-inch pans. Bake at 350° for 25 to 30 minutes.

Fiction isn't an ivory tower. It isn't a dodge from real life. It can be where we most completely encounter "real life."

Millions knew that slavery was wrong. Thousands had heard escaped slaves speak movingly of what they had suffered. Their memoirs were widely read.

Harriet Beecher Stowe drew upon some of these memoirs in *Uncle Tom's Cabin*. In her fictional story—acknowledged to be wooden, wordy, and poorly plotted—she hammered away at the separation of families. Thousands of fathers and mothers, reading this book aloud by their firesides, looked down at the listening faces of their own children and knew that they could no longer be indifferent to slavery.

When he met Stowe, President Abraham Lincoln greeted her as "the little woman who wrote the book that made this great war." He ascribed the Civil War to the effect of her book.

ᴥ᷍ **Susan Shaughnessy,** *Walking on Alligators*

Sponge Cake

ᴄᴍᴧᴑ

Once more Isobel drifted back into that illusion of timelessness in which she had been lost before Verena's interruption. She thought again of old Lady Balmerino, who used to sit here, as she and Verena sat, reading a novel or peacefully sewing her tapestry. Everything now as nice as once it had been. Perhaps in a moment there would come a discreet tap on the door and Harris the butler would enter, pushing before him the mahogany trolley laid with the silver teapot and the eggshell china cups, the covered dishes of scones, fresh from the oven, the bowl of cream, the strawberry jam, the lemon sponge-cake, and the dark, sticky gingerbread.

ᴥ᷍ **Rosamunde Pilcher,** *September*

As soon as the men had left the next morning, Hanna started making a sponge cake, generous with both butter and sugar, and tasting until the mixture was smooth and sweet. Then she took the cake to the smithy where Lame-Malin almost swooned with surprise.

"I thought," said Hanna, "we neighbors should stay friends."

Malin was so astonished, she never even got around to putting on the coffee. Hanna was grateful for that, for she found it difficult to bear the filth and bad air in the smith's house. She talked for a while about Malin's boys, who were shaping up well, she said. And about the winter that refused to go.

Then she went home and said to Him up there in the heavens that now she'd done what she could. Now it was His turn to do something for her.

◖ Marianne Fredriksson, *Hanna's Daughters*

Lemon Sponge Cake

∾

1 cup cake flour
1¼ teaspoons baking powder
¼ teaspoon salt
1 cup ultrafine sugar or sifted
    granulated sugar
2 teaspoons fresh grated lemon
    zest

3 eggs, at room temperature,
    separated
¼ cup boiled water, cooled to
    warm
1 tablespoon lemon juice
Powdered sugar or Lemon Icing

Sift together the flour, baking powder, and salt and set aside. Combine the sugar and lemon zest and set aside. In a large bowl, beat the egg yolks until thick and light. Gradually beat in the sugar with lemon zest. Beat in the water. Beat in the lemon juice. Gradually stir in the flour mixture with a whisk. Beat egg whites in a separate bowl until stiff but not dry. Gently fold the egg whites into the batter with a whisk. Pour the batter into an ungreased aluminum tube pan. Make sure the tube pan is clean and free of grease. Tube pans with removable bottoms work best. Drag a spoon through the batter to eliminate any large air pockets. Bake at 350° for about 45 minutes. Invert pan to cool. Top with powered sugar to taste, or drizzle with Lemon Icing.

Lemon Icing

2 tablespoons butter or margarine
1 tablespoon lemon juice
½ teaspoon orange juice

¾ cup powdered sugar
¼ teaspoon cream of tartar
1 teaspoon water

Melt the butter in a saucepan over low heat. Add the lemon juice and orange juice. Stir in the powdered sugar and cream of tartar. Add 1 teaspoon water, more or less as needed, to make a thin icing that will drizzle off a spoon over the cake while warm.

What are we doing when we are telling stories? It seemed to me that we are uttering a kind of prayer, and we are uttering it to the angel on the roof.

The angel on the roof [the title of his collection of short stories] is a figure—the Muse, maybe, or a genie, or an angel that makes us better, smarter, more honest than we might be otherwise in the telling of a story.

Russell Banks

Marmalade Cake

On Tuesday, he had breakfast with Olivia Davenport, and allowed her to drive him to the office in a rain so heavy they could scarcely see the lights of oncoming cars along Main Street.

"Did you hear what happened at the lay readers meeting last night?" Emma asked as he removed his raincoat.

"Esther Bolick did her impersonation of the bishop?"

"Worse than that. Somebody stole her famous orange marmalade cake out of the parish hall fridge."

"Stole it?"

"Just cracked open that cake carrier and cleaned it out, crumbs an' all."

"I don't understand."

"Everybody brought a little somethin' for refreshments. After meetin' in the nursery where it was warm, they went to the kitchen to pour tea, and the cake was gone. Hilda Lassister said she'd been waitin' two years for a taste of that marmalade cake, and when they couldn't find it, she said she like to cried."

He scratched his head. "I don't understand why they couldn't find it."

"The point," she said impatiently, "is that it wasn't in the refrigerator where Esther left it. It was gone. Kaput. Zip. Outta there."

"They put the cake in the refrigerator and went back after the meeting and it was gone?"

"That's what I'm tryin' to tell you. But whoever stole it didn't even touch Marge Houck's pineapple upside down."

"Now there's something I can understand," he said.

Jan Karon, *At Home in Mitford*

Esther's Orange-Marmalade Layer Cake

CAKE:

3 cups cake flour

½ teaspoon baking soda

½ teaspoon salt

1 cup unsalted butter, softened

2¼ cups sugar

3 large eggs, at room temperature, beaten lightly

1 tablespoon fresh grated orange zest

1½ teaspoons vanilla

1 cup buttermilk, at room temperature

1 cup fresh-squeezed orange juice

1 cup orange marmalade

ESTHER'S FROSTING:

¾ cup heavy cream

3 tablespoons sugar

¾ cup well-chilled sour cream

Preheat oven to 325°. Butter two 9-inch round cake pans, line with parchment paper, and butter and flour the paper, shaking out the excess.

In a bowl, sift the flour, baking soda, and salt. Set aside.

In a bowl with an electric mixer, beat the butter until smooth. Add 2 cups sugar, a little at a time, beating until light and fluffy. Beat in the eggs, orange zest, and vanilla. Beat in ⅓ of the sifted dry ingredients alternately with ½ of the buttermilk until combined well. Add half the remaining sifted dry ingredients and the remaining buttermilk and beat until combined well. Finally, beat in the remaining sifted dry ingredients until mixture is smooth.

Evenly divide the batter between the pans, smooth the surface, rap each pan on the counter to expel any air pockets or bubbles, then transfer to the oven. Bake for 45 minutes or until a cake tester inserted in the center comes out clean. Transfer to racks and cool in the pans for 20 minutes.

Stir the orange juice and ¼ cup sugar together in a bowl until sugar is dissolved. With a toothpick or wooden skewer, poke holes at ½-inch intervals in the cake layers and spoon the syrup over each layer, allowing the syrup to be completely absorbed before adding the remaining liquid. Let layers cool completely.

In a small saucepan set over moderate heat, heat the marmalade until just melted. Let cool 5 minutes. While it cools, make frosting.

Whisk the heavy cream with 3 tablespoons sugar until it forms firm peaks. Add the sour cream, a little at a time, and whisk until of spreading consistency.

Arrange one of the layers on a cake plate, carefully peel off the parchment paper, then spread ⅔ of the marmalade over the top, smoothing it into an even layer. Invert the remaining layer onto the top of the first layer, peel off the waxed paper, and spoon the remaining marmalade onto the center of it, leaving a 1¼-inch border around the edge. Frost the sides and top of the border with the frosting, leaving the marmalade on top of the cake exposed. Or if you prefer, frost the entire cake, adding the marmalade as a garnish on top. Chill for at least 2 hours before serving.

—Recipe was originally created by Scott Peacock and published in *Victoria* magazine (July 1998). This recipe is accepted by all Mitford and Jan Karon fans as Esther's cake.

H̲ow do I know what I think until I write it?
& W. H. Auden

Bread Pudding

"Wait till you taste Ada June's bread pudding. She's famous for it," I said. When I saw Ada June blush, I knew she'd made it in honor of Rita, so I laid it on as thick as cream. "Bread pudding's like quilting. Ada June and I can take the same pattern and the same material, but our quilts are as different as the sun and moon. I use stale bread and milk and eggs, but my bread pudding's as dull as Jell-O, while Ada June's is fine enough to take first prize at the state fair. It would if the fair had a category for bread pudding, that is. You know what I mean?"

Sandra Dallas, *The Persian Pickle Club*

Bread Pudding

Bread pudding is my favorite dessert, and I've got loads of recipes for it. I'm enclosing one from my grandmother's Modern Priscilla Standard Cook Book. *My grandmother, Faye Dallas, is Mrs. Ritter in* Persian Pickle. *And the Dallas farm is the Ritter farm. Grandma was a wonderful cook. I remember driving back to the farm in Harveyville (we lived in Denver) at Thanksgiving and arriving after dark to find the old farmhouse kitchen filled with wonderful smells. Grandma always had something simmering on the back of the cookstove, and after we ate supper, she tucked us into feather beds upstairs, and we slept under handmade quilts.—Sandra Dallas*

1½ cups breadcrumbs	Pinch of salt
3 cups milk	¼ teaspoon cinnamon or allspice
⅓ cup sugar	⅛ teaspoon nutmeg
2 eggs, beaten	½ cup raisins (optional)

Scald milk by bringing it barely to a boil over medium heat, stirring constantly. Cool slightly. Soak the breadcrumbs in the warm, scalded milk until they are very moist. Stir in the sugar, eggs, salt, and desired spices. Add raisins, if desired. Pour into a large, greased casserole dish. Bake at 325° until firm, about 45 minutes. Makes 5 servings.

—Recipe contributed by Sandra Dallas

A book is the purest essence of the human soul.

   Thomas Carlyle

Rice Pudding

One January night in 1996 I dreamed that I jumped into a swimming pool filled with rice pudding, where I swam with the grace of a porpoise. It's my favorite dessert—rice pudding, that is, not porpoise. I love it so much so that in 1991, in a restaurant in Madrid, I ordered four servings, and then a fifth for dessert. I ate them down without blinking, with the vague hope that that nostalgic dessert from my childhood could help me bear the anguish of seeing my daughter so ill. Neither my soul nor my daughter improved, but rice pudding remains associated in my memory with spiritual comfort. There was nothing, however, elevating about the dream: I dived in, and that delicious creaminess caressed my skin, slipped into all the crevices of my body, filled my mouth. I awoke feeling happy and threw myself on my husband before the poor man realized what was happening to him. The next week I dreamed I was arranging a naked Antonio Banderas on a Mexican tortilla; I slathered on guacamole and salsa, rolled him up, and wolfed him down. That time I woke up in terror. And a few days later, I dreamed . . . well, there's no point in going on with the list, it's not enough to say that when I told my mother of these cruelties, she advised me to see a physiatrist—or a cook. You're going to get fat, she added, and so I decided to confront the problem with the only solution I know for my obsessions: writing.

   Isabel Allende, *Aphrodite*

Arroz con Leche
(Spiritual Solace Rice Pudding)

⌒∿⌒

This recipe will serve 8 normal people, but in my eyes it's a crime to make less. I am capable of devouring it at one sitting without blinking an eye, and I don't see why it should be any different in your case, my dear reader. But if you can't finish, you can keep it in the refrigerator, then, should you be in a good mood, you can cover your lover from head to foot with this mouthwatering arroz con leche and slowly lick it off. On such an occasion the calories are justified.—Isabel Allende

1 cup rice	2 cups sugar
4 cups warm water	1 piece lemon zest
10 cups milk	1 tablespoon cinnamon
1 cinnamon stick	

Soak the rice in the warm water for 30 minutes. Drain. Cook the rice with the milk and cinnamon stick until the rice begins to soften, about 30 minutes. Add the sugar and lemon zest and simmer over very low heat, stirring from time to time to prevent the rice from sticking. In about 30 minutes the mixture will thicken. Place in a bowl, cool in the refrigerator, and sprinkle with cinnamon just before serving.

—Recipe from Isabel Allende, *Aphrodite*

The words that enlighten the soul are more precious than jewels.

   Hazrat Inayat Khan

Holiday Pudding

ەرى

There never was such a goose. Bob said he didn't believe there ever was such a goose cooked. Its tenderness and flavor, size and cheapness, were the themes of universal admiration. Eked out by apple sauce and mashed potatoes, it was a sufficient dinner for the whole family; indeed, as Mrs. Cratchit said with great delight (surveying one small atom of a bone upon the dish), they hadn't ate it all at last! Yet every one had enough, and the youngest Cratchits in particular were steeped in sage and onion to the eyebrows! But now, the plates being changed by Miss Belinda, Mrs. Cratchit left the room alone—too nervous to bear witness—to take the pudding up, and bring it in.

Suppose it should not be done enough! Suppose somebody should have got over the wall of the back yard, and stolen it, while they were merry with the goose—a supposition at which the two young Cratchits became livid! All sorts of horrors were supposed.

Hallo! A great deal of steam! The pudding was out of the copper. A smell like a washing-day! That was the cloth. A smell like an eating-house and a pastry-cook's next door to each other, with a laundress's next door to that! That was the pudding! In half a minute Mrs. Cratchit entered—flushed but smiling proudly—with the pudding, like a speckled cannon-ball, so hard and firm, blazing in half of half a quartern of ignited brandy, and bedight with Christmas holly stuck into the top.

Oh, a wonderful pudding! Bob Cratchit said, and calmly, too, that he regarded it as the greatest success achieved by Mrs. Cratchit since their marriage. Mrs. Cratchit said that, now the weight was off her mind, she would confess she had her doubts about the quantity of flour. Everybody had something to say about it, but nobody said or thought it was at all a small pudding for a large family. It would have been flat heresy to do so. Any Cratchit would have blushed to hint at such a thing.

 Charles Dickens, *A Christmas Carol*

Carrot Pudding

1½ cups grated carrots

1 cup nuts

2 teaspoons baking powder

1 cup shortening

1 cup milk

½ teaspoon salt

2 cups all-purpose flour

½ cup candied citrus peel, any
   variety

2 eggs, beaten

1 package seedless raisins

¼ cup dark molasses

½ teaspoon cinnamon

1 cup brown sugar

¾ cup white sugar

¼ teaspoon ground cloves

1 cup dry breadcrumbs

1 teaspoon soda

½ teaspoon allspice

TOPPING:

2 tablespoons butter

¾ cup light brown sugar

2 cups boiling water

2 tablespoons cornstarch

⅛ teaspoon nutmeg

1 teaspoon vanilla

Pinch of salt

SAUCE:

1 cup sugar mixed with
   2 tablespoons cornstarch

2 cups boiling water

4 tablespoons butter

Combine all the pudding ingredients in a large bowl and stir well. Pour the batter into greased pudding molds or a casserole dish, no more than two-thirds full. Cover with lids or aluminum foil. Place on rack in a large kettle containing about 2 inches of water, using a rack high enough so that molds or dish does not sit in the water. Bring water to a gentle boil and steam pudding for 2 to 3 hours, until pudding is firm. Monitor water level every 30 minutes and add more when necessary to maintain about 2 inches.

To prepare topping, melt the butter with brown sugar in a saucepan over low heat until it bubbles. Add boiling water. Dissolve the cornstarch in about 1 teaspoon of water and stir in. Add the nutmeg and salt. Mix all ingredients together in the saucepan until thickened. Stir in vanilla.

To prepare sauce, mix the sugar, cornstarch, and water together in a saucepan. Boil for about 1 minute, stirring constantly. Stir in the butter until melted and mix well. Remove from heat and stir in one of the following flavorings: 2 teaspoons vanilla, 2 teaspoons fresh-squeezed lemon juice with fresh grated zest of 1 lemon, or 2 teaspoons nutmeg.

Spread the topping on the cooked pudding before serving. Then top with sauce.

MAKES 12 SERVINGS

I just like the way words sound and collide, combine, fade into the sentence, and combine again.

᳚   Viken Berberian

Custard Pudding

ↄ丿ↄ

Readers of J. K. Rowling's *Harry Potter and the Chamber of Secrets* will remember Aunt Petunia's levitating cream-covered, violet-topped custard—the elegant creation that crashes and covers Harry with dessert, thanks to Dobby, the house elf, who has appeared to warn Harry not to return to the Hogwarts School of Witchcraft and Wizardry.

Caution: Use Hover Charm at own risk.

Aunt Petunia's Baked Custard Pudding

1 8-ounce package cream cheese,
    cut into chunks
2 cups half-and-half
1 cup sugar

⅛ teaspoon salt
4 eggs, beaten
1 teaspoon vanilla

Combine all the ingredients in a blender and process for about 2 minutes on high speed or until very smooth. Strain the mixture and pour into a 2-quart glass casserole coated with cooking spray. Place the casserole in a larger pan and fill pan with boiling water, to within 1 inch of the top of the dish.

For individual custards, strain mixture and pour the strained mixture into 8 custard cups (6 ounces each) coated with cooking spray. Place the individual custard cups in 2 cake pans. Fill pans with boiling water to within 1 inch of the cup tops.

Steam in a 325° oven for about 70 minutes for individual puddings and about 90 minutes for a large pudding. Pudding is done when it is firm and a knife inserted into the center comes out clean. Chill thoroughly. Serve with whipped cream and garnish with sugar cake decorations.

MAKES 8 SERVINGS

Writing fiction is a solitary occupation but not really a lonely one. The writer's head is mobbed with characters, images and language, making the creative process something like eavesdropping at a party for which you've had the fun of drawing up the guest list.

   Hilma Wolitzer

Chocolate Pudding and
Chocolate Soufflé

ᔇ

Dearest Emily,

Did you ever wonder what the difference is between chocolate soufflé and chocolate pudding? I know the question sounds crazy, but stay with me on this one and you will soon understand.

In college I took a job at David Angela's, a restaurant in the ritzy part of town. While most of the desserts we served were purchased frozen from a supplier, thawed, and then presented as if fresh, we did actually make our own chocolate soufflé. It was an old family recipe and a house specialty. It was served on a white plate drizzled with raspberry and chocolate syrup. Belgian chocolate was grated on top with just a sprinkle of powdered sugar. It was always made from scratch and it was a sight to behold. While I was there, I actually learned how to prepare it. Can you believe that? Your grandpa in the kitchen cooking. Just the thought scared Kathryn. After we got married, she kicked me out of the kitchen. She said it was 'cause I never cleaned up my mess, but I knew it was because my chocolate soufflé put her to shame.

Anyway, one day I picked up Kathryn who was getting her hair done—something I've honestly never understood. Why would you pay someone to make your hair look funny, so you can't sleep normally for days afraid you'll mess it up? Strange custom. Anyway, her hair wasn't finished, so while I waited, I scanned several of the magazines on the table. There were no outdoor magazines, so I picked up one about cooking and started to flip through its pages. In my flipping, I came across a recipe for chocolate pudding. Yes, chocolate pudding. Not the instant kind, the homemade kind, but chocolate pudding nonetheless. I stared at the recipe and realized the ingredients were exactly the same as the chocolate soufflé I had made at the restaurant. The only real difference between the two was the time and manner in which the ingredients were put together and the way it was presented.

It dawned on me right then and there, Emily, that life is very much like gourmet cooking. The ingredients we are given are often very much the same as those that others receive. It is how those ingredients are put together—the detail, the time, and the presentation—

that make the difference. While some make pudding, others take just a bit more time, go to a little extra trouble, present their creations properly, and create something sumptuous.

So go to the kitchen, Emily, take the ingredients you've been given in life and make your grandpa a chocolate soufflé.

Love,

Grandpa Harry

Camron Steve Wright, *Letters for Emily*

Chocolate Pudding

1 cup sugar

2 tablespoons cornstarch *or*

    ¼ cup all-purpose flour

¼ teaspoon salt

2 cups milk

2 1-ounce squares of

    unsweetened chocolate

2 slightly beaten egg yolks *or*

    1 well-beaten egg

2 tablespoons butter

1 teaspoon vanilla

In a double-boiler, blend sugar, cornstarch (or flour), and salt; add milk and chocolate squares. Cook and stir over medium heat until thick and bubbly. Continue to cook for 2 additional minutes. Remove from heat.

Stir a small amount of hot mixture into yolks (or whole egg), then return to hot mixture. Cook and stir 2 minutes more. Remove from heat. Blend in butter and vanilla. Pour into dessert dishes and chill.

MAKES 4 OR 5 SERVINGS

—Recipe contributed by Camron Steve Wright

Or, Chocolate Soufflé

3 eggs, separated

2 tablespoons butter

2 tablespoons all-purpose flour

¼ teaspoon salt

¾ cup milk

2 1-ounce squares unsweetened
    chocolate, melted and cooled
    slightly

½ cup sugar, divided

2 tablespoons hot water

¼ teaspoon vanilla

Sweetened whipped cream

Beat egg yolks until thick, then set aside. In saucepan, melt butter. Stir in flour and salt. Add milk all at once. Cook, stirring constantly, until mixture is thickened and bubbly. Stir a moderate amount of the hot mixture in with the egg yolks and mix well. Return to the remaining hot mixture and cook for 2 minutes, stirring constantly. Remove from heat.

Stir together unsweetened chocolate (melted and cooled), ¼ cup sugar, and hot water. Stir chocolate mixture into egg mixture.

Beat egg whites and vanilla until soft peaks form. Gradually add ¼ cup sugar, until stiff peaks form. Fold egg whites into chocolate mixture. Turn into a 1½-quart greased soufflé dish. Bake at 325° until a knife comes out clean, about an hour.

Top with whipped cream. Serve immediately. May also be garnished with grated chocolate, powdered sugar, and/or raspberry or chocolate sauce drizzled on the serving plate.

MAKE 6 SERVINGS

—Recipe contributed by Camron Steve Wright

Words are a form of action, capable of influencing change.

    Ingrid Bengis

Applesauce

Ruth was home safely, and now they would eat a well-balanced meal, Amanda told herself, spooning red cabbage onto Ruth's plate. Everything was all right, then. Everything was as it should be, she thought, surveying the table, except for one detail. "Do you think we should have applesauce, Ruth? There's some in the icebox. Why don't you get it?"

"I don't need applesauce."

"Well, but I think we should have it. It's just in the icebox, in the little green dish."

"I really don't want applesauce tonight."

"But I think we should have it. Otherwise, we don't have any fruit, and fruit is very important. Let's have it on the table, at least, in case we change our minds."

    Christina Schwarz, *Drowning Ruth*

Applesauce, Just as It Should Be

6 cups tart cooking apples,
     peeled, cored, and chopped
⅓ to ½ cup granulated sugar
½ teaspoon ground cinnamon

Pinch of ground nutmeg
½ cup water
2 teaspoons lemon juice

Place all the ingredients together in a medium, heavy-bottomed pot. Stir well to mix evenly, cover, and cook over low heat for about 30 minutes or until the apples are very tender. Stir often during cooking. Remove from heat. Cool slightly and process until somewhat smooth in a food processor. Serve warm or cool.

MAKES 8 TO 10 SERVINGS

Each writer has a particular book that unlocked the desire to write. For me, I think *Ethan Frome* was that book. I read it when I was a junior in high school. I consider it a nearly perfect novel. It's a framed story and contains within it the delicate thread of literary suspense.

◖   Anita Shreve

Popovers

My uncle ordered popovers
from the restaurant's bill of fare.
And, when they were served,
he regarded them
with a penetrating stare . . .
Then he spoke great Words of Wisdom
as he sat there on that chair:
"To eat those things," said my uncle,
"you must exercise great care.
You may swallow down what's solid . . .
BUT . . . you must spit out the air!"

And . . . as you partake of the world's
bill of fare

that's darned good advice to follow.
Do a lot of spitting out the hot air.
And be careful what you swallow.

 Dr. Seuss, "My Uncle Terwilliger on the Art of Eating Popovers," from
Seuss-isms: Wise and Witty Prescriptions for Living from the Good Doctor

Uncle Terwilliger's Artful Popovers

A perfect popover is crisp on the outside, tender and moist inside. The secret of success is simple—do not over-beat batter, and be sure the popovers are thoroughly baked when you take them from the oven.

½ cup flour (do not use self-rising
    flour)
¼ teaspoon salt
½ cup milk

1 egg
Shortening or vegetable cooking
    spray

Heat oven to 450°. (For higher popovers, heat muffin tins or oven-glass cups in oven before filling with batter.) Beat all the ingredients together in a large bowl just until blended (lumps are okay). Pour the batter into well-greased, deep muffin cups (¾ full) or oven-glass cups (½ full). If using glass cups, place them on a cookie sheet or shallow casserole for stability. If any sections of muffin tins are empty, fill them half full with water for even baking. Pour the batter into alternating cups so that they do not touch as they bake.

Bake for 25 minutes. Lower oven temperature to 350° and bake for 15 to 20 minutes longer or until deep golden brown. Do not open oven at all during the baking process or they will fall.

Poke a small hole into side of each popover with a toothpick to allow steam to escape. Immediately remove from pan with spatula and serve hot. Break and spread with desired topping (honey butter, fruit, preserves, etc.) or fill crusty hollow shell with creamed seafood or meat.

MAKES 4 POPOVERS

Variations:
Sprinkle bottom of each cup or tin with grated Parmesan cheese (distribute ¼ cup cheese among the containers).
Add ¼ cup shredded cheddar cheese to batter.
Add ¼ cup cooked, crisp, diced bacon to batter.

A child's dreams blueprint his future, and it's a wise child whose instincts (unwarped by ignorant elders) lead him to fill his dream house with the riches of idea and emotion that the great books offer.

✍   T. Morris Longstreth

Peaches

"Stop!" Aunt Spiker said quickly. "Hold everything!" She was staring up into the branches with her mouth wide open and her eyes bulging as though she had seen a ghost. "Look!" she said. "*Look*, Sponge, *look!*"

"What's the matter with you?" Aunt Sponge demanded.

"It's *growing!*" Aunt Spiker cried. "It's getting bigger and bigger!"

"What is?"

"The peach, of course!"

"You're joking!"

"Well, look for yourself!"

"But my dear Spiker, that's perfectly ridiculous. That's impossible. That's—that's—that's—Now, wait *just* a minute—No—No—that can't be right—No—Yes—Great Scott! The thing really *is* growing!"

"It's nearly twice as big already!" Aunt Spiker shouted.

"It can't be true!"

"It *is* true!"

"It must be a miracle!"

"Watch it! Watch it!"

"I *am* watching it!"

"Great Heavens alive!" Aunt Spiker yelled. "I can actually see the thing bulging and swelling before my very eyes!"

✍ Roald Dahl, *James and the Giant Peach*

It was a large hole, the sort of thing an animal about the size of a fox might have made.

James knelt down in front of it and poked his head and shoulders inside.

He crawled in.

He kept on crawling.

This isn't just a hole, he thought excitedly. *It's a tunnel!*

The tunnel was damp and murky, and all around him there was the curious bittersweet smell of fresh peach. The floor was soggy under his knees, the walls were wet and sticky, and peach juice was dripping from the ceiling. James opened his mouth and caught some of it on his tongue. It tasted delicious.

He was crawling uphill now, as though the tunnel were leading straight toward the very center of the gigantic fruit. Every few seconds he paused and took a bite out of the wall. The peach flesh was sweet and juicy, and marvelously refreshing.

✍ Roald Dahl, *James and the Giant Peach*

Marvelously Refreshing Peach Juice

∽

1 16-ounce can peaches in fruit
    juice, or 6 fresh peaches,
    skinned and pitted

1 5-ounce can mangos, or half a
    mango
Juice of 1 lemon

Pureé all ingredients until liquefied. Add ice cubes and serve immediately.

MAKES 4 TO 6 SERVINGS

—From *Roald Dahl's Revolting Recipes*

James's Ginger Peaches

∽

¼ cup sugar with ¼ teaspoon
    cinnamon
4 peaches, sliced, skin removed
2 tablespoons butter or
    margarine

1 tablespoon crystallized ginger,
    chopped

Sprinkle the sugar mixture over the peaches in a saucepan and let sit for 2 hours. Add the butter and ginger. Heat peaches over medium heat, melting the butter. Stir continuously to coat peaches with sugary mixture. Heat until peaches are warmed through, about 3 to 5 minutes. Serve topped with whipped cream.

MAKES 4 SERVINGS

Great Heavens!
Peach-Cranberry Crisp

4 peaches, skins and pits
   removed, and sliced
½ to ¾ cup sugar
½ cup all-purpose flour, divided
1½ cup fresh cranberries
¼ cup orange juice

½ cup sugar
2 teaspoons cornstarch
2 tablespoons butter or margarine
¼ cup brown sugar
¼ cup quick-cooking oats

Combine the peaches, ½ to ¾ cup sugar, and ¼ cup flour in a medium-sized bowl. Toss to coat. Set aside.

Place the cranberries, orange juice, and ½ cup sugar in a medium pot. Bring to a boil, then reduce heat to low and simmer for no more than one minute. Remove from heat and stir in cornstarch. Add cranberry mixture to peaches and stir to combine. Pour peach-cranberry filling into a 9-inch pie pan.

Combine butter, brown sugar, ¼ cup flour, and ¼ cup oats in a bowl, and mix with fork or pastry blender until crumbly, then sprinkle over dessert. Bake at 375° for about 30 minutes.

MAKES 6 SERVINGS

Some books are to be tasted, others to be swallowed, and some few to be chewed and digested.

‹‹© **Francis Bacon**

Apples

AFTER APPLE-PICKING

My long two-pointed ladder's sticking through a tree
Toward heaven still,
And there's a barrel that I didn't fill
Beside it, and there may be two or three
Apples I didn't pick upon some bough.
But I am done with apple-picking now.
Essence of winter sleep is on the night,
The scent of apples: I am drowsing off.
I cannot rub the strangeness from my sight
I got from looking through a pane of glass
I skimmed this morning from the drinking trough
And held against the world of hoary grass.
It melted, and I let it fall and break.
But I was well
Upon my way to sleep before it fell,
And I could tell
What form my dreaming was about to take.
Magnified apples appear and disappear,
Stem end and blossom end,
And every fleck of russet showing clear.
My instep arch not only keeps the ache,
It keeps the pressure of a ladder-round.
I feel the ladder sway as the boughs bend.
And I keep hearing from the cellar bin
The rumbling sound
Of load on load of apples coming in.
For I have had too much

Of apple-picking: I am overtired
Of the great harvest I myself desired.
There were ten thousand thousand fruit to touch,
Cherish in hand, lift down, and not let fall.
For all
That struck the earth,
No matter if not bruised or spiked with stubble,
Went surely to the cider-apple heap
As of no worth.
One can see what will trouble
This sleep of mine, whatever sleep it is.
Were he not gone,
The woodchuck could say whether it's like his
Long sleep, as I describe its coming on,
Or just some human sleep.

Robert Frost

Wassail
(Hot Spiced Cider)

1 teaspoon whole cloves	½ cup sugar
1 stick cinnamon	3 cups pineapple juice
2 quarts apple cider	1 cup lemon juice
2 cups orange juice	

Wrap cloves and cinnamon stick snugly in a small piece of clean cheese-cloth and tie it with string. Combine other ingredients in a large saucepan. Add the spice bag and simmer for 30 to 45 minutes. Remove spice bag and serve hot.

MAKES 12 SERVINGS

Harvest-Time Baked Apples

Baking apples of choice
  (Macintosh or Jonathan)
¼ cup brown sugar
⅛ teaspoon nutmeg

½ teaspoon cinnamon
2 tablespoons butter or
  margarine, melted, per apple

Preheat oven to 375°. Mix brown sugar, nutmeg, and cinnamon in a bowl. Remove cores from the number of apples desired per person, leaving bottom of each apple intact. Also, peel skin from top quarter of each apple. Pour ½ to 1 tablespoon butter into each apple center, and drizzle the remainder over the outside of the apple. Add ½ tablespoon sugar mixture to each apple center and sprinkle additional sugar mixture over the upper peeled quarter of apple. Place apple(s) in a shallow pan filled with about ¼-inch depth of water. Bake apple(s) about 35 to 45 minutes, until tender.

Serve warm. Use spoons to scoop out baked fruit.

EACH APPLE MAKES 1 SERVING

Poetry is the journal of the sea animal living on land, wanting to fly in the air. Poetry is a search for syllables to shoot at the barriers of the unknown and the unknowable. Poetry is a phantom script telling how rainbows are made and why they go away.

  Carl Sandburg

Strawberries

Etta grew tired, gut weary, of strawberries: she didn't even like to eat them. Her husband was a true lover of the fruit, but Etta couldn't feel anything for it. To him strawberries were a holy mystery, jewels of sugar, deep red gems, sweet orbs, succulent rubies. He knew their secrets, the path they took, the daily responses they made to sunlight. The rocks between the rows collected heat, he said, and kept his plants warmer at night than they would otherwise have been—but to this sort of thing she made no answer.

◄ **David Guterson,** *Snow Falling on Cedars*

Island Strawberries and Cream

1 quart strawberries   1 cup heavy cream
¼ cup sugar   ¼ cup powdered sugar

Clean, hull, and slice strawberries. Place them in a medium-sized bowl, and sprinkle them with sugar. Set aside for 1 to 2 hours. Whip cream and sugar together into soft peaks. Serve strawberries with a dollop of the whipped cream.

MAKES 6 TO 8 SERVINGS

One of the gifts of being a writer is that it gives you an excuse to do things, to go places and explore. Another is that writing motivates you to look closely at life, at life as it lurches by and tramps around.

◄ **Anne Lamott**

Black Cows

ᴄᴠᴐ

My favorite memory—the one I went back to the most—happened the year July was so hot you sweated standing still. I was seven. Matt, my brother, and I, and May and Elmer were drinking black cows in the kitchen after supper. Elmer, scooping up refills, missed my glass, and this splat of ice cream landed on my head.

It is crystal clear. We are a family, laughing our heads off, and I'm laughing too, because the ice cream feels cold dripping down my hot skin, and I'm making faces, twisting up my tongue to get the drops. Everyone's howling at me and I'm cracking up because I know I'm funny. I have my eyes crossed. May doesn't try to wipe off my head. The flesh on her bare arms is shaking and she has tears coming down her face. She can't breathe. Elmer stands behind me with his hands on my shoulders, patting me. He has a deep laugh with spaces between, like he has to remind himself every few seconds what's so funny. And the best part is Matt. He reaches out to touch my arm. Suddenly I'm a celebrity.

◅ɢ   **Jane Hamilton,** *The Book of Ruth*

Refreshing Black Cows

ᴄᴠᴐ

Perfect for scenes of family discord.—Jane Hamilton

1 scoop vanilla ice cream	Whipped cream
1 tablespoon chocolate syrup	Maraschino cherry
8 to 12 ounces root beer or cola	

Chill a tumbler. Add the vanilla ice cream and chocolate syrup. Slowly pour in cold soda until the glass is full. Garnish with whipped cream and a cherry. Serve with a straw and a long-handled spoon.

MAKES 1 SERVING

ALGERNON: Oh! it is absurd to have a hard and fast rule about what one should read and what one shouldn't. More than half of modern culture depends on what one shouldn't read.

   Oscar Wilde, *The Importance of Being Earnest*

Jam Roly Poly

The plates were big ones, and they were literally heaped with food: boiled potatoes, lamb stew and beans cut that day from the garden, ladled in huge portions. In spite of the muted groans and sounds of disgust, everyone including Stu polished his plate clean with bread, and ate several slices more spread thickly with butter and native gooseberry jam. Fee sat down and bolted her meal, then got up at once to hurry to her worktable again, where into big soup plates she doled out great quantities of biscuit made with plenty of sugar and laced all through with jam. A river of steaming hot custard sauce was poured over each, and again she plodded to the dining table with the plates, two at a time. Finally, she sat down with a sigh; this she could eat at her leisure.

"Oh, goodie! Jam roly-poly!" Meggie exclaimed, slopping her spoon up and down in the custard until the jam seeped through to make pink streaks in the yellow.

"Well, Meggie girl, it's your birthday, so Mum made your favorite pudding," her father said, smiling.

There was no complaining this time; no matter what the pudding was, it was consumed with gusto. The Clearys all had a sweet tooth.

   Colleen McCullough, *The Thorn Birds*

Fee's Jam Roly Poly

⅓ cup shortening

2 cups all-purpose flour

¼ cup sugar

3 teaspoons baking powder

1 teaspoon salt

¾ cup buttermilk

2 cups strawberry jam or fruit
  preserves of choice

1 teaspoon sugar

Combine shortening, flour, ¼ cup sugar, baking powder, and salt with pastry blender until mixture has the consistency of fine crumbs. Stir in buttermilk until just blended. Place dough on lightly floured surface and gently form into a ball. Knead 25 to 30 times. Grease sides and bottom of an 8 × 11-inch cake pan.

Gently pat ⅔ of the dough into the bottom of the pan until surface is flat and smooth. Spread jam on dough to within 1 inch of edges. Roll remaining dough ¼ inch thick. Cut into 2-inch squares. Place squares randomly over jam layer, allowing jam to show through to produce a marbled effect. Sprinkle the top dough squares lightly with 1 teaspoon of sugar. Bake at 450° for 20 to 25 minutes. Serve warm with vanilla sauce.

MAKES 8 SERVINGS

SAUCE:

1 cup sugar mixed with
  2 tablespoons cornstarch

2 cups boiling water

4 tablespoons butter

2 teaspoons vanilla

Mix the sugar, cornstarch, and water together in a saucepan. Boil for about 1 minute, stirring constantly until slightly thickened. Stir in the butter until melted and mix well. Remove from heat and stir in vanilla.

I want a poem to hit me on the solar plexus. I want good imagery. I only ask one thing from a poem: that it irretrievably changes my life.

◂ David Lee

Coffee

ᴏⅤ♂

COFFEE WITH THE MEAL

A gentlemanly gentleman, as mild as May,
Entered a restaurant famed and gay.
A waiter sat him in a draughty seat
And laughingly inquired what he'd like to eat.
"Oh I don't want venison, I don't want veal,
But I do insist on coffee with the meal.
Bring me clams in a chilly group,
And a large tureen of vegetable soup,
Steak as tender as a maiden's dream,
With lots of potatoes hashed in cream,
And a lettuce and tomato salad, please,
And crackers and a bit of Roquefort cheese,
But waiter, the gist of my appeal,
Is coffee with, coffee with, coffee with the meal."
The waiter groaned and he wrung his hands;
"Perhaps the headwaiter understands."
Said the sleek headwaiter, like a snobbish seal,

"What, monsieur? Coffee with the meal?"
His lip drew up in scornful laughter;
"Monsieur desires a demitasse after!"
The gentleman's eyes grew hard as steel,
He said, "I'm ordering coffee with the meal.
Hot black coffee in a great big cup,
Fuming, steaming, filled right up.
I don't want coffee iced in a glass,
And I don't want a miserable demitasse,
But what I'll have, come woe, come weal,
Is coffee with, coffee with, coffee with the meal."
The headwaiter bowed like a poppy in the breeze;
"Monsieur desires coffee with the salad or the cheese?"
Monsieur said, "Now you're getting warmer;
Coffee with the latter, coffee with the former;
Coffee with the steak, coffee with the soup,
Coffee with the clams in a chilly group;
Yes, and with a cocktail I could do,
So bring me coffee with the cocktail, too.
I'll light to the death for my bright ideal,
Which is coffee with, coffee with, coffee with the meal."
The headwaiter swiveled on a graceful heel;
"Certainly, certainly, coffee with the meal!"
The waiter gave an obsequious squeal,
"Yes, sir, yes, sir, coffee with the meal!"
Oh, what a glow did Monsieur feel
At the warming vision of coffee with the meal,
One hour later Monsieur, alas!
Got his coffee in a demitasse.

  Ogden Nash, *The Face Is Familiar*

Irish Coffee

1 cup brewed coffee

1 tablespoon orange juice

1 teaspoon lemon juice

1½ ounces Irish whiskey

Whipped cream

Mix first four ingredients. Top with whipped cream.

MAKES 1 SERVING

Coffee Mocha

1 cup brewed coffee

2½ tablespoons cocoa powder

1 cup milk

¼ teaspoon vanilla

Whipped cream

Cinnamon

In saucepan combine coffee with cocoa powder and milk. Stir over medium heat until simmering. Remove from heat and add vanilla. Pour into cups and top with whipped cream sprinkled with cinnamon.

MAKES 2 SERVINGS

Language is the raw material that makes a poem float.

Lorraine Healy

Tea

ᏯᏴᏗ

Few hours in life [are] more agreeable than the hour dedicated to the ceremony known as afternoon tea.

᎑᎐   Henry James, *The Portrait of a Lady*

We did not always sit below in the library. Sometimes she would ask me to go with her upstairs, to aunt Phoebe's boudoir, and we would spread out the books and plans of gardens upon the floor. I was host in the library down below, but here in her boudoir she was host-ess. I am not sure I did not like it better. We lost formality. Seacombe did not bother us— by some measure of tact she had got him to dispense with the solemnity of the silver tea tray—and she would brew tisana for us both instead, which she said was a continental cus-tom and much better for the eyes and skin.

᎑᎐   Daphne du Maurier, *My Cousin Rachel*

Mrs. Albert Forrester, confident in the judgment of posterity, could afford to be disinter-ested. With these elements then it is no wonder that she had succeeded in creating some-thing as near the French salon of the eighteenth century as our barbarous nation has ever reached. To be invited to "eat a bun and drink a cup of tea on Tuesday" was a privilege that few failed to recognize; and when you sat on your Chippendale chair in the discreetly lit but austere room, you could not but feel that you were living literary history. The American am-bassador once said to Mrs. Albert Forrester:

"A cup of tea with you, Mrs. Forrester, is one of the richest intellectual treats which it has ever been my lot to enjoy."

It was indeed on occasion a trifle overbearing. . . . For my part I found it prudent to for-tify myself with a cocktail or two before I exposed myself to the rarefied atmosphere of her society. Indeed, I very nearly found myself for ever excluded from it, for one afternoon, pre-senting myself at the door, instead of asking the maid who opened it: "Is Mrs. Albert For-rester at home?" I asked: "Is there Divine Service to-day?"

᎑᎐   W. Somerset Maugham, "The Creative Impulse" from *The Complete Short Stories of W. Somerset Maugham, Vol. 1*

An Agreeable Cup (or Two) of Tea
Apple-Ginger Tea

2 cups water
¼ cup chopped crystallized
    ginger
2 cinnamon sticks

2 tablespoons sugar
1 bag lemon herb tea
1 bag apple-cinnamon herb tea
1½ cups apple juice

Combine the water, ginger, cinnamon sticks, and sugar in a small saucepan and bring to a boil. Reduce heat to low and simmer for 7 minutes. Remove from heat, add tea bags, and steep for 5 minutes. Discard tea bags, strain, and return beverage to pan. Add juice, heat through, and serve.

MAKES 4 SERVINGS

Ginger-Raspberry Tea

3¼ cups water
¼ cup chopped crystallized
    ginger

5 cranberry herb tea bags
2 cups cranberry-raspberry juice
3 tablespoons sugar

Bring water to a boil in a saucepan. Remove from heat. Add the ginger and tea bags, cover, and steep for 5 minutes. Discard tea bags. Add juice and sugar and return to medium heat, stirring until sugar dissolves. Discard ginger and serve.

MAKES 5 SERVINGS

Orange Tea

6 cups water
4 bags orange-spice herbal tea
1 cup sugar

2 teaspoons chopped crystallized
   ginger
2 cinnamon sticks
2 cups orange juice

In saucepan bring water to a boil. Add the tea bags, sugar, ginger, and cinnamon sticks; cover and simmer for 5 to 7 minutes. Strain into a pitcher and cool to room temperature. Add the orange juice. Serve with ice.

MAKES ABOUT 8 SERVINGS

But Kino's brain burned, even during his sleep, and he dreamed that Coyotito could read, that one of his own people could read him the truth of things. And in his dream, Coyotito was reading from a book as large as a house, with letters as big as a dog, and the words galloped and played on the book.

John Steinbeck, *The Pearl*

COOKIES
AND OTHER
SWEETS

If there is no happy ending . . . make one out of cookie dough.

COOPER EDENS, *IF YOU'RE AFRAID OF THE DARK, REMEMBER THE NIGHT RAINBOW*

Cookies

⌀⌀

Because my grandma had nothing much to put in her huge bedroom closet, I kept my dolls there, four of them, two with their own little cribs and two in a baby buggy. Way in the back in a shadow lived the dolls' other mother, a girl just like me. She never came out. I tried leaving votive offerings—chewing gum when I had an extra piece, but she never chewed it. One day she ate a cookie, which proved to me that she existed.

◖ Shirley Abbott, *The Bookmaker's Daughter*

Delightful Banana Chocolate Chip Cookies

⌀⌀

½ small ripe banana, mashed

½ cup butter or margarine, softened

½ cup shortening

¾ cup sugar

¾ cup packed brown sugar

2 eggs

2 teaspoons vanilla extract

2½ cups all-purpose flour

1 teaspoon baking soda

½ teaspoon salt

½ cup sweetened, flaked coconut

1 12-ounce bag semisweet chocolate chips

Preheat oven to 375°. Cream the banana, butter, shortening, sugars, eggs, and vanilla in a large mixing bowl. Add the dry ingredients and mix well. Stir in coconut and chocolate chips. Scoop tablespoon-sized amounts onto a greased cookie sheet. Bake 9 to 11 minutes, until golden brown.

MAKES ABOUT 4 DOZEN COOKIES

I never wrote to Hanna. But I kept reading to her. When I spent a year in America, I sent cassettes from there. When I was on vacation or was particularly busy, it might take longer for me to finish the next cassette; I never established a definite rhythm, but sent cassettes sometimes every week or two weeks, and sometimes only every three or four weeks. I didn't worry that Hanna might not need my cassettes now that she had learned to read by herself. She could read as well. Reading aloud was my way of speaking to her, with her.

Bernhard Schlink, *The Reader*

Peanut Butter

"Hey, shouldn't we be heading out to the woods?" asked Joel, breaking into my reverie. For a fanatic, he seemed to be remarkably moderating.

Everyone agreed, including myself, that it was long past time they hit the road. I surprised them by dashing off to the kitchen and returning with sack lunches. "They're all the same," I said pointedly. "Oatmeal batter bread sandwiches with strawberry preserves, and peanut butter cookies."

"Better not be any eggs in here," growled Jeanette.

"Did you use organic peanut butter in the cookies?" asked Linda.

I smiled benevolently. "Of course, dear." I wasn't lying, either. I'd checked my dictionary before going to bed the night before. According to Webster, organic things were those that were, or had been, alive and that contained carbon. Even the off-brand of peanut butter I bought used peanuts that had once been alive and contained carbon. Of course, it is quite possible that Linda meant to ask if the peanuts had been grown by the aid of organic fertilizer and without pesticides. But that's not what she said, was it?

Tamar Myers, *Too Many Crooks Spoil the Broth*

The popularity of [Tamar] Myers' series is rising like sticky bun dough.

Allentown Morning Call

Possibly Organic Peanut Butter Cookies

½ cup white sugar

½ cup brown sugar

½ cup butter or margarine, softened

½ cup peanut butter (do not use reduced-fat peanut butter)

1 egg, beaten

3 tablespoons milk

1¾ cups all-purpose flour

½ teaspoon salt

1 teaspoon baking soda

Cream the sugars and butter together in a large bowl. Add the peanut butter, egg, and milk and combine well. Stir in the dry ingredients until dough is well blended. Form dough into 1-inch balls. Place the balls on a greased cookie sheet and flatten each ball with the bottom of a glass. Make cross marks on top of each cookie with a damp fork dipped in sugar. Bake at 350° for about 10 minutes.

MAKES 3 DOZEN COOKIES

Rolled Holiday

December 18, 1919
Dallas

Dear Papa and Mavis,

The closer we get to Christmas, the harder it is for me to live in the present. I am besieged by memories of last Christmas. The war was over and Rob was home again. Never was a holiday so filled with joy. Though I will never know such happiness again, at least I knew it once, and only some mind-shattering illness can keep it from being mine forever.

Children fortunately approach each holiday as if it were happening for the first time, and they are eagerly looking forward to all that Christmas will bring.

Annie's husband, Hans, has secured by means we decided not to question a pine tree from the woods of East Texas and we have decorated it with iced sugar cookies and candy canes (the advantage of edible ornaments is that they do not have to be stored).

Elizabeth Forsythe Hailey, *A Woman of Independent Means*

That morning Pippi was busy making a *pepparkakor*—that's a kind of Swedish [cookie]. She had made an enormous amount of dough and rolled it out on the kitchen floor.

"Because," said Pippi to her little monkey, "what earthly use is a baking board when one plans to make at least five hundred cookies?"

Astrid Lindgren, *Pippi Longstocking*

Rolled Sugar Cookies with Icing

½ cup butter or margarine

½ cup sugar

½ cup light brown sugar

1 egg, beaten

1¾ cups all-purpose flour

1 teaspoon baking powder

¼ teaspoon salt

2½ tablespoons rice milk or milk

½ teaspoon vanilla

Cream together the butter and sugars, then add the egg and mix well. Add the remaining ingredients and mix until dough is thick and smooth. Refrigerate the dough for at least 2 hours.

Heat the oven to 375°. Roll out the dough ⅜ inch thick on a lightly floured surface and cut cookies as desired. Place the cut cookies on an ungreased cookie sheet.

Bake for about 10 to 12 minutes. Remove the cookies from the sheet and cool on a cooling rack. Decorate with icing, as desired.

MAKES ABOUT 2 DOZEN COOKIES

ICING:

2 cups powdered sugar   Food coloring, if desired
Water

Gradually add water, a few drops at a time, to the sugar. Mix until the icing is a smooth, thick liquid that drips off spoon. Spread the icing over cooled cookies. Place the cookies on waxed paper until the icing dries.

A good book is the best of friends, the same today and forever.

   Martin Tupper

Giving Cookies

If you give a mouse a cookie, he's going to ask for a glass of milk.

   Laura Joffe Numeroff, *If You Give a Mouse a Cookie*

A NOTE FROM LAURA NUMEROFF: My mother taught home economics to junior high school girls. She tried to teach me how to cook, but all I wanted to do was read, write stories and draw.

When I offered to make dinner for my first boyfriend, my mother cooked everything and left. The next time, I tried it myself. The eggplant was crunchy and the salad was absolutely awful.

Since then, almost nothing I've made from a recipe ever came out good enough to try again (except for these cookies). Now I rely on eating in restaurants, take-out food and my boyfriend who makes several yummy things.

Speaking of cookies, maybe it's a good thing I cared more about books than food or I might not have written If You Give a Mouse a Cookie*!*

Tempting Oatmeal-Raisin Cookies

3 egg whites
½ cup applesauce
¼ cup butter or margarine,
   softened
1 cup brown sugar
1 cup sugar
1 teaspoon vanilla extract
1 teaspoon ground cinnamon

Pinch of nutmeg
1½ cups all-purpose flour
1 cup whole-wheat flour
2 teaspoons baking soda
1 teaspoon salt
2 cups quick-cooking oats
1½ cups raisins
½ cup sweetened, flaked coconut

Preheat oven to 350°. Mix together the egg whites, applesauce, butter or margarine, sugars, and vanilla extract in a large bowl. Add the spices, flours, baking soda, and salt and mix well. Stir in the oats. Stir in the raisins and coconut.

Scoop tablespoon-sized amounts onto a greased cookie sheet. Bake for about 12 to 14 minutes, or until lightly browned. Serve with milk, if desired.

MAKES ABOUT 4 DOZEN COOKIES

Grandma's Oatmeal Cookies

1 cup shortening
1 cup brown sugar
1 cup sugar
2 eggs, beaten
1 teaspoon vanilla

1½ cups all-purpose flour
1 teaspoon salt
1 teaspoon baking soda
3 cups quick-cooking oats
½ cup chopped nuts

Cream together the shortening and sugars in a large bowl. Add the eggs and vanilla. Beat well. Combine the flour with the salt and baking soda, and then mix into the batter. Mix in the oats and nuts. Shape the dough into long rolls that are about 2½ inches in diameter. Wrap dough rolls in aluminum foil and freeze for several hours. To bake, cut the dough into ¼-inch-thick slices. Place the slices on a greased cookie sheet and bake at 350° for 10 minutes until barely brown on the bottom.

MAKES ABOUT 4 DOZEN CRISP WAFER-TYPE COOKIES

Rereading, we contemplate and admire; we look back, not ahead; we burrow deeper into the writer's words. Surely most writers dream of being read this way.

Laura Green

Tea Cakes

"We haven't met for many years," said Daisy, her voice as matter-of-fact as it could ever be. "Five years next November."

The automatic quality of Gatsby's answer set us all back at least another minute. I had them both on their feet with the desperate suggestion that they help me make tea in the kitchen when the demoniac Finn brought it in a tray.

Amid the welcome confusion of cups and cakes a certain physical decency established itself. Gatsby got himself into a shadow and, while Daisy and I talked, looked conscientiously from one to the other of us with tense, unhappy eyes. However, as calmness wasn't an end in itself, I made an excuse at the first possible moment, and got to my feet.

"Where are you going?" demanded Gatsby in immediate alarm.

F. Scott Fitzgerald, *The Great Gatsby*

Reacquainting Tea Cakes

⁕

1 cup butter or margarine, softened	2 cups all-purpose flour
1 teaspoon vanilla	1 cup chopped nuts (any type)
¾ cup powdered sugar	¼ teaspoon salt
	About 1 cup powdered sugar

Mix all the ingredients together, except 1 cup powdered sugar, in a large bowl and form into balls about 1 inch in diameter. Bake for 10 minutes at 400° on a greased cookie sheet. Cookies should be set but not brown. Roll the warm cookies in powdered sugar, and repeat when cool.

MAKES ABOUT 3 DOZEN TEA CAKES

When you reread a classic, you do not see more in the book than you did before; you see more in you than there was before.

   Clifton Fadiman

Gingerbread and Torte

⁕

The Vermont midwives, all of whom knew my mother, rallied around her like Secret Service agents around a president who's been shot. They brought her casseroles and stews; they left in our kitchen absolutely mammoth tureens of gazpacho, escabèche, or sweet pea and spinach soup. They baked multigrain breads and blueberry muffins, gingerbread cookies and decadent chocolate tortes. They wrote my mother poems. They penned editorials for the opinion pages of Vermont newspapers; they wrote letters to legislators and the state's at-

torney. They conducted "teach-ins" to explain home birth at public libraries in St. Johns-
bury and Montpelier. Cheryl Visco and Donelle Folino organized a quilt sale to raise money
for my mother's legal defense fund, while Molly Thompson and Megan Blubaugh wrote
hundreds of fund-raising letters on her behalf. Midwife Tracy Fitzpatrick's sister and
brother-in-law owned a vegetarian restaurant in Burlington, and she convinced them to
have a special fund-raising dinner one night, with all of the proceeds going toward my
mother's defense.

⍩   **Chris Bohjalian,** *Midwives*

Soft Gingerbread Creams

⅓ cup shortening or margarine	1 teaspoon ginger
½ cup sugar	½ teaspoon salt
1 egg	½ teaspoon baking soda
½ cup molasses	½ teaspoon nutmeg
½ cup water	½ teaspoon cloves
2 cups all-purpose flour	½ teaspoon cinnamon

Mix the shortening, sugar, egg, molasses, and water in a large bowl. Add
the remaining ingredients, mix well, and refrigerate for 1 hour. Heat the
oven to 400°. Scoop tablespoon-sized amounts of cookie dough onto an
ungreased cookie sheet. Bake for 8 minutes or until no imprint remains
when touched.

Cool and frost with Butter Frosting.

MAKES 3 DOZEN COOKIES

W hen I want to read a novel, I write one.
⍩   **Benjamin Disraeli**

Butter Frosting

2½ tablespoons butter, softened   ¾ teaspoon vanilla
1½ cups powdered sugar   1 tablespoon milk

Mix all the ingredients in a large bowl until smooth. Spread the frosting on cooled cookies.

Chocolate Almond Torte

4 ounces semisweet chocolate,   1 teaspoon almond extract
   finely chopped   ½ teaspoon vanilla extract
½ cup cocoa   4 egg whites
¾ cup sugar, divided   ¼ teaspoon cream of tartar
½ cup boiling water   ⅓ cup all-purpose flour
½ cup almonds, finely chopped   Powdered sugar
3 egg yolks   ½ pint fresh raspberries

Spray the sides of an 8-inch round springform cake pan that is about 3 inches deep with cooking spray. Place a piece of parchment paper (cut to size) in the bottom of pan.

Combine the chocolate, cocoa, half of the sugar, and boiling water in a large bowl. Whisk until smooth. Stir in the almonds, egg yolks, and extracts. Set aside.

In a separate bowl, beat the egg whites and cream of tartar into soft peaks. Gradually add the remaining sugar while continuing to beat at high speed until stiff peaks form.

Add the flour to the chocolate mixture and whisk until well blended. Whisk 1 cup of the beaten egg whites into the chocolate mixture to lighten the batter. Fold in the remaining egg whites.

Scoop the batter into the pan and smooth the top with a rubber spatula. Bake at 350° for 30 to 35 minutes, or until a toothpick retains only a few moist crumbs after being inserted in the center. Place the torte on a rack to cool, leaving it in the pan.

Slide a knife around the inner edge of the pan. Remove the sides and bottom of the springform pan. Sprinkle the torte with powdered sugar (shaking the sugar through a sieve works best). Top with fresh raspberries.

MAKES 10 SERVINGS

Gingerbread

We decided to have a country Christmas, without any help from town. I had wanted to get some picture books for Yulka and Ántonia; even Yulka was able to read a little now. Grandmother took me into the ice-cold storeroom, where she had some bolts of gingham and sheeting. She cut squares of cotton cloth and we sewed them together into a book. We bound it between pasteboards, which I covered with brilliant calico, representing scenes from a circus. For two days I sat at the dining-room table, pasting this book full of pictures for Yulka. We had files of those good old family magazines which used to publish coloured lithographs of popular paintings, and I was allowed to use some of these. I took "Napoleon Announcing the Divorce to Josephine" for my frontispiece. On the white pages I grouped Sunday-School cards and advertising cards which I had brought from my "old country." Fuchs got out the candle-moulds and made tallow candles. Grandmother hunted up her fancy cake-cutters and baked gingerbread men and roosters, which we decorated with burnt sugar and red cinnamon drops.

≈ **Willa Cather,** *My Ántonia*

One morning an old woman decided to bake something special.

"I think I'll make a gingerbread man," she said.

She gave him round candy buttons, a red licorice grin, and crinkly raisin eyes.

Then she put him in the hot oven to bake.

While he baked she sat in her favorite rocking chair and knitted him a stocking hat.

But when the old woman opened the oven door for a peek, the gingerbread man hopped up and ran out the door, saying "Run, run, as fast as you can, you can't catch me, I'm the gingerbread man!"

 "The Gingerbread Man" (folktale)

Gingerbread Men

½ cup sugar

¼ cup butter or margarine,
 softened

¼ cup applesauce

½ cup molasses

¼ cup water

2½ cups all-purpose flour

¾ teaspoon salt

¾ teaspoon ginger

½ teaspoon baking soda

¼ teaspoon allspice

Raisins or red cinnamon candies
 (for decorating)

Beat the sugar, butter, applesauce, and molasses in a large bowl. Add the water and remaining dry ingredients and beat at medium speed until well blended. Cover and refrigerate for 2 hours.

When ready to bake, heat oven to 375°. Roll out the dough on a floured surface ¼ inch thick and cut out cookies. Place the cookies on an ungreased cookie sheet. Decorate the cookies with raisins or cinnamon candies. Bake for 8 to 10 minutes. Cool. Decorate with lemon or vanilla icing.

MAKES 3 DOZEN COOKIES

ICING:

1 cup powdered sugar   ½ teaspoon lemon or vanilla
Water   extract

Mix powdered sugar and extract in a bowl, adding water a few drops at a time and stirring until smooth and lightly creamy.

> We are trying to communicate that which lies in our deepest heart, which has no words, which can only be hinted at through the means of a story. And somehow, miraculously, a story that comes from deep in my heart calls from a reader that which is deepest in his or her heart, and together from our secret hidden selves we create a story that neither of us could have told alone.
>
>   Katherine Paterson

Gingersnaps and Sugar Cookies

As Levi lugged in his trays, his eyes kept hopping over the double stand opposite the Zendt location. There Peter Stoltzfus was opening a family stall which had almost as long a history as the Zendts'. Three generations had created a reputation for fruit pies and stollen, lebkuchen and shoofly and the best crunchy bread in the area. Stoltzfus himself was laying out large trays of gingersnaps and sugar cookies, enticingly arranged, and he waved a greeting to Levi.

   James A. Michener, *Centennial*

Gingersnaps

½ cup molasses

2 tablespoons water

2 tablespoons brown sugar

¼ cup shortening

1½ teaspoons ginger

¼ teaspoon cinnamon

Pinch of ground cloves

1½ cups all-purpose flour

½ teaspoon baking soda

¼ teaspoon salt

¾ teaspoon lemon extract

½ cup sugar

Combine the molasses, water, and sugar together in a medium saucepan. Cook over low heat, stirring continuously with wooden spoon, until it reaches the boiling point. Remove from heat and add the shortening and spices. Stir until the shortening is melted and spices are combined. Combine the flour, baking soda, and salt, and stir into the heated sugar mixture with the lemon extract. Dough will be thick. Refrigerate for about ½ hour.

Shape the dough into 1-inch-diameter balls and roll in sugar to coat. Flatten them with the bottom of a drinking glass. Place the balls on a greased baking sheet. Bake at 375° for about 8 minutes.

MAKES 2 DOZEN COOKIES

VARIATION: A marshmallow topping can be added. Halfway through the baking time, remove the baking sheet from the oven, top each cookie with half a marshmallow, cut side down, and return the baking sheet to the oven to finish baking. At end of bake time, remove the marshmallow from each cookie and discard, leaving behind a thin layer of melted fluff.

Soft Sugar Cookie Drops

2 cups all-purpose flour

1 teaspoon baking powder

¼ teaspoon salt

½ cup butter or margarine,
softened

½ cup sugar

½ cup brown sugar

1 large egg

¼ cup rice milk or regular milk

½ teaspoon vanilla

Preheat oven to 375°. Combine the dry ingredients together and set aside. Cream the butter and sugars together in a large bowl. Beat in the egg. Add the dry ingredients, milk, and vanilla; mix well. Drop tablespoon-sized amounts of the dough onto a lightly greased baking sheet. Bake for 10 to 12 minutes, or until no imprint remains when touched.

MAKES ABOUT 3½ DOZEN COOKIES

I love my main characters. If I don't, how can I expect a reader to truly believe in them?

◁ Barbara Taylor Bradford

Lemon Butter Wafers

I flipped through Tom's cards for apple cheese tart and Chocolate Truffle Cheesecake. Ladies' luncheons do better with cookies for dessert, I'd discovered long ago, for a couple of reasons. The dieters can take only a few and not feel cheated. Unlike cake, where the public taking of more than one piece is viewed as piggish, the nondieters can have numerous cookies in unobtrusive fashion. I would offer two types, I figured, one with chocolate and one without. For the chocolatey ones, I decided on Canterbury Jumbles, a chocolate-chip-and-nut affair that had such a wonderful Anglican name the women would feel duty-bound to eat them. I mixed up that batter, put it in the cooler, and then flipped through Tom's recipes until I came to Lemon Butter Wafers. On the side of the card, Tom had written, *B. - Dinner - Captain.*

There was that *B.* again. *B.* for what? *B. - Read - Judas.* In the dinner context, it looked less like someone's name. Before? British? Bring? Big? I had no idea.

In any event, the Lemon Butter Wafers called for ingredients I had on hand, so I softened unsalted butter and wielded my zester over plump lemons. A fine mist of fragrant oil from the golden citrus fruit sprayed my face. I closed the door to the kitchen so as not to wake Arch and Julian, then pulverized almonds in a small food processor and carefully mixed the ingredients together. I did a trial batch: The first hot cookie was buttery, crunchy, and as lemony as a meringue pie. It melted in my mouth. I set the rest of the batter in to chill and mentally thanked Tom for his culinary expertise. The churchwomen would think their dessert was sent from heaven.

Diane Mott Davidson, *The Last Suppers*

Lemon Butter Wafers

1¼ cups unsalted butter
1 cup sugar
2 large eggs
1¼ cups sifted flour

2 tablespoons very finely minced
lemon zest (see note)
⅓ cup ground almonds (see note)

In the large bowl of an electric mixer, beat the butter until smooth and add the sugar, beating until creamy. Beat in the eggs, scraping down the sides of the bowl. Add the flour, beating just until combined. Add the lemon zest and almonds, stirring until well incorporated. Cover the bowl with plastic wrap and place in the refrigerator until well chilled, at least 3 hours.

Preheat the oven to 350°. Butter a nonstick cookie sheet. Using a ½-tablespoon measure, spoon out level ½ tablespoons of chilled cookie dough onto the cookie sheet, placing them 3 inches apart. Bake for about 10 minutes or until the cookies have just flattened and are lightly browned around the edges. Cool the cookies on racks. Store in a covered tin.

MAKES 64

Note: It is best to grind the almonds and mince the lemon zest in a small electric grinder such as a coffee grinder. The result is superior to that obtained with an ordinary food processor.

VARIATION: Spread 1 tablespoon best-quality seedless raspberry jam on the bottom of one cookie, then place the bottom of another cookie on top. This makes a delicious lemon-raspberry cookie sandwich.

MAKES 32

—Recipe of Diane Mott Davidson from *The Last Suppers*

> What I really liked as a child were atlases and encyclopedias. I spent long hours dreamily combing their pages in an utterly purposeless way.
>
> ᴥ **David Guterson**

Hazelnuts

ᴥ

Caddie picked furiously, filling her skirt. It was not often that she got more nuts than Tom. To-day she would have more than anybody. An evening stillness crept through the golden woods. Suddenly Caddie knew that she had better go or supper would be begun. To be late for a meal was one of the unpardonable sins in the Woodlawn family. Clutching the edges of her heavy skirt, she began to run. A thorn reached out and tore her sleeve, twigs caught in her tangled hair, her face was dirty and streaked with perspiration, but she didn't stop running until she reached the farmhouse. In fact, she didn't stop even then, for the deserted look of the yard told her that they were all at supper. She rushed on, red and disheveled, and flung open the dining-room door.

There she stopped for the first time, frozen with astonishment and dismay. It wasn't an ordinary supper. It was a company supper! Everybody was calm and clean and sedate, and at one end of the table sat the Circuit Rider! Paralyzed with horror, Caddie's fingers let go her skirt, and a flood of green hazelnuts rolled all over the floor. In a terrible lull in the conversation they could be heard bumping and rattling to the farthest corners of the room.

"How do you do, Caroline Augusta?" said the Circuit Rider in his deep voice—that voice which filled the schoolhouse with the fervor of his praying. The Circuit Rider was the only person who bothered to remember that Caddie was really Caroline Augusta and that Hetty was Henrietta. He turned his dark, deep-set eyes on Mrs. Woodlawn, who sat beside him at the end of the long table.

"When are you going to begin making a young lady out of this wild Indian, Mrs. Woodlawn?" he inquired.

☙ **Carol Ryrie Brink**, *Caddie Woodlawn*

Caddie's Hazelnut Squares

½ cup powdered sugar

2 cups all-purpose flour

1 cup unsalted butter, softened

Dash of salt

8 ounces cream cheese, softened

2 eggs, beaten

½ cup honey

3 tablespoons cream

½ cup brown sugar

1 teaspoon vanilla

3 cups hazelnuts, chopped

Grease a 9 × 12-inch pan. Stir the sugar, flour, and salt together in a bowl. Cut in the butter, using a fork or pastry blender, until crumbly. Press the crust into the prepared baking pan. Bake at 350° for about 20 minutes or until lightly browned. Cool for about 15 minutes.

Mix the cream cheese, eggs, honey, cream, brown sugar, and vanilla in a bowl. Stir in the hazelnuts until they are coated thoroughly. Spread the batter on top of the cooled crust. Return the pan to the oven and bake for about 25 minutes at 350° or until topping is bubbling slightly. Cool completely before cutting into squares.

Or, Caroline Augusta's Toffee Hazelnut Bars

½ cup butter or margarine, softened
1 mashed ripe banana
1½ cups brown sugar, packed
2 large eggs, beaten
2 teaspoons vanilla extract
2½ cups all-purpose flour

1½ teaspoons baking powder
1 teaspoon salt
1 11-ounce package white baking chips
½ cup hazelnuts, chopped
¼ cup sweetened, flaked coconut (optional)

Beat the butter, banana, brown sugar, eggs, and vanilla together until smooth. Add the dry ingredients and mix well. Stir in the chips, nuts, and coconut. Spread the batter in a greased and floured 9 × 13-inch pan. Bake at 350° for about 30 minutes. Cool completely, cut into squares.

VARIATION: For a low-fat treat, applesauce can be substituted for butter.

It is imperative for me to take a vacation from twentieth-century America and look at life through other eyes. Indeed, most of my writing has been a series of such excursions.

🔖 Jean Fritz

Strawberry Fudge

∾

"Keep calm!" cried Mr. Wonka. "Keep calm, my dear lady, keep calm. There is no danger! No danger whatsoever! Augustus has gone on a little journey, that's all. A most interesting little journey. But he'll come out of it just fine, you wait and see."

"How can he possibly come out just fine!" snapped Mrs. Gloop. "He'll be made into marshmallows in five seconds!"

"Impossible!" cried Mr. Wonka. "Unthinkable! Inconceivable! Absurd! He could never be made into marshmallows!"

"And why not, may I ask?" shouted Mrs. Gloop.

"Because that pipe doesn't go to the Marshmallow Room!" Mr. Wonka answered. "It doesn't go anywhere near it! That pipe—the one Augustus went up—happens to lead directly to the room where I make a most delicious kind of strawberry-flavored chocolate-coated fudge."

🔖 **Roald Dahl,** *Charlie and the Chocolate Factory*

Mr. Wonka's Strawberry-Flavored Chocolate-Coated Fudge

2 cups sugar

½ cup unsalted butter

4 ounces evaporated milk

2 ounces strawberry syrup

(Hershey's, if available)

4 ounces melted semisweet

chocolate for dipping

Line an 8 × 10-inch shallow baking pan with buttered wax paper.

Put the sugar, butter, evaporated milk, and strawberry syrup into a large, heavy-bottomed saucepan and place over low heat. Stir occasionally. Once the sugar has dissolved, bring the mixture to a boil gently, stirring constantly to prevent sticking and burning on the bottom of the pan. Boil gently until a little of the mixture dropped into cold water forms a soft ball, about 5 minutes. (Or you can place a warmed candy thermometer in the saucepan and boil the mixture until it reaches 234°F.)

Take the pan off the heat and stir until the bubbles subside. Beat rapidly with a wooden spoon until the mixture thickens and becomes granular, about 3 minutes.

Pour the fudge into the lined baking pan and let set. If necessary, smooth with a spatula dipped in boiling water.

With shaped cutters, cut out the fudge, and dip one side into the melted chocolate; or decorate with piped chocolate, creating different patterns.

Makes enough for 10 greedy children.

—From *Roald Dahl's Revolting Recipes*

When school ends, millions of children will head for the beach or will climb into the family station wagon for a trip to Grandmother's. But none will travel farther than the child with a book who goes only to his own room or to the shade beneath a back-yard tree.

The books of childhood are always with us. Lost in their pages, a child may swim the bluest sea, rise on the highest swing, engage in the grandest adventure.

 Gene Shalit

Chocolates

Simpsons Basement used to be bargain clothes and wrenches. Now it's resplendent. There are pyramids of imported chocolates, an ice cream counter, aisles and aisles of fancy cookies and canned gourmet food, ticking away like little clocks toward the obsolescence dates stamped on their packages. There's even an espresso counter. It's all very world-class down here, where I used to buy cheap nighties in high school with my tiny allowance, on sale at that and a size too large. I'm overwhelmed by all the chocolates. Just looking at them reminds me of Christmas and the sticky feeling after eating too many, the surfeit and glut.

 Margaret Atwood, *Cat's Eye*

Chocolate-Covered Coconut Balls

1 pound powdered sugar
14 ounces sweetened, flaked
    coconut
½ cup butter or margarine
1 14-ounce can sweetened
    condensed milk

1 12-ounce package semisweet
    chocolate chips
2 tablespoons vegetable oil

Mix the first four ingredients together and roll the candy filling into 1-inch balls. Refrigerate overnight.

In a double boiler, melt the chocolate chips and oil. Stir regularly.

Dip the chilled coconut balls in the melted chocolate, place on wax paper, and let set for about 10 minutes.

MAKES 8 DOZEN CHOCOLATES

Chocolate-Covered Peanut Butter Balls

2 cups powdered sugar
½ cup margarine
1 cup peanut butter

1 12-ounce package semisweet
    chocolate chips
2 tablespoons vegetable oil

Mix first three ingredients together and roll the candy filling into 1-inch balls. Refrigerate overnight.

In a double boiler, melt the chocolate chips and oil. Stir regularly.

Dip the chilled peanut butter balls in the melted chocolate, place on wax paper, and let set for about 10 minutes.

MAKES 4 DOZEN CHOCOLATES

The best fiction is where art, philosophy, and adventure all meet.

   Norman Mailer

Fudge

Then I look at everyone in the eyes and say: "Now it is official: we are from here on out to be known as Ya-Yas!" And everybody starts clapping.

"Some of that kind of sounds like it came from the Bible," Necie says.

"Do not question the Mistress of Legend," I say.

"Yeah," Teensy chimed in. "The Bible doesn't *own* those words."

"Never mind," Necie says. "Would yall care for some fudge?"

"Why, thank you, Mistress of Refreshment," I say.

And we all bite into big chunks of chocolate pecan fudge.

"I hate those old alligators," Caro says, then looks in the direction of the bayou.

"Uh," Necie says. "Yall don't think there are any alligators in this bayou, do you?"

"*Maman* put a *gris-gris* on all the alligators behind our house," Teensy says. "We don't have to worry. *Maman* is the one who gave us our name! She's the one always saying, 'Gumbo Ya-Ya, gumbo ya-ya!' "

"That's us," Necie says.

"*Exactement!*" Teensy says. "From here on out to the end of time, we will be known as The Ya-Yas! Nobody can take our name away!"

   Rebecca Wells, *Divine Secrets of the Ya-Ya Sisterhood*

Chocolate Pecan Fudge

⚬⌇⚬

1 12-ounce package semisweet
   chocolate chips
1 14-ounce can sweetened
   condensed milk

1 teaspoon vanilla
1½ cups pecans, finely chopped
Pinch of salt

Heat all ingredients, except nuts, in a double boiler until melted. Stir in nuts. Spread mixture in a greased 8-inch square pan. Cool to room temperature, and refrigerate for 2 hours before cutting.

MAKES ABOUT 60 BITE-SIZED TREATS

All of the spiritual growth, emotional maturity, and intellectual alertness that we seek in life is exercised and strengthened by writing.

⚬⌇   Tina Welling

Honey

⚬⌇⚬

Pooh always liked a little something at eleven o'clock in the morning, and he was very glad to see Rabbit getting out the plates and mugs; and when Rabbit said, "Honey or condensed milk with your bread?" he was so excited that he said, "Both," and then, so as not to seem greedy, he added, "but don't bother about the bread, please."

⚬⌇   A. A. Milne, *The Complete Tales of Winnie-the-Pooh*

Pooh's Honey Kisses

1 package brown sugar (1 pound)
1 cup honey
½ teaspoon salt

1 cup water
¼ cup butter
1 teaspoon vanilla

Boil all ingredients except vanilla until they reach the hard ball stage, where a little bit of the hot mixture dropped into cold water forms a ball that has lost almost all plasticity (about 250° to 268°). Stir in vanilla. Pour the candy mixture into an 8-inch square pan lined with greased aluminum foil. Cool until solidified. Cut into bite-sized pieces and wrap in waxed paper.

MAKES ABOUT 60 TREATS

The thought that I could write something and 100 years from now someone will be reading it—that's like sending a space probe to Mars.

🔖 Ian Frazier

Turkish Delight

"It is dull, Son of Adam, to drink without eating," said the Queen presently. "What would you like best to eat?"

"Turkish Delight, please, your Majesty," said Edmund.

The Queen let another drop fall from her bottle on to the snow, and instantly there appeared a round box, tied with green silk ribbon, which, when opened, turned out to contain several pounds of the best Turkish Delight. Each piece was sweet and light to the very centre and Edmund had never tasted anything more delicious. He was quite warm now, and very comfortable.

While he was eating the Queen kept asking him questions. At first Edmund tried to remember that it is rude to speak with one's mouth full, but soon he forgot about this and thought only of trying to shovel down as much Turkish Delight as he could, and the more he ate the more he wanted to eat, and he never asked himself why the Queen should be so inquisitive.

✍ **C. S. Lewis,** *The Lion, the Witch and the Wardrobe*

Turkish Delight

∞

3 tablespoons gelatin	Fresh grated zest of 1 lemon
½ cup cold water	Fresh grated zest of 1 orange
2 cups sugar	½ cup hot water
2 tablespoons fresh-squeezed	Red food coloring (optional)
orange juice	Powdered sugar
2 tablespoons fresh-squeezed	
lemon juice	

Combine gelatin and cold water, and set aside. Combine sugar, juices, grated zests, and hot water. While stirring, heat to boiling over medium-high heat. Reduce heat slightly to keep mixture at a low boil for 10 minutes. Add gelatin and simmer slowly for another 10 minutes. Add food coloring, if desired. Strain into an 8-inch square cake pan lined with lightly greased aluminum foil. Chill until firm. Cut into squares. Remove squares from foil and roll in powdered sugar.

MAKES ABOUT 60 SMALL TREATS

I entered Francie's world [in Betty Smith's *A Tree Grows in Brooklyn*] like any good reader would, and, more importantly, she entered mine.

⤷ Dorianne Laux

Moon Pie

⟳

"I've got something else to tell you too," Lindsey said, delighted in the surprise she had in store for her grandmother. In fact, Lindsey had told Gabby that if hearing they had met Ben didn't rate a will-wonders-never-cease from Sarah, then hearing about their upcoming New England road trip—which Gabby insisted on calling a tour—would. Especially when she found out that Lindsey was going to stay on for a couple of weeks at the end.

"Sugar Creek has decided to take a road trip through New England. We're going to take a leave from our day jobs. We've got a little saved up, and we can camp out, crash with friends, crash with you when we're close enough by, and we might even make some money hawking our CD. And I've already told them I want some time off at the end to spend with you. Which will work great because Trisha and Billy Earl's baby will be due about the time we finish, and Gabby has to be a bridesmaid in a bunch of weddings, and J.J. says if he doesn't get some fishing in he's going to forget how."

But again, there was no wonders-never-ceasing from her grandmother. Instead Sarah Frost simply said, "It'll do you good to get home and get some real food for a change. Every time I call and get your roommate, she tells me what you live on. And tell me," Sarah Frost asked, "what exactly is a Moon Pie?"

⤷ M. L. Rose, *The Road to Eden's Ridge*

Lindsey's Favorite Food*

¾ cup all-purpose flour

1 cup graham flour

¼ teaspoon baking soda

½ teaspoon baking powder

¼ teaspoon salt

¼ cup shortening

½ cup brown sugar

¼ cup granulated sugar

1 egg

½ teaspoon vanilla

¼ cup milk

1 small jar marshmallow crème

12 ounces semisweet chocolate
   chips

¼ cup butter or margarine

2 tablespoons water

Combine first five dry ingredients and set aside. Beat the shortening and sugars together until smooth. Mix in the egg and vanilla. Mix in the dry ingredients with the milk. Chill dough in refrigerator for at least 2 hours. After dough is chilled, roll it out to a ⅜-inch thickness on a floured countertop. Use a round cutter to cut circles from dough that are about 1½-inches to 2-inches in diameter. Bake on a greased cookie sheet at 350° for about 10 to 12 minutes, until no imprint remains at the touch. Cool.

After the cookies have cooled, prepare cookie sandwiches by spreading about 1 tablespoon of marshmallow crème between 2 cookies. The marshmallow crème should be spread to about ¼-inch thickness.

To prepare the chocolate coating, melt the chocolate chips with the butter or margarine and water in the top of a double boiler over high heat, stirring continuously until smooth. Dip each cookie in the melted chocolate, flipping at least once to coat completely. Remove cookie sandwich immediately from chocolate (to prevent the marshmallow crème from melting), and set on a cooling rack. Waxed paper or aluminum foil should be placed under the cooling rack to catch chocolate drippings. Chill in refrigerator to complete the setting of the chocolate.

MAKES ABOUT 20 TREATS

* The Chattanooga Bakery in Tennessee invented Moon Pies® in the early 1900s. A popular southern treat, Moon Pies® are still made by the bakery today. This recipe is our version of Lindsey's favorite treat in The Road to Eden's Ridge by M. L. Rose.

Moon Pie Delight

An easy, no-fuss Moon Pie® and ice cream dessert.—M. L. Rose

4 Chattanooga Chocolate Moon
    Pies® or 10 of Lindsey's
    Favorite Food
½ gallon of vanilla ice cream

1 12-ounce package of mini
    chocolate chips
½ cup pecans, finely chopped

Soften one half-gallon of vanilla ice cream to a spreadable consistency, but do not allow it to melt. Finely chop or crumble Moon Pies® and spread them in the bottom of a 13 x 9-inch freezer-proof dish. Spoon ice cream over the top of the Moon Pie® crust and spread it into a smooth layer (use more or less ice cream to make the dessert as thick as you like). Sprinkle half of the chocolate chips and all of the chopped pecans over the ice cream layer. Return to the freezer for at least 2 hours. Remove the dessert from the freezer ten to fifteen minutes before serving. Melt the remaining chocolate chips in a plastic bag in hot water. Snip a small corner off the plastic bag of chips and drizzle the top of the dessert with the melted chocolate. Serve and enjoy.

—Recipe contributed by M. L. Rose

I was born with a reading list I will never finish.

Maud Casey

CREDITS

Excerpt from BACK ROADS by Tawni O'Dell, copyright © 2000 by Tawni O'Dell. Used by permission of Viking Penguin, a division of Penguin Group (USA) Inc.

Excerpt from A YEAR DOWN YONDER by Richard Peck, copyright © 2000 by Richard Peck. Used by permission of Dial Books for Young Readers, a division of Penguin Young Readers Group, a member of Penguin Group (USA) Inc., 345 Hudson St., New York, NY 10014. All rights reserved.

Excerpt from PLAIN TRUTH by Jodi Picoult, copyright © 2000 by Jodi Picoult. Reprinted with the permission of Atria Books, an imprint of Simon & Schuster Adult Publishing Group.

Excerpt from SEPTEMBER by Rosamunde Pilcher, copyright © 1991 by Rosamunde Pilcher. Reprinted by permission of St. Martin's Press, LLC

Excerpt from THE HEART OF THE SEA by Nora Roberts, copyright © 2000 by Nora Roberts. Used by permission of Berkley Publishing Group, a division of Penguin Group (USA) Inc.

Excerpt from WORD FOR WORD by Andrew A. Rooney, copyright © 1984, 1985, 1986 by Essay Production, Inc. Used by permission of G.P. Putnam's Sons, a division of Penguin Group (USA) Inc.

Excerpt from THE ROAD TO EDEN'S RIDGE by M. L. Rose, copyright © 2002 by Myra McLarey and Linda Weeks. Used by permission of Rutledge Hill Press, Nashville, Tennessee.

Excerpts from THE VERSE BY THE SIDE OF THE ROAD by Frank Rowsome Jr., copyright © 1965 by Frank Rowsome. Foreword copyright © 1990 by Robert Dole. Used by permission of The Stephen Green Press, an imprint of Penguin Group (USA) Inc.

Excerpt from ICY SPARKS by Gwyn Hyman Rubio, copyright © 1998 by Gwyn Hyman Rubio. Used by permission of Viking Penguin, a division of Penguin Group (USA) Inc.

Excerpt from SEUSS-ISMS: WISE AND WITTY PRESCRIPTIONS FOR LIVING FROM THE GOOD DOCTOR by Dr. Seuss, copyright © 1997 by Dr. Seuss Enterprises, L.P. Used by permission of Random House Children's Books, a division of Random House, Inc.

Excerpt from WALKING ON ALLIGATORS: A BOOK OF MEDITATIONS FOR WRITERS by Susan Shaughnessy, copyright © 1992 by Susan Shaughnessy. Reprinted by permission of HarperCollins Publishers Inc.

"Pancake" from WHERE THE SIDEWALK ENDS by Shel Silverstein, copyright © 1974 by Evil Eye Music, Inc. Used by permission of HarperCollins Publishers.

Excerpt from THE NOTEBOOK by Nicholas Sparks (Warner Books 1996), used with permission.

Excerpts from THE GRAPES OF WRATH by John Steinbeck, copyright 1939, renewed 1967 by John Steinbeck. Used by permission of Viking Penguin, a division of Penguin Group (USA) Inc.

Excerpts from THE PEARL by John Steinbeck, copyright © 1945 by John Steinbeck, renewed 1973 by Elaine Steinbeck, Thom Steinbeck and John Steinbeck IV. Used by permission of Viking Penguin, a division of Penguin Group (USA) Inc.

Excerpt from pages 7, 8, and 32 from COOK-A-DOODLE-DOO!, copyright © 1999 by Janet Stevens and Susan Stevens Crummel, reprinted by permission of Harcourt, Inc.

"Millions of Strawberries" by Genevieve Taggard, copyright © 1986. Originally published in *The New Yorker*. Used by permission of Judith Benét Richardson.

Excerpts from THE HIDING PLACE by Corrie ten Boom with John and Elizabeth Sherrill, copyright 1971 by Corrie ten Boom with John and Elizabeth Sherrill. Reprinted by permission of Chosen Books, Chappaqua, NY.

Excerpts from "Edith's Wardrobe" and "Herb's Book" in HERB'S PAJAMAS by Abigail Thomas, copyright © 1998 by Abigail Thomas. Reprinted by permission of Algonquin Books of Chapel Hill, a division of Workman Publishing.

INDEX

yams, 23–24
Year Down Yonder, A (Peck), 220
yellow cake, 229–30
yogurt, Persian cucumber and, 73
Yumoto, Kazumi, 150

Zinsser, William, 115
zucchini:
  bread, 13
  bread, chocolate, 14
  lasagne, 78–79

THE

BOOK LOVER'S
COOKBOOK

A Reader's Guide

Shaunda Kennedy Wenger

& Janet Kay Jensen

A Conversation with
Shaunda Kennedy Wenger and Janet Kay Jensen

Q: How did you come up with the idea for *The Book Lover's Cookbook*?

Shaunda Kennedy Wenger: In the fall of 1999, the idea for a literary cookbook took shape while I was reading a specific novel, Sue Miller's *While I Was Gone*. Set in the East, this story's setting mirrored my memories of off-campus living in a three-story Victorian at college. By the time the main character made chili with her housemate, Eli (a.k.a. murder suspect #1), the combination of vivid imagery and strong feelings of nostalgia left me feeling as if Miller had set her characters in my old house, in my old kitchen, with my old recipe—chili happened to be my specialty when I shared meals with my housemates.

Naturally, I got up and looked for that old recipe, remembering that a housemate had written it down one evening while I prepared it several years before. Because I'm such a foodie, someone who would never dream of throwing away a recipe, I found it tucked in one of my cookbooks. Almost immediately, I began to wonder if authors routinely fed their characters well, and certain books that I'd read recently came to mind: Toni Morrison's *The Bluest Eye*. Isabel Allende's *Daughter of Fortune*. Barbara Kingsolver's *The Bean Trees*.

Q: How did the cookbook become a coauthored project?

SKW: From the moment the idea for the cookbook took shape, I believed this project begged for a coauthor—the very nature of reading and cooking leads to sharing with others, and good books and great recipes are almost always passed along to receptive hands.

I shared the idea with my local group of writing colleagues in an e-mail to see if they thought the project was plausible. Out of the handful of responses, Janet's included suggestions of several pertinent authors whose novels contained classic scenes pivoting around food: Charles Dickens's *Oliver Twist* and *David Copperfield*. Mark Twain's *The Adventures of Huckleberry Finn*. Margaret Mitchell's *Gone with the Wind*. Lewis Carroll's *Alice in Wonderland*. Victor Hugo's *Les Misérables*.

Her enthusiasm was contagious, and our e-mails quickly bounced back and forth, listing possibilities of recipes and novels. I knew I'd found a kindred spirit and asked Janet if she'd like to step on board.

Q: Out of all the excerpts from books that you found during your research, did you get a sense of a unifying theme?

SKW: Food creates such vivid imagery for the reader that our minds can add details that aren't even described by the author. We can smell the onions in Sue Miller's *While I Was Gone*. We see the flaky frosting of Effie Belle's coconut cake in *Cold Sassy Tree* (by Olive Anne Burns). We can hear the clink of the spoon against the soup bowl in George Eliot's *Middlemarch*, and feel the butter coating our fingers from a hot ear of sweet corn in Sandra Brown's *The Alibi*. With our senses turned on, it's easy to step into the scene. And once we've stepped into it, we've opened ourselves up to making an emotional connection with the characters.

Overall, I believe many of the passages we selected for this cookbook are hinged on emotional undercurrents. They stir up tension or show insight into a character's desires. Although many aren't centered on the emotional firestorm of a climax, they fan the emotional embers of character interaction and plot development. Ultimately, these scenes, set against familiarity, keep the pages turning.

Q: You've also included over a hundred quotes about reading and books. What led you to do that?

SKW: In doing our research, we found great quotes about books in literature and magazines. We decided to sprinkle them throughout the cookbook to share an overall excitement for books with our readers.

Q: Out of all you included, do you have a favorite quote?

SKW: At one of her readings in a California library, Isabel Allende said, "The library is inhabited by spirits that come out of the pages at night."

I just love the thought of stories having lives of their own, lives that might carry on after the book is finished, the cover closed.

Janet Kay Jensen: Maud Casey said, "I was born with a reading list I will never finish."

When I travel, I spend more time choosing the books I want to take than the clothes I need to pack!

Q: What is your favorite passage in *The Book Lover's Cookbook*?

SKW: Each time I visit the cookbook my favorite changes. Today, during this hot, summer day in July, I'm drawn to Barbara Kingsolver's excerpt about green beans, green tomatoes, and green tomato pies from *The Bean Trees*. It's been my favorite before—because like the character, Mattie, I have a couple of gardens, and right now mine are bursting with blueberries, raspberries, and gooseberries, as well as green beans, carrots, and herbs. Soon I'll be harvesting broccoli, tomatoes, tomatillos, okra, watermelon, and corn. I can fully appreciate Mattie's satisfaction in outthinking nature's frost and utilizing every nugget offered up by her garden. By the end of this passage, sometimes I wish I knew my way to her apartment, so I could stop by for a visit to smell and see what treats Mattie might be baking.

JKJ: One of mine takes place in Roxanna's kitchen in Leif Enger's *Peace Like a River*, an allegorical story of a family's journey to reconnect with one another and ultimately heal from the tragedies that have pursued them.

In 1962, widowed Jeremiah Land and two of his children embark on a trek across wintry Minnesota and North Dakota in an Airstream trailer. In the excerpt we chose, Jeremiah, Reuben and Swede are stranded in a blizzard and taken in by Roxanna, a strong, capable woman with an intriguing history of her own. As they gather around a tempting meal of roasted chicken in Roxanna's kitchen, a compelling scene unfolds: a strong and growing attraction between a man and a woman, a motherless boy's longing for family and a stable home, and the safety and comfort of being inside while a blizzard rages outside.

Q: What are the most enjoyable recipes you developed in the course of writing the book?

SKW: "Turkish Delight" piqued my interest many years ago when I read C. S. Lewis's *The Lion, the Witch, and the Wardrobe*. Being a chocolate lover, I wrongly assumed at the time that this insatiable treat was something chocolatey. It's actually a popular European, citrus-flavored gelatin dessert—harder than Jell-O, softer than hard candy. The most exciting part for me was discovering that eating it produced the same effect as Lewis described for Edmund:

"Each piece was sweet and light to the very centre and Edmund had never tasted anything more delicious . . . the more he ate the more he wanted to eat. . . ."

It's a pleasure everyone should experience.

JKJ: I wasn't a fan of chilled soups until I met Forney, Billie Letts's librarian/cook in *Where the Heart Is*. "Forney's Orange-Almond Bisque" resulted after a number of experimental batches. The cantaloupe balances the citrus nicely, and the yogurt gives it a creamy texture.

I spent several days experimenting with custards until I was satisfied with "Aunt Petunia's Baked Custard Pudding," based on the levitating dessert described in *Harry Potter and the Chamber of Secrets*. Fortunately, the house elf Dobby wasn't around to work the Hover Charm.

Q: Did you develop all of the recipes, or did some of the authors create recipes for the book?

SKW: We developed most of them, but some were contributed directly from the author whose passage we featured: Elizabeth Berg's "Thanksgiving Spinach Casserole," Jim Fergus's "Nostalgic Coq au Vin," Jodi Picoult's "Amish Chicken and Dumplings" and "1-2-3-4 Cake," Camron Steve Wright's "Chocolate Pudding" and "Chocolate Soufflé," Judith Guest's "Chocolate Pecan Pie," Barbara Kingsolver's "First Frost Green Tomato Pie," Carolyn Campbell's "Celebration Potatoes," and M. L. Rose's "Moon Pie Delight."

We also have a few recipes that involved working together with the contributing author on fine-tuning the recipe through correspondence, like Maeve Binchy's "Almond-Bacon Wraps," Kay Chorao's "Chocolate Swirl Fudge Cake," Connie May Fowler's "Tomato Pie," and Patricia Gaffney's "Curried Shrimp with Snow Peas and Apples."

The enthusiasm and assistance from these authors was fantastic.

JKJ: Other recipes were derived directly from the text of the novel, like John Grisham's " 'Good Life' Veal Piccata" in *The Firm*, Louisa May Alcott's "A Little Woman's Butternut Bevy" in *Little Women*, and Patricia Cornwell's "No-Fuss Crab Cakes" in *Unnatural Exposure*, where by following the character Bev's instruction, I discovered that she's a good cook! There also seems to be a trend for some authors (i.e., Fannie Flagg and Diane Mott Davidson) to include actual recipes in their books, an invitation for readers to be even more engaged with the characters and the story.

Q: If you could dine with an author, who would it be, and what would you have to eat?

SKW: That would have to be Elizabeth Berg. While reading *Open House*, as soon as Samantha raised her glass higher at King's table for more wine and thought, *This is my favorite restaurant*, I said, "Take me there!" I'd love to pull up a chair at Berg's table.

I'd bring the wine—maybe a bottle of Robert Mondavi Coastal Sauvignon Blanc and a Louis Jadot Pinot Noir Bourgogne—and dessert, which would depend on the season. A honeydew melon Italian ice if it's warm, or an apple-raisin-crumb pie if it's chilly. And guests?! Maybe Barbara Kingsolver or Patricia Gaffney would be available.

JKJ: I'd like to break bread with Victor Hugo (*Les Misérables*), who said, "If a writer wrote merely for his time, I would have to break my pen and throw it away." I can imagine him instructing Madame Magloire to bring in the silver candlesticks. She would serve a simple meal: a marvelous fresh vegetable soup from her garden with hearty rye bread. I would love to paddle a raft on the Mississippi to join Mark Twain, Huck, and Jim (*Huckleberry Finn*) for some tender pork roast, cabbage, and cornbread, but I'd pass on the after-dinner corncob pipe. Then it would be on to Minnesota to meet Garrison Keillor (*We Are Still Married*) to ask him to make me a perfect Lutheran apple pie. It would be a treat to spend a week in Diane Mott Davidson's kitchen in Evergreen, Colorado, tasting, taking notes, and watching her create the tempting recipes she includes in her culinary mysteries—in this case, *The Last Suppers*. Goldie, a feisty heroine with a wry sense of humor, is a caterer who on an average day stumbles onto at least one crime scene but never, ever burns her cookies, which she selects according to the scruples of her clients. For example, her "Canterbury Jumbles," which she serves at a church social, "had such a wonderful Anglican name the women would feel duty-bound to eat them."

Q: How did you name the recipes?

JKJ: We tried to link the recipe directly to the plot, setting, a character, or a line of dialogue in the selected passage.

SKW: Naming recipes was the best part of writing the cookbook. Coming up with a suitable recipe title really cinched the connection between recipe and novel.

Q: Let's explore this topic a little more. What are some examples of recipe titles that are tied into the plot or events in a novel?

JKJ: Although Bridget Jones (*Bridget Jones's Diary* by Helen Fielding) gets drunk while making her "Third-World–style ethnic family party" shepherd's pie, we chose to name ours "Sober Shepherd's Pie."

SKW: That was intentional, of course. For the safety of our readers, we'd hate to promote reckless behavior, outside of fiction. Cooking is serious business. And with alcohol, even more so. [*smile*]
And similar situations occurred with recipe titles such as "Specialty Omelet" (*Little Women*) and "Eli and Jo's Innocent Vegetarian Chili" (*While I Was Gone*). In *Little Women*, Jo brings a burned breakfast to her mother, who's ill. And in *While I Was Gone*, Eli is a suspect in the murder of one of his housemates. We didn't want to suggest that our recipes would lead to disasters depicted in the stories we excerpted, although in the kitchen anything is possible. [*smile*]

Q: What are some examples of recipe titles that refer to a novel's setting?

SKW: "Tianjin Dumplings" are named for a favorite meal that writer Adeline Yen Mah ate in China, before her childhood took a dreadful turn (*Falling Leaves*).

JKJ: Because James Michener's *Centennial* is set in Colorado, we included the region's geography in naming "Rocky Mountain Sourdough Starter" and "Rocky Mountain Sourdough Biscuits."

Q: What are some examples of recipes that were named for specific characters?

JKJ: We couldn't imagine another name for "Mrs. Liebowitz's Lentil-Vegetable Soup" when we read the scene in Frank McCourt's *Angela's Ashes* where a compassionate neighbor brings hot soup to Frankie's hungry, impoverished family. Frankie thinks it's so delicious, he wonders if he can swap mothers with Freddie Liebowitz. He's even willing to throw his little brothers in for free.

"Brandy's Tomato-Beef Soup" is named after one of veterinarian James Herriot's favorite patients, a dog named Brandy who periodically raids the dustbin and gets a tomato soup can stuck on his nose. "Brandy the Dustbin Dog" is found in James Herriot's *Favorite Dog Stories*.

SKW: In reviewing our list, I see many recipes are named for specific characters. I suppose the reason for this is that these novels introduced us to memorable characters. Naturally, we leaned toward naming the recipes after those who made them: "Miss Maudie's Lane Cake" from *To Kill a Mockingbird* by Harper Lee, "Emma's Curried Shrimp with Snow Peas and Apples" from *The Saving Graces* by Patricia Gaffney, "Ruby's Potato Salad" from *Cold Mountain* by Charles Frazier, "Effie Belle's Coconut Cake" from *Cold Sassy Tree* by Olive Ann Burns, and "Queen Nacha's Tamales" from Laura Esquivel's *Like Water for Chocolate*.

Q: What are you reading?

SKW: Looking at my shelf, I can see it's stacked—well, overstocked—with novels I can't wait to get to. *Deafening* by Frances Itani. *The Virgin Blue* by Tracy Chevalier. *The Little Friend* by Donna Tartt. *The Seduction of Water* by Carol Goodman. *These Is My Words* by Nancy E. Turner. Right now, all these books are waiting for me to finish a great novel: *Angry Housewives Eating Bon Bons* by Lorna Landvik.

JKJ: As we each contributed different excerpts to the book, there are works represented in *The Book Lover's Cookbook* that I haven't read yet, so it's my reading guide for the next couple of years. In addition, I just finished Mary Webb's lovely and poetic *Precious Bane*. On deck are *A Midwife's Tale: The Life of Martha Ballard, Based on Her Diary* by Laurel Thatcher Ulrich and *The Stone Diaries* by Carol Shields.

Q: What fostered your love of reading and literature?

SKW: My mother. She loved to read us bedtime stories. She read them from a large, bound book filled with classic tales and poems. It had more words than pictures, but it still held our attention. My brother and I would crawl into her lap, tuck ourselves under the blankets, and listen to the story play out in the sound of her voice. As we came to know each story by heart, we followed along with the words that floated across my mother's fingertips. Before long, the words jumped out at us, familiar, like old friends, and the routine changed, with us reading the stories aloud to our mother. By the time I stood chest-high to the kitchen counter, I was also reading cookbooks with her, standing at her side while she cooked.

JKJ: My mother was a librarian and my father was a teacher; both of them were well-read. Memorizing classic poetry was part of their generation's curriculum, so our exposure to great literature was early and continuous, too. That's a wonderful legacy to share with your children.

SHAUNDA KENNEDY WENGER enjoys creative cooking and writing, and her essays on these topics are occasionally featured on Utah public radio. She is currently writing a novel. Her work has been published in *Babybug*, *The Writer*, *American Careers*, *Family History Magazine*, and *Short-Short Stories for Reading Aloud* (The Education Center, 2000). Her first children's book will be published by Richard Owen Publishers. She regards her monthly book club meeting as one of life's essential ingredients.

JANET KAY JENSEN is published in *Healing Ministry Journal*, *ByLine*, *Everton's Family History Magazine*, and *The Magic of Stories*. She has received awards for essays, poetry, and short stories, including seven *ByLine* honorable mentions and third place in the 2004 Association for Mormon Letters fiction contest. A speech-language pathologist, she holds degrees from Utah State University and Northwestern University. She is writing a novel, has taught creative writing to jail inmates, and is a literacy tutor. She is married and the mother of three college student sons.